HARRAP'S ENGLISH–FRENCH
DICTIONARY OF DATA PROCESSING

HARRAP'S ENGLISH–FRENCH DICTIONARY OF DATA PROCESSING

by

CLAUDE CAMILLE

and

MICHEL DEHAINE

HARRAP   LONDON

First published in Great Britain 1970
by GEORGE G. HARRAP & CO. LTD
182–184 High Holborn, London WC1V 7AX

Second edition 1976

© *Claude Camille and Michel Dehaine* 1970

ISBN 0 245 52293 X

Set in 10 pt. Photon Times, printed by photolithography,
and bound in Great Britain at The Pitman Press, Bath

FOREWORD TO THE SECOND EDITION

The progress of data processing as a technique, since its beginnings about twenty years ago, has been extremely rapid. With the advent of this new branch of industry, the specialized vocabulary required to accommodate its many new concepts has developed at an ever-increasing rate—first in English, since the great majority of the giants of this industry are to be found in the United States; and subsequently in other languages including French. The same striking features have appeared in both languages: the emergence of completely new terms, and the use, in a new context, of words already in existence.

The first edition of this dictionary, which appeared in 1970, aimed primarily at taking stock of the situation as it was then and providing a working tool for those who, in one way or another, were concerned with data processing. With the help of several glossaries published by leading manufacturers and certain international standards associations, an extensive list of terms was compiled.

So swift has been the evolution of this branch of technical knowledge, however, that a second edition incorporating the more recent terminology was imperative to keep the work up to date. While the content of the first edition has been substantially retained, numerous additions have been made so that the dictionary now reflects the comprehensive range of the vocabulary of data processing as it is today. The new style of presentation is designed to assist the user to find the information required more readily.

The scope of this new edition, as with the first, includes utilization methods, in particular programming, and the related fields of electrical engineering, electronics, and telecommunications.

C.C.
M D
January 1976

AVANT-PROPOS A LA DEUXIEME EDITION

L'informatique est une science qui a fait des progrès très rapides depuis sa naissance, il y a une vingtaine d'années. Le vocabulaire spécialisé qui sert à exprimer les concepts propres à cette nouvelle discipline s'est lui aussi développé à grands pas, tout d'abord en langue anglaise car c'est surtout des Etats-Unis, où se trouvent la majorité des grosses entreprises de ce secteur, que nous vient la terminologie originale, puis par la suite en d'autres langues dont le français. Dans les deux langues qui nous intéressent ici on constate donc les mêmes phénomènes: apparition de termes entièrement inédits et attribution d'acceptions nouvelles à des mots déjà connus.

La première édition de ce dictionnaire, parue en 1970, avait surtout pour objet de faire le point et de faciliter la tâche de ceux qui, de près ou de loin, s'occupaient d'informatique. Nous avions établi une liste alors exhaustive de termes recueillis dans les glossaires et lexiques des principaux constructeurs et de certains organismes internationaux de normalisation.

Mais l'informatique évolue à un tel rythme que la liste complète d'hier est aujourd'hui pleine de lacunes; aussi une seconde édition, revue et mise à jour, s'imposait-elle. Nous y avons conservé la majeure partie des termes de la première édition et ajouté de nombreux termes nouveaux. Ce dictionnaire reflète donc fidèlement le vocabulaire très riche de l'informatique tel qu'il existe à l'heure actuelle. Nous avons modifié sa disposition pour permettre à l'utilisateur de trouver plus facilement et plus rapidement le terme recherché.

Comme la précédente, cette deuxième édition embrasse le champ des méthodes d'utilisation, en particulier la programmation, et des domaines connexes de l'électrotechnique, de l'électronique et des télécommunications.

C.C.
M.D.
Janvier 1976

ACKNOWLEDGEMENTS

The material for this work has been drawn from a number of sources, and we are happy to acknowledge the following standards institutions, associations, and companies whose publications have been of help in our compilation:

American National Standards Institute, Inc.
British Standards Institution
International Telecommunications Union
International Federation for Information Processing
International Computation Centre
International Business Machines Corporation
Honeywell Ltd.
Honeywell-Bull
Association Française de Normalisation

REMERCIEMENTS

Les auteurs se sont servis de termes et expressions provenant de sources très variées pour la compilation de ce dictionnaire, et ils souhaitent remercier les associations de normalisation, les organisations et compagnies mentionnées ci-dessus dont les ouvrages leur ont permis de mener à bien cette tâche.

C.C.
M.D.

HOW TO USE THE DICTIONARY

1. SINGLE WORD.   If there are several equivalent translations in French, the order does not indicate any priority; alternatively, the translation is accompanied by a number if the word has several different meanings in French.

   e.g. **allocate (to),**   allouer, affecter

       record,   1. enregistrement *m*; 2. article *m*; 3. rubrique *f*; 4. fiche *f*; 5. relevé *m*;

2. EXPRESSION COMPRISING TWO TERMS.   This type of expression appears twice in the dictionary. It is translated under both terms.

3. EXPRESSION COMPRISING MORE THAN TWO TERMS.   In most cases, this will only appear in the dictionary under the first and the last terms.

   e.g. **binary to decimal conversion**
      (a) under **binary**
         b. to decimal conversion,   conversion *f* binaire (à) décimal
      (b) under **conversion**
         binary to decimal c.,   conversion binaire (à) décimal

If the key-word has, on its own, no meaning in the context of data processing, then it will only be translated when combined with other terms. Finally, in some composite expressions, the key-word may not clearly stand out, as for instance the word **mode** in the following example:

simultaneous mode of working   mode *m* (d'exploitation) simultané

Abbreviations and special signs used in the dictionary

    m masculine
    f feminine
  adj adjective
(*Am.*) American—this indicates that the term preceding this abbreviation is
         more commonly used in the United States, and a different term is used in
         Great Britain.
OCR optical character recognition
  ( ) Parentheses may indicate:
  (1) that the whole or part of the term inside them is optional
         e.g. **conditional (control) transfer**
  (2) the verb form in English
         e.g. **transfer (to)**
  (3) combined with *or* (or *ou*), an alternative expression (in French or in English)
         e.g. **acoustic store (*or* storage)**
           amplificateur à une sortie (*ou* à sortie simple)
  (4) combined with the sign =, the explanation in full of an abbreviation
         e.g. **a.c. (= alternating current)**

UTILISATION DU DICTIONNAIRE

1. MOT SIMPLE. Si plusieurs traductions équivalentes existent en français, l'ordre n'indique aucune priorité; par ailleurs, les traductions seront différenciées par un chiffre si ce mot peut avoir plusieurs sens en français.

    Ex. **allocate (to),** allouer, affecter

    record, 1. enregistrement *m*; 2. article *m*; 3. rubrique *f*; 4. fiche *f*; 5. relevé *m*;

2. EXPRESSION COMPOSÉE DE DEUX TERMES. Ce type d'expression paraît en deux endroits dans le dictionnaire. La traduction est donnée sous les deux termes.

3. EXPRESSION COMPORTANT PLUS DE DEUX TERMES. Dans la plupart des cas, elle ne paraîtra dans le dictionnaire que sous les premier et dernier termes.

    Ex. **binary to decimal conversion**
    (a) sous **binary**
        b. to decimal conversion, conversion *f* binaire (à) décimal
    (b) sous **conversion**
        binary to decimal c., conversion binaire (à) décimal

Si le mot-clé n'a pas, par lui-même, de signification dans le contexte de l'informatique, sa traduction ne sera donnée que pour les combinaisons de ce mot avec d'autres termes. Enfin, dans certaines expressions composées, le mot-clé peut être difficile à distinguer comme indiqué par l'exemple suivant:

simultaneous mode of working mode *m* (d'exploitation) simultané

Abréviations et signes particuliers utilisés dans le dictionnaire

    m masculin
    f féminin
  adj adjectif
(*Am.*) américain—signale que le terme précédant cette abréviation est plus
      particulièrement utilisé aux Etats-Unis, un terme différent étant employé
      en Grande-Bretagne.
OCR reconnaissance optique de caractères
  ( ) Les parenthèses peuvent indiquer:
  (1) que le terme ou partie de terme inclus est facultatif
      Ex. **conditional (control) transfer**
  (2) la forme verbale en anglais
      Ex. **transfer (to)**
  (3) en combinaison avec *ou* (ou *or*), autre version d'une expression (en français ou en anglais)
      Ex. **acoustic store (or storage)**
        amplificateur à une sortie (*ou* à sortie simple)
  (4) en combinaison avec =, l'explication en toutes lettres d'une abréviation
      Ex. **a.c. (= alternating current)**

A

abacus, abaque *m*.
aberration, aberration *f*.
abnormal, anormal *adj*.; **a. exit**, sortie anormale.
abort (to), abandonner (*un programme*).
aborting, **a. procedure**, procédure *f* d'abandon.
abrasiveness, abrasivité *f*.
abscissa, abscisse *f*.
absolute, absolu *adj*.; réel (-elle) *adj*.; **a. address**, adresse absolue, adresse réelle; **a. addressing**, adressage absolu, adressage réel; **a. code**, code réel (*en langage machine*); **a. coding**, codage absolu; **a. error**, erreur absolue; **a. instruction**, instruction réelle; **a. language**, langage *m* machine; **a. value**, valeur absolue; **a. value computer**, calculateur *m* à valeurs réelles.
absorbency, absorptivité *f*.
abstract, abstrait *adj*.; **a. symbol**, symbole abstrait.
abstract, résumé *m*, abrégé *m*, sommaire *m*; **automatic a.**, résumé automatique, auto-résumé *m*; **descriptive a.**, résumé descriptif.
abstract (to), résumer, abréger.
a.c. (= **alternating current**), courant alternatif; **a.c. coupled flip-flop**, bascule *f* à couplage alternatif (*ou* capacitif); **a. c. dump**, coupure *f* de courant alternatif.
acceleration, **a. time**, temps *m* d'accélération.
acceptance, réception *f*; **a. test**, essai *m* de réception.
accepting, **a. station**, station *f* de réception.
acceptor, 1. accepteur *m*; 2. accepteur (-trice) *adj*.; **a. impurity**, impureté acceptrice.
access, accès *m*; **direct a.**, accès direct, accès sélectif; **immediate a.**, accès immédiat, accès instantané, accès direct; **instantaneous a.**, accès instantané, accès immédiat, accès direct; **multiple a.**, accès multiple; **parallel a.**, accès parallèle; **queued a.**, accès par file d'attente; **random a.**, accès aléatoire, accès sélectif; **remote a.**, accès à distance; **sequence a.**, accès séquentiel; **sequential a.**, accès séquentiel; **serial a.**, accès en série; **simultaneous a.**, accès

simultané; **a. arm**, bras *m* d'accès; **a. conflict**, conflit *m* d'accès; **a. cycle**, cycle *m* d'accès; **a. mechanism**, mécanisme *m* d'accès; **a. method**, méthode *f* d'accès; **a. mode**, mode *m* d'accès; **a. time**, temps *m* d'accès.
account, compte *m*; **a. form**, imprimé *m* de relevé de compte.
accounting, comptabilité *f*; **a. machine**, 1. machine *f* comptable; 2. tabulatrice *f*.
accumulate (to), 1. accumuler; 2. totaliser.
accumulated, **a. total punching**, total *m* de contrôle perforé.
accumulator, 1. accumulateur *m*; 2. accumulateur (-trice) *adj*.; **running a.**, accumulateur circulant; **a. jump instruction**, instruction *f* de saut fonction de l'accumulateur; **a. register**, registre *m* accumulateur; **a. shift instruction**, instruction *f* de décalage dans l'accumulateur; **a. transfer instruction**, instruction *f* de saut fonction de l'accumulateur.
accuracy, exactitude *f*, précision *f*, justesse *f*; **a. control character**, caractère *m* de contrôle de précision; **a. control system**, système *m* de contrôle de précision.
ACK (=**acknowledge character**), (caractère *m*) accusé *m* de réception (positif).
acknowledge, **a. character**, (caractère *m*) accusé *m* de réception (positif).
acknowledgement, accusé *m* de réception; **a. signal**, signal *m* (d')accusé de réception.
acorn, **a. tube**, tube *m* gland.
acoustic, acoustique *adj*.; **a. coupling**, couplage *m* acoustique; **a. delay line**, ligne *f* à retard acoustique; **a. memory**, mémoire *f* acoustique; **a. store** (*or* **storage**), mémoire *f* acoustique.
acquisition, **data a.**, collecte *f* de données, rassemblement *m* de données, saisie *f* de données.
acronym, sigle *m*.
active, actif (-ive) *adj*.; **a. element**, élément actif; **a. file**, fichier actif, fichier vivant; **a. page**, page active; **a. store**, mémoire active; **a. transducer**, transducteur actif.
activity, activité *f*; **a. ratio**, taux *m* d'activité.
actual, réel (-elle) *adj*.; effectif (-ive) *adj*.; **a. address**, adresse absolue, adresse réelle; **a.**

code, code réel (*en langage machine*); **a. coding,** codage absolu; **a. instruction,** instruction réelle; **a. key,** adresse réelle (*en COBOL*); **a. length,** longueur réelle.

actuating, a. mechanism, dispositif *m* de commande, mécanisme *m* de commande.

actuator, dispositif *m* de commande, mécanisme *m* de commande.

A.C.U. (=**automatic calling unit**), dispositif *m* automatique d'appel.

acyclic, acyclique *adj.*; **a. feeding,** alimentation *f* acyclique.

adapter, adapt(at)eur *m*; **line a.,** adapt(at)eur de ligne(s).

adapting, (auto-)adaptatif (-ive) *adj.*; auto-adaptateur (-trice) *adj.*

adaptive, a. control système, *m* à auto-contrôle.

A.D.C. (=**analog to digital converter**), convertisseur *m* analogique-numérique.

add, addition *f*; **Boolean a.,** réunion *f* logique, mélangeur *m*; **false a.,** addition sans report(s); **logical a.,** réunion *f* logique, mélangeur *m*; **a. instruction,** instruction *f* d'addition; **a. operation,** opération *f* d'addition; **a.-subtract time,** durée *f* d'addition/soustraction; **a. time,** durée *f* d'addition; **a. without carry gate,** circuit OU exclusif.

add (to), additionner, ajouter, totaliser.

addend, cumulateur *m*, second terme d'une somme.

adder, additionneur *m*; **analog a.,** additionneur analogique; **binary half a.,** demi-additionneur binaire; **digital a.,** additionneur numérique; **full a.,** additionneur (complet); **half a.,** demi-additionneur; **one-digit a.,** demi-additionneur; **parallel full a.,** additionneur parallèle; **parallel half a.,** demi-additionneur parallèle; **serial full a.,** additionneur série; **serial half a.,** demi-additionneur série; **three-input a.,** additionneur à trois entrées; **two-input a.,** additionneur à deux entrées.

adder-subtracter, additionneur/soustracteur *m*.

adding, addition *f*; **a. machine,** machine *f* à additionner.

addition, addition *f*; **destructive a.,** addition avec effacement; **non-destructive a.,** addition sans effacement; **a. circuit,** circuit *m* d'addition; **a. record,** enregistrement *m* supplémentaire; **a. table,** table *f* d'addition; **a. without carry,** exclusion *f* réciproque, opération *f* de non-équivalence.

additional, a. character, caractère spécial.

additive, additif *m*.

address, adresse *f*; **absolute a.,** adresse absolue, adresse réelle; **actual a.,** adresse absolue, adresse réelle; **arithmetic a.,** adresse arithmétique; **base a.,** adresse de base, adresse origine; **binary coded a.,** adresse codée (en) binaire; **calculated a.,** adresse calculée; **direct a.,** adresse directe, adresse réelle; **effective a.,** adresse effective; **explicit a.,** adresse explicite; **external page a.,** adresse externe de page; **first-level a.,** adresse directe, adresse réelle; **floating a.,** adresse flottante; **four-a.,** à quatre adresses; **four-plus-one a.,** à quatre adresses d'opérande et une adresse de commande; **generated a.,** adresse générée; **immediate a.,** adresse immédiate, adresse directe; **indexed a.,** adresse indexée; **indirect a.,** adresse indirecte; **instruction a.,** adresse d'instruction; **invalid a.,** adresse invalide; **machine a.,** adresse machine, adresse directe; **multi-a.,** à adresses multiples; **multilevel a.,** adresse indirecte; **multiple-a.,** à adresses multiples; **n-level a.,** à n niveaux d'adressage; **one-a.,** à une adresse; **one-level a.,** adresse directe, adresse réelle; **one-plus-one a.,** à une adresse d'opérande et une adresse de commande; **original a.,** adresse d'origine; **presumptive a.,** adresse de base, adresse origine; **reference a.,** adresse de base, adresse origine; **relative a.,** adresse relative; **relocatable a.,** adresse relogeable, adresse translatable; **return a.,** adresse de retour; **second-level a.,** adresse indirecte à deux niveaux; **seek a.,** adresse de recherche; **single-a.,** à une adresse; **single-level a.,** adresse directe, adresse réelle; **specific a.,** adresse absolue, adresse réelle; **symbolic a.,** adresse symbolique; **synthetic a.,** adresse générée; **third-level a.,** adresse indirecte à trois niveaux; **three-a.,** à trois adresses; **three-level a.,** adresse indirecte à trois niveaux; **three-plus-one a.,** à trois adresses d'opérande et une adresse de commande; **two-a.,** à deux adresses; **two-level a.,** adresse indirecte à deux niveaux; **two-plus-one a.,** à deux adresses d'opérande et une adresse de commande; **variable a.,** adresse indexée; **virtual a.,** adresse virtuelle; **zero-level a.,** adresse immédiate, adresse directe; **zero-relative a.,** adresse calculée par rapport à zéro; **a. code,** code *m* d'adresse; **a. computation,** calcul *m* d'adresse; **a. constant,** adresse de base, adresse origine; **a. conversion,** calcul *m* d'adresses (réelles); **a. format,** format *m* d'adresse; **a. generation,** génération *f* d'adresses; **a. modification,** modification *f* d'adresse; **a. part,** partie *f* adresse (*d'une instruction*); **a. register,** registre *m* d'adresse; **a. selection,** sélection *f* d'adresse; **a. substitution,** substitution *f* d'adresses; **a. track,** piste *f* d'adresses.

address (to), adresser.

addressable, adressable *adj.*; **a. store,** mémoire *f* adressable.

addressed, adressé *adj.*; **a. system,** système adressé.

addressee, destinataire *m ou f.*

addressing, adressage *m*; **absolute a.,** adressage absolu, adressage réel; **deferred a.,** adressage indirect à plusieurs niveaux; **direct a.,** adressage direct; **group a.,** adressage de groupe; **immediate a.,** adressage immédiat, adressage direct; **implied a.,** adressage à progression automatique avancée; **indirect a.,** adressage indirect; **multilevel a.,** adressage indirect; **one-ahead a.,** adressage à progression automatique avancée; **relative a.,** adressage relatif; **repetitive a.,** adressage à progression automatique; **second-level a.,** adressage indirect à deux niveaux; **specific a.,** adressage absolu, adressage réel; **stepped a.,** adressage à progression automatique avancée; **symbolic a.,** adressage symbolique; **three-level a.,** adressage indirect à trois niveaux; **two-level a.,** adressage indirect à deux niveaux; **zero-level a.,** adressage immédiat, adressage direct; **a. level,** niveau *m* d'adressage; **a. system,** système *m* d'adressage.

addressless, sans adresse; **a. instruction format,** format *m* d'instruction sans adresse.

adjacency, proximité *f*; **a. matrix,** matrice *f* d'incidence.

adjacent, adjacent *adj.*; **a. channel,** voie adjacente; **a. channel interference,** interférence adjacente; **a. channel selectivity,** sélectivité adjacente; **a. vertex,** sommet adjacent.

adjust (to), ajuster, régler.

adjustable, ajustable *adj.*; réglable *adj.*; **a. point,** virgule *f* réglable.

administrative, administratif (-ive) *adj.*; **a. data processing,** informatique *f* de gestion, traitement *m* de l'information en gestion; **a. information,** information *f* de gestion.

admittance, admittance *f*; **transfer a.,** admittance de transfert.

A.D.P. (=**automatic data processing**), traitement *m* automatique de l'information, traitement *m* automatique des données.

A.D.U. (=**automatic dialling unit**), dispositif *m* automatique de sélection.

advance, item a., balayage *m* d'articles (*en mémoire*).

aerial, 1. antenne *f*; **2.** aérien (-enne) *adj.*; **a. cable,** câble aérien, fil aérien.

AF (=**audio frequency**), basse fréquence (BF), fréquence *f* acoustique, fréquence *f* audible, audiofréquence *f*.

ageing, vieillissement *m*.

aids, aides *f*; **programming a.,** aides à la programmation.

air, air *m*; **a. conditioning,** conditionnement *m* d'air, climatisation *f*; **a. gap,** entrefer *m*.

alarm, audible a., (signal *m* d')alarme *f* sonore.

aleatory, aléatoire *adj.*

alert, alerte *f*, incident *m*; **read a.,** incident de lecture.

alf, alpha.

algebra, algèbre *f*; **Boolean a.,** algèbre booléenne; **matrix a.,** algèbre matricielle.

algebraic, algébrique *adj.*; **a. function,** fonction *f* algébrique; **a. language,** langage *m* algébrique.

ALGOL (=**ALGorithmic Oriented Language**), ALGOL.

algorithm, algorithme *m*; **translation a.,** algorithme de traduction (*de langages*); **a. translation,** traduction *f* algorithmique.

algorithmic, algorithmique *adj.*; **a. language,** langage *m* algorithmique; **a. routine,** programme *m* algorithmique.

alias, étiquette équivalente.

aligner, dispositif *m* d'alignement,

mécanisme *m* d'alignement; **a. area,** piste *f* d'alignement.

alignment, alignement *m*; **contact a.,** alignement de contacts; **document a.,** alignement de documents.

allocate (to), allouer, affecter.

allocation, allocation *f*, affectation *f*; **direct a.,** allocation fixe; **dynamic a.,** allocation dynamique; **dynamic store (or storage) a.,** allocation dynamique de mémoire; **group a.,** répartition *f* des groupes primaires; **store (or storage) a.,** allocation de mémoire; **supergroup a.,** répartition *f* des groupes secondaires.

all-purpose, universel (-elle) *adj.*; polyvalent *adj.*; **a.-p. computer,** calculateur universel, calculateur polyvalent; **a.-p. meter,** polymètre *m*, multimètre *m*, appareil *m* de mesure universel.

all-relay, a.-r. system (*Am.*), système *m* automatique tout à relais.

alpha, alpha.

alphabet, alphabet *m*; **telegraph a.,** alphabet télégraphique.

alphabetic(al), alphabétique *adj.*; **a. character set,** jeu *m* de caractères alphabétiques; **a. character subset,** jeu partiel de caractères alphabétiques; **a. code,** code *m* alphabétique; **a. coded character set,** jeu *m* de caractères codés alphabétiques; **a. data code,** code *m* alphabétique; **a. signal,** signal *m* alphabétique; **a. string,** chaîne *f* (de caractères) alphabétique(s); **a. word,** mot *m* alphabétique.

alphameric, alphanumérique *adj.*; **a. code,** code *m* alphanumérique.

alphanumeric, alphanumérique *adj.*; **a. character set,** jeu *m* de caractères alphanumériques; **a. character subset,** jeu partiel de caractères alphanumériques; **a. code,** code *m* alphanumérique; **a. coded character set,** jeu *m* de caractères codés alphanumériques; **a. data,** données *f* alphanumériques; **a. data code,** code *m* alphanumérique; **a. information,** information *f* alphanumérique; **a. instruction,** instruction *f* alphanumérique; **a. machine,** machine *f* alphanumérique; **a. sorting,** tri *m* alphanumérique.

alteration, modification *f*, changement *m*; **a. switch,** inverseur *m*.

alternate, a. operation, exploitation *f* à l'alternat; **a. routing,** voie *f* de déroutement, déviation *f*.

alternating, alternatif (-ive) *adj.*; **a. current (a.c.),** courant alternatif.

alternation, opération *f* OU; **tape a.,** travail *m* en bascule sur dérouleurs; **a. gate,** circuit *m* OU.

alternative, a. denial, opération *f* NON-ET; **a. denial gate,** circuit *m* NON-ET.

A.L.U. (=arithmetic and logical unit), unité *f* arithmétique et logique.

AM (=amplitude modulation), modulation *f* d'amplitude; **AM detector,** détecteur *m* AM (*ou* MA).

ambient, ambiant *adj.*; **a. noise,** bruit ambiant.

ambiguity, ambiguïté *f*; **a. error,** erreur *f* d'ambiguïté.

amendment, a. file, fichier *m* (des) mouvements, fichier *m* (de) détail; **a. record,** enregistrement *m* (de) mouvement, enregistrement *m* (de) détail; **a. tape,** bande *f* (des) mouvements.

ammeter, ampèremètre *m*.

amphibolous, ambigu (-uë) *adj.*; équivoque *adj.*

amphiboly, ambiguïté *f*.

amplification, amplification *f*; **a. factor,** facteur *m* d'amplification.

amplifier, 1. amplificateur *m*; 2. amplificateur (-trice) *adj.*; **audio a.,** amplificateur BF (*ou* basse fréquence); **buffer a.,** amplificateur tampon, amplificateur intermédiaire; **chopper-stabilized a.,** amplificateur à découpage; **computing a.,** amplificateur calculateur; **differential a.,** amplificateur différentiel; **differentiating a.,** amplificateur différentiateur; **direct current a.,** amplificateur à couplage direct; **directly coupled a.,** amplificateur à couplage direct; **double-ended a.,** amplificateur push-pull, amplificateur symétrique; **drift-corrected a.,** amplificateur à compensation de dérive; **feedback a.,** amplificateur à réaction; **high-gain a.,** amplificateur à gain élevé (*ou* à grand gain); **integrating a.,** amplificateur intégrateur; **inverting a.,** amplificateur inverseur (*ou* changeur) de signe; **multirange a.,** amplificateur multigain; **operational a.,** amplificateur calculateur; **pulse a.,**

amplificateur d'impulsions; **push-pull a.**, amplificateur push-pull, amplificateur symétrique; **relay a.**, amplificateur-relais *m*; **resistance-coupled a.**, amplificateur à couplage par résistance; **sign-changing a.**, amplificateur inverseur (*ou* changeur) de signe; **sign-reversing a.**, amplificateur inverseur (*ou* changeur) de signe; **single-ended a.**, amplificateur à une sortie (*ou* à sortie simple); **summing a.**, amplificateur de sommation; **telephone a.**, répéteur *m* téléphonique; **torque a.**, coupleur synchronisé; **wideband a.**, amplificateur à large bande; **a. circuit**, circuit amplificateur; **a. gain**, gain *m* d'un amplificateur; **a. tube,** tube amplificateur, lampe amplificatrice; **a. valve,** tube amplificateur, lampe amplificatrice.

amplitude, amplitude *f*; **pulse a.**, amplitude d'impulsion; **a.-change signalling,** (formation *f* des signaux par) modulation *f* d'amplitude; **a. distortion,** distorsion *f* d'amplitude; **a. modulation (AM),** modulation *f* d'amplitude.

analog, analogique *adj.*; **network a.,** réseau *m* d'étude analogique; **a. adder,** additionneur *m* analogique; **a. channel,** voic *f* analogique; **a. comparator,** comparateur *m* analogique; **a. computer,** calculateur *m* analogique; **a. data,** données *f* analogiques; **a. demodulation,** démodulation *f* analogique; **a. device,** dispositif *m* analogique; **a. divider,** diviseur *m* analogique; **a. integration,** intégration *f* analogique; **a. multiplier,** multiplicateur *m* analogique; **a. network,** réseau *m* analogique; **a. representation,** représentation *f* analogique; **a. to digital converter,** convertisseur *m* analogique-numérique; **a. transmission,** transmission *f* analogique.

analyser, 1. analyseur *m*; **2.** programme *m* analyseur; **differential a.,** analyseur différentiel, calculateur analogique différentiel; **digital differential a. (d.d.a.),** analyseur différentiel numérique, calculateur numérique différentiel; **electronic differential a.,** analyseur différentiel électronique; **mechanical differential a.,** analyseur différentiel mécanique; **network a.,** simulateur *m* (d'étude) de réseaux.

analysis, analyse *f*; **contour a.,** suivi *m* des contours; **critical path a.,** analyse de chemin critique; **information flow a.,** analyse de circulation de l'information; **logic a.,** analyse logique; **matrix a.,** analyse matricielle; **numerical a.,** analyse numérique; **operations a.,** recherche opérationnelle; **stroke a.,** analyse par traits élémentaires (*ou* segments) (*OCR*); **systems a.,** analyse de systèmes.

analyst, analyste *m ou f*; **systems a.,** analyste de systèmes.

analytical function, a.f. generator, générateur *m* de fonctions analytiques.

anchorage, adhérence *f*.

ancillary, auxiliaire *adj.*; d'appoint, secondaire *adj.*; **a. equipment,** matériel *m* auxiliaire.

AND, ET, conjonction *f*, affirmation *f* connexe, intersection *f* logique; **AND circuit,** circuit *m* ET; **AND element,** élément *m* ET, intersecteur *m*; **AND gate,** circuit *m* ET; **AND operation,** opération *f* ET; **AND operator,** opérateur *m* ET; **AND unit,** élément *m* ET.

angle, angle *m*; **a. modulation,** modulation *f* d'angle.

annotate (to), annoter.

annotation, annotation *f*.

annular, annulaire *adj.*; **a. magnet,** aimant *m* torique.

annunciator, annonciateur *m*.

answer, réponse *f*; **a. lamp,** lampe *f* de réponse; **a. signal,** signal *m* de réponse.

answerback, réponse *f*; **a. code,** indicatif *m*; **a. unit,** émetteur *m* automatique d'indicatif.

answering, unattended a., réponse *f* automatique; **a. jack,** jack *m* de réponse.

antiblocking, antibourrage *m*.

anticoincidence, a. circuit, circuit *m* de non-équivalence; **a. element,** élément *m* de non-équivalence, élément OU exclusif; **a. gate,** circuit *m* de non-équivalence, circuit OU exclusif; **a. unit,** circuit *m* de non-équivalence.

antijamming, antibourrage *m*.

antisetoff, a. powder, poudre *f* anti-maculage (*OCR*).

aperiodic, apériodique *adj.*

aperture, ouverture *f*, trou *m*; **a. card,** carte *f* à fenêtre; **a. plate,** plaque *f* à trous.

apostrophe, apostrophe *f*.

apparatus, appareil *m*; **duplex a.,** appareil

duplex; **start–stop a.,** appareil arythmique.

apparent, apparent *adj.*; **a. power,** puissance apparente.

application, application *f*; **computer a.,** application de l'ordinateur; **inquiry a.,** consultation *f* (de fichier); **slave a.,** application en mode asservi; **standby a.,** application avec système(s) auxiliaire(s) (*ou* de secours); **a. study,** étude *f* d'application.

approach, heuristic a., méthode *f* heuristique.

arbitrary, a. function generator, générateur *m* de fonctions polyvalent; **am sequence computer,** calculateur séquentiel à enchaînement arbitraire.

area, zone *f*; **aligner a.,** piste *f* d'alignement; **cell a.,** surface *f* élémentaire d'analyse (*OCR*); **clear a.,** zone à ne pas marquer; **common (storage) a.,** zone commune de mémoire; **constant a.,** zone de constantes; **dynamic a.,** zone dynamique; **input a.,** zone d'entrée, zone d'introduction; **input/output a.,** zone d'entrée-sortie; **instruction a.,** zone (de stockage) d'instruction(s), zone de programme; **local service a.,** zone de taxation urbaine (*ou* locale); **non-dynamic a.,** zone statique, partie *f* statique; **operating a.,** zone de travail, zone de manœuvre; **output a.,** zone de sortie, zone d'extraction; **reserved a.,** zone réservée; **seek a.,** zone de recherche (accélérée); **storage a.,** zone de mémoire, zone de stockage; **working a.,** zone de travail, zone de manœuvre; **a. search,** recherche *f* de zone.

argument, 1. argument *m*; **2.** variable indépendante; **3.** mantisse *f* (*en représentation à virgule flottante*).

arithmetic, arithmétique *f*; **double-precision a.,** arithmétique en double précision; **external a.,** fonction *f* de calcul externe; **fixed-point a.,** arithmétique à virgule fixe; **floating decimal a.,** arithmétique à virgule flottante; **floating-point a.,** arithmétique à virgule flottante; **internal a.,** arithmétique interne; **multiple a.,** calcul *m* à plusieurs résultats; **multiple-length a.,** fonctionnement *m* en longueur multiple; **multi-precision a.,** arithmétique à précision multiple; **parallel a.,** arithmétique (en) parallèle; **partial a.,** calcul *m* à un seul résultat; **serial a.,** arithmétique (en) série.

arithmetic(al), arithmétique *adj.*; **a. address,** adresse *f* arithmétique; **a. and logical unit (A.L.U.),** unité *f* arithmétique et logique; **a. check,** contrôle *m* arithmétique; **a. computer,** calculateur *m* arithmétique; **a. instruction,** instruction *f* arithmétique; **a. operation,** opération *f* arithmétique; **a. organ,** unité *f* arithmétique; **a. point,** virgule *f*; **a. product,** produit *m* arithmétique; **a. register,** registre *m* arithmétique; **a. section,** unité *f* arithmétique; **a. shift,** décalage *m* arithmétique; **a. sum,** somme *f* arithmétique; **a. unit,** unité *f* arithmétique.

arm, bras *m*; **access a.,** bras d'accès; **picker a.,** bras d'alimentation; **positioning a.,** bras de positionnement.

array, 1. tableau *m*; **2.** rangée transversale; **3.** matrice *f* (*ou* plan *m*) (*de mémoire*); **core a.,** matrice de tores; **data a.,** arrangement *m* de données; **a. pitch,** pas longitudinal, interligne *m*.

artificial, artificiel (-elle) *adj.*; **a. intelligence,** intelligence artificielle; **a. language,** langage artificiel; **a. line,** ligne artificielle; **a. load,** circuit *m* de charge fictif; **a. perception,** perception artificielle.

ascending, a. order, ordre croissant.

ASCII, =USASCII.

A.S.R. (=**automatic send/receive**), téléimprimeur *m* automatique d'émission-réception.

assemble (to), assembler, compiler.

assembled, a. card deck, paquet *m* de cartes-programme en langage machine.

assembler, assembleur *m*, programme *m* d'assemblage; **one-to-one a.,** assembleur un(e) pour un(e).

assembly, 1. ensemble *m*; **2.** assemblage *m*; **brush a.,** ensemble porte-balais; **job a.,** préparation *f* des travaux; **work a.,** préparation *f* des travaux; **a. language,** langage *m* d'assemblage; **a. list,** liste *f* d'assemblage; **a. listing,** impression *f* d'assemblage; **a. program,** assembleur *m*, programme *m* d'assemblage; **a. routine,** assembleur *m*, programme *m* d'assemblage; **a. system,** système *m* d'assemblage; **a. unit, 1.** unité *f* d'assemblage; **2.** segment *m* (de programme) assemblable.

assign (to), affecter, allouer.

assignment, affectation *f.*
associative, a. store (*or* **storage**), mémoire associative.
assumed, a. decimal point, virgule *f* implicite.
astable, a. multivibrator, multivibrateur *m* astable.
asymmetrical, asymétrique; **a. distortion,** distorsion *f* dissymétrique; **a. sideband transmission,** transmission *f* à bandes latérales asymétriques, transmission *f* avec bande latérale partiellement supprimée.
asynchronous, asynchrone *adj.*; **a. computer,** calculateur *m* asynchrone, calculateur *m* arythmique; **a. device,** dispositif *m* asynchrone; **a. machine,** machine *f* asynchrone; **a. mode,** mode *m* asynchrone; **a. operation,** fonctionnement *m* asynchrone; **a. transmission,** transmission *f* asynchrone; **a. working,** fonctionnement *m* asynchrone.
asyndetic, asyndétique *adj.*
attended, a. station, station surveillée.
attention, a. device, dispositif *m* d'appel d'attention.
attenuate (to), atténuer.
attenuation, atténuation *f*, affaiblissement *m*; **crosstalk a.,** affaiblissement diaphonique; **echo a.,** atténuation d'échos, affaiblissement des courants d'échos; **signal a.,** atténuation de signaux; **a. coefficient,** constante *f* d'affaiblissement, affaiblissement linéique; **a. distortion,** distorsion *f* d'affaiblissement; **a. equalizer,** compensateur *m* d'affaiblissement; **a. pad,** atténuateur *m* fixe.
attenuator, atténuateur *m.*
attribute, attribut *m*, caractéristique *f*; **default a.,** attribut par défaut.
audible, a. alarm, (signal *m* d')alarme *f* sonore.
audio, a. amplifier, amplificateur *m* BF (*ou* basse fréquence); **a. frequency,** basse fréquence (BF), fréquence *f* acoustique, fréquence *f* audible, audiofréquence *f*; **a. response unit,** unité *f* de réponse vocale.
audit, vérification *f*; **a. list,** liste *f* de contrôle.
augend, cumulande *m*, premier terme d'une somme.
auto-abstract, auto-résumé *m*, résumé *m* automatique.

auto-answer, auto-réponse *f.*
autobalance, mécanisme *m* différentiateur.
autocode, autocode *m.*
autocoder, autocodeur *m.*
autocorrelation, autocorrélation *f.*
auto-index, auto-répertoire *m*, auto-index *m.*
auto-man, automatique-manuel (-elle) *adj.*
automata, a. theory, théorie *f* des automates.
automated, automatisé *adj.*; **a. data medium,** support *m* exploitable sur machine; **a. management,** gestion automatisée; **a. production management,** gestion *f* de production automatisée.
automatic, automatique *adj.*; **a. abstract,** résumé *m* automatique; **a. calling unit,** dispositif *m* automatique d'appel; **a. carriage,** chariot *m* automatique; **a. check,** contrôle *m* automatique; **a. code,** code *m* automatique; **a. coding,** codage *m* automatique; **a. computer,** calculateur *m* automatique; **a. control,** commande *f* automatique, contrôle *m* automatique, régulation *f* automatique; **a. control engineering,** automatique *f*; **a. controller,** unité *f* de commande (*ou* de contrôle *ou* de régulation) automatique; **a. data processing,** traitement *m* automatique de l'information, traitement *m* automatique des données; **a. data processing equipment,** matériel *m* de traitement automatique des données (*ou* de l'information); **a. data processing system,** système *m* automatique de traitement de l'information; **a. data switching centre,** centre *m* de prise en charge automatique de données; **a. dialling unit,** dispositif *m* automatique de sélection; **a. dictionary,** dictionnaire *m* automatique; **a. error correction,** correction *f* d'erreurs automatique; **a. error detection,** détection *f* d'erreurs automatique; **a. exchange,** central *m* automatique, centre *m* automatique; **a. feed punch,** perforateur *m* à alimentation automatique (de cartes); **a. message switching,** commutation *f* automatique de messages; **a. message switching centre,** centre *m* automatique de commutation de messages; **a. numbering transmitter,** numéroteur *m* automatique; **a. programming,** programmation *f* automatique; **a.**

punch, perforateur *m* automatique; **a. repetition,** répétition *f* automatique; **a. reset,** rétablissement *m* automatique; **a. routine,** programme *m* automatique; **a. send/receive,** téléimprimeur *m* automatique d'émission-réception; **a. sequence-controlled calculator,** calculateur *m* automatique à séquence contrôlée; **a. sequential operation,** fonctionnement séquentiel automatique; **a. signalling, 1.** signalisation *f* automatique; **2.** transmission *f* automatique des signaux; **a. stop,** arrêt *m* automatique; **a. store,** mémoire *f* interne; **a. switching centre,** centre *m* de commutation automatique; **a. switching equipment,** matériel *m* de commutation automatique; **a. system,** système *m* automatique; **a. tape punch,** perforateur *m* de bande automatique; **a. tape relay,** retransmission *f* automatique par bande perforée; **a. telegraphy** (*Am.*), transmission *f* automatique; **a. teleprinter service,** liaison *f* automatique par téléimprimeur; **a. telex exchange,** central *m* télex automatique; **a. telex facilities,** service *m* automatique télex; **a. transmission,** transmission *f* automatique; **a. transmitter,** émetteur *m* automatique, transmetteur *m* automatique; **a. typesetting,** composition *f* automatique (des textes); **a. verifier,** vérificatrice *f* automatique; **a. volume-contractor,** compresseur *m*; **a. volume-expander,** extenseur *m*, expanseur *m*.

automatically, a. programmed tools, machines-outils *f* à programme (*ou* à commande) automatique.

automatics, automatique *f*.

automation, automatisation *f*; **design a.,** automatisation d'étude; **source data a.,** automatisation des données de base.

automatization, automatisation *f*.

automonitor, auto-contrôle *m*.

autonomous, autonome *adj.*; **a. working,** fonctionnement *m* autonome.

autopolling, appel sélectif automatique.

auxiliary, auxiliaire *adj.*, d'appoint, secondaire *adj.*; **a. data,** données *f* auxiliaires; **a. equipment,** matériel *m* auxiliaire; **a. operation,** opération *f* auxiliaire; **a. route,** voie *f* auxiliaire; **a. routine,** programme *m* auxiliaire; **a. station, 1.** station *f* auxiliaire; **2.** station téléalimentée; **a. store (or**

storage),** mémoire *f* auxiliaire.

availability, disponibilité *f*; **a. ratio,** taux *m* de disponibilité.

available, disponible *adj.*; **a. power,** puissance *f* (maximum) disponible; **a. time,** temps *m* disponible.

average, a. calculating operation, opération *f* de calcul moyenne; **a. data-transfer rate,** vitesse effective de transfert de données, débit effectif; **a.-edge line,** ligne *f* de contour moyenne; **a.-effectiveness level,** niveau *m* d'efficacité moyenne; **a. operation time,** temps moyen d'exploitation; **a. transmission rate,** vitesse effective de transfert de données, débit effectif.

awaiting, a. repair time, (temps *m* d')attente *f* de dépannage.

axis, reference a., axe *m* de référence.

azimuth, azimut *m*.

B

back (of a card), verso *m* (d'une carte), dos *m* (d'une carte); **card b.,** verso d'une carte, dos d'une carte.

background, arrière-plan *m*; **b. noise,** bruit *m* de fond; **b. printing,** impression *f* du fond (*OCR*); **b. processing,** traitement *m* non prioritaire; **b. program,** programme *m* non prioritaire; **b. reflectance,** réflectance *f* de fond (*OCR*).

backgrounding, traitement *m* non prioritaire.

backing, b. store (*or* storage), mémoire *f* auxiliaire.

backlash, jeu *m*.

backlog, arriéré *m* (de travail).

backspace, espace *m* arrière, retour *m* arrière; **b. character,** caractère *m* espace arrière.

backspace (to), effectuer un retour arrière.

backward, b. channel, voie *f* de retour; **b. sort,** tri décroissant.

badge, jeton *m*, «badge» *m*, plaque *f* d'identification; **b. reader,** lecteur *m* de jetons, lecteur *m* de «badges».

balance, balance *f*, solde *m*; **b. error,** erreur *f* d'équilibrage.

balanced, équilibré *adj.*; **b. circuit,** circuit

équilibré, circuit *m* symétrique; **b. error range,** plage *f* d'erreurs à valeur moyenne nulle; **b. line,** ligne équilibrée; **b. transmission line,** ligne équilibrée.

balancing, b. network, réseau *m* d'équilibrage, équilibreur *m*.

banana, b. plug, fiche *f* banane.

band, 1. piste *f*; 2. bande *f* (de fréquence); **calling b.,** bande d'appel; **clear b.,** zone *f* à ne pas marquer; **frequency b.,** bande de fréquences; **guard b.,** bande de garde; **pass b.,** bande passante; **voice-frequency b.,** bande de fréquence vocale; **b. elimination filter** (*Am.*), filtre *m* à élimination de bande; **b.-pass filter,** filtre *m* passe-bande; **b. rejection filter,** filtre *m* à élimination de bande; **b.-stop filter,** filtre *m* à élimination de bande.

bandwidth, largeur *f* de bande; **nominal b.,** largeur de bande nominale.

bank, core b., bloc *m* de mémoire (à tores); **data b.,** banque *f* de données.

bar, barre *f*, barreau *m*; **fixed type b.,** barre d'impression fixe; **interchangeable b.,** barre d'impression amovible; **print b.,** barre d'impression; **type b.,** barre d'impression, barre porte-caractères; **b. magnet,** barreau aimanté, aimant droit; **b. printer,** imprimante *f* à barres.

bar-code, b.-c. scanner, analyseur *m* de code à bâtonnets.

barrel, print b., cylindre *m* d'impression; **b. printer,** imprimante *f* à la volée.

barrier, b. layer, couche *f* d'arrêt.

base, 1. base *f* (des puissances); 2. (*of a notation*) base *f* (de numération); **complement b.,** base du complément; **corporate data b.,** base de données de l'entreprise; **data b.,** base de données; **floating-point b.,** base de séparation flottante, base (de numération) à virgule flottante; **napierian b.,** base des logarithmes népériens; **time b.,** base de temps, rythme *m*; **b. address,** adresse *f* de base, adresse *f* origine; **b. notation,** numération *f* à base; **b. register,** registre *m* de base.

baseband, bande *f* de base.

based, b. variable, variable pointée (*PL/1*).

BASIC (=**Beginner's All-purpose Symbolic Instruction Code**), BASIC.

basic, de base; **b. access method,** méthode *f* d'accès de base; **b. code,** code réel (*en langage machine*); **b. coding,** codage *m* de base; **b. control (BC) mode,** mode *m* de base, mode BC, mode 360; **b. language,** langage non évolué; **b. linkage,** liaison *f* de base; **b. operating system,** système *m* d'exploitation de base; **b. signal,** signal *m* de base; **b. telecommunication access method (B.T.A.M.),** méthode *f* d'accès de base en télétraitement.

batch, lot *m* (de données); **b. processing,** 1. traitement *m* par lots, traitement différé; 2. traitement *m* en série; **b. total,** total *m* par groupe.

batching, groupement *m*, groupage *m*.

Batten, B. check, contrôle visuel.

battery, station b., alimentation *f* (en électricité) d'une station.

baud, baud *m*.

Baudot, B. code, code *m* Baudot.

bay, 1. bâti *m*; 2. armoire *f*; 3. section *f*.

B box, registre *m* d'index.

B.C.D. (=**binary coded decimal**), décimal codé binaire.

BC mode (=**basic control mode**), mode *m* de base, mode BC, mode 360.

bead, ferrite b., tore *m* de ferrite; **b. memory,** mémoire *f* à tores de ferrite.

beam, faisceau *m*; **electron b.,** faisceau électronique; **holding b.,** faisceau d'accumulation, faisceau de régénération; **b. store,** mémoire *f* à faisceau(x).

beat, battement *m*.

bed, card b., chemin *m* de cartes.

beginning, b. of information mark(er), marque *f* de début d'information (sur bande); **b. of tape mark(er),** marque *f* de début de bande.

bel, bel *m*.

BEL (=**bell character**), caractère *m* sonnerie, caractère *m* appel.

belt, courroie *f*; **drive b.,** courroie d'entraînement, courroie de transmission; **picker b.,** courroie d'alimentation.

benchmark, 1. point *m* de référence; 2. banc *m* d'essai; **b. problem,** problème *m* de référence, problème *m* d'évaluation comparative.

B-H curve, courbe *f* de magnétisation.

bias, 1. écart *m*; 2. (tension *f* de) polarisation *f*; **ordering b.,** 1. écart d'ordre; 2. séquence préexistante (*dans un tri*); **b. check,** contrôle *m* par marges, test *m* de marges; **b.**

distortion, distorsion *f* dissymétrique; **b. test(ing),** test *m* de marges, contrôle *m* par marges.

bibliography, bibliographie *f.*

biconditional, b. gate, circuit NI exclusif; **b. operation,** opération *f* d'équivalence.

bidirectional, b. flow, transfert bilatéral.

bigit, bit *m*, chiffre *m* binaire, poids *m* binaire.

bin, 1. puits *m*; 2. récipient *m*.

binary, binaire *adj.*; **Chinese b.,** binaire par colonne; **column b.,** binaire par colonne; **normal b.,** binaire pur; **ordinary b.,** binaire pur; **regular b.,** binaire pur; **row b.,** binaire par rangée; **straight b.,** binaire pur; **b. arithmetical operation,** opération *f* binaire arithmétique; **b. Boolean operation,** opération booléenne diadique; **b. card,** carte *f* binaire; **b. cell,** élément *m* binaire; **b. character,** caractère *m* binaire; **b. chop,** recherche *f* dichotomique; **b. code,** code *m* binaire; **b. coded address,** adresse codée (en) binaire; **b. coded character,** caractère codé (en) binaire; **b. coded decimal (B.C.D.),** décimal codé binaire; **b. coded decimal notation,** notation (*ou* numération) décimale (codée en) binaire; **b. coded decimal number,** nombre décimal codé binaire; **b. coded decimal representation,** numération décimale (codée en) binaire, représentation *f* (en) décimal codé binaire; **b. coded decimal system,** système décimal codé binaire; **b. coded notation,** représentation codée en binaire; **b. coded octal,** octal codé binaire; **b. coding,** codage *m* binaire; **b. column,** colonne *f* (en) binaire; **b. counter,** compteur *m* binaire; **b. deck,** jeu *m* de cartes en binaire; **b. digit,** bit *m*, chiffre *m* binaire, poids *m* binaire; **b. dump,** vidage *m* (en) binaire; **b. element,** élément *m* binaire, binon *m*; **b. element string,** chaîne *f* d'éléments binaires; **b. equivalent,** équivalent *m* binaire d'une combinaison alphabétique; **b. half adder,** demi-additionneur *m* binaire; **b. image,** image *f* binaire; **b. incremental representation,** représentation *f* par accroissements binaires; **b. mode,** mode *m* binaire; **b. notation,** notation *f* binaire; **b. number,** nombre *m* binaire; **b. number system,** système *m* de nombres binaires; **b. numeral,** nombre *m* binaire; **b. one,** «un» binaire; **b. operation,** opération *f* binaire; **b. pair,** bascule *f*; **b. point,** virgule *f* (en) binaire; **b. representation,** représentation *f* binaire; **b. scale,** notation *f* binaire; **b. search,** recherche *f* binaire, recherche *f* dichotomique; **b.-state variable,** variable *f* binaire; **b. to decimal conversion,** conversion *f* binaire (à) décimal; **b. unit,** unité *f* binaire; **b. variable,** variable *f* binaire; **b. weight,** poids *m* (d'une position) binaire; **b. zero,** zéro *m* binaire.

bionics, bionique *f.*

bipolar, bipolaire *adj.*

biquinary, biquinaire *adj.*; **b. code,** code *m* biquinaire; **b. coded decimal number,** nombre décimal codé biquinaire; **b. notation,** notation *f* biquinaire; **b. number,** nombre *m* biquinaire.

bistable, bistable *adj.*; **b. multivibrator,** bascule *f*; **b. (trigger) circuit,** bascule *f.*

bit, bit *m*, chiffre *m* binaire, poids *m* binaire; **check b.,** bit de contrôle; **erroneous b.,** bit erroné; **information b.,** bit d'information; **overhead b.,** bit supplémentaire; **parity b.,** bit de parité; **presence b.,** bit indicateur de présence; **service b.,** bit de service; **sign b.,** bit de signe; **stop b.,** élément *m* d'arrêt; **zone b.,** bit (d'information) complémentaire; **b. configuration,** configuration *f* binaire; **b. density,** densité *f* en (nombre de) bits; **b. error rate,** taux *m* d'erreurs sur les bits; **b. location,** emplacement *m* (de stockage) d'un bit; **b. pattern,** profil *m* binaire; **b. position,** position *f* binaire; **b. rate,** débit *m* binaire, vitesse *f* de transmission de bits; **b. stream,** signal *m* binaire; **b. string,** chaîne *f* de chiffres binaires.

bits, framing b., bits *m* de synchronisation; **sync. b.,** bits *m* de synchronisation.

blank, 1. vierge *adj.*; 2. disponible *adj.*; 3. blanc *m*; **b. card,** carte *f* vierge; **b. character,** caractère *m* espace; **b. coil,** bobine *f* de bande non perforée; **b. column,** colonne *f* vierge; **b. column detector,** détecteur *m* de colonnes vierges; **b. deleter,** suppresseur *m* d'espaces; **b. form,** imprimé *m* vierge; **b. instruction,** instruction *f* factice, instruction *f* de remplissage; **b. medium,** support *m* vierge; **b. paper tape coil,** bobine *f* de bande non perforée; **b. spool,** bobine *f* (*de bande perforée*) sans enregistrement; **b. tape,** bande *f* vierge.

blind (to), interdire (la transmission de

données), inhiber.

B line, registre *m* d'index.

blister, verrue *f* (de programme).

block, 1. bloc *m*; **2.** zone *f*; **control b.,** zone de contrôle (*p.ex.* du système d'exploitation); **data control b.,** zone de contrôle (de transfert de données); **erroneous b.,** bloc erroné; **input b.,** zone d'entrée, zone d'introduction; **output b.,** zone de sortie, zone d'extraction; **queue control b.,** zone de contrôle de file d'attente; **standby b.,** bloc de réserve, bloc de secours; **storage b.,** zone de mémoire; **table b.,** subdivision *f* de table; **task control b.,** zone de contrôle (d'enchaînement) de travaux; **variable b.,** bloc à longueur variable; **b. cancel character,** caractère *m* de rejet de bloc, caractère *m* d'annulation de bloc; **b. check,** contrôle *m* par bloc; **b. diagram,** schéma fonctionnel, schéma *m* synoptique; **b. error rate,** taux *m* d'erreurs sur les blocs; **b. gap,** espace *m* inter-blocs; **b. ignore character,** caractère *m* de rejet de bloc, caractère *m* d'annulation de bloc; **b. length,** longueur *f* de bloc; **b. loading,** chargement groupé; **b. mark,** marque *f* de bloc; **b. multiplexor channel,** canal *m* multiple par blocs; **b. sort,** tri *m* par sous-groupes (d'indicatif); **b. transfer,** transfert *m* de bloc(s).

block (to), 1. grouper (en blocs); **2.** bloquer (un programme).

blockette, partie *f* de bloc.

blocking, 1. groupement *m*, groupage *m*; **2.** blocage *m*; **record b.,** groupage d'enregistrements; **b. circuit,** circuit *m* de blocage; **b. factor,** facteur *m* de groupage.

board, 1. tableau *m*; **2.** table *f*; **plotting b.,** table traçante, table de report; **printed circuit b.,** (plaque(tte) *f* à) circuit imprimé; **problem b.,** tableau de connexions; **program b.,** tableau de connexions; **test b.** (*Am.*), table d'essais; **wiring b.,** tableau de connexions; **b.-wired,** à tableau de connexions.

book, run b., dossier *m* d'exploitation; **b. message,** message *m* à plusieurs adresses.

book-keeping, comptabilité *f*; **b.-k. operation,** opération *f* de service, opération *f* auxiliaire.

Boolean, de Boole, booléen (-enne) *adj.*; **B. add,** réunion *f* logique, mélangeur *m*; **B. algebra,** algèbre booléenne; **B. complementation,** opération *f* NON; **B. connective,** opérateur booléen; **B. operation,** opération booléenne; **B. operation table,** tableau *m* d'opération booléenne; **B. operator,** opérateur booléen; **B. variable,** variable booléenne.

bootstrap, amorce *f*, programme *m* d'amorçage, séquence *f* de démarrage; **b. input program,** programme d'amorçage; **b. loader,** chargeur *m* d'instructions initiales.

border, b.-punched card, carte *f* à perforations marginales.

bore, diamètre intérieur.

borrow, retenue *f*.

B.O.S. (= **basic operating system**), système *m* d'exploitation de base.

both-way, b.-w. circuit, circuit exploité dans les deux sens.

bound, tape-b., subordonné au débit (binaire) des dérouleurs.

boundary, character b., limite *f* de caractère.

box, boîte *f*; **B b.,** registre *m* d'index; **connection b., 1.** boîte de connexion; **2.** boîte de jonction; **decision b.,** aiguillage *m*; **stunt b.,** coffret *m* de commande.

brackets, round b., parenthèses *f*; **square b.,** crochets *m*.

branch, 1. branchement *m*; **2.** dérivation *f*; **conditional b.,** branchement conditionnel, saut conditionnel; **unconditional b.,** branchement inconditionnel, branchement «toujours»; **b. cable,** câble *m* de dérivation; **b. instruction,** instruction *f* de branchement, instruction *f* de saut.

branch (to), 1. raccorder, connecter; **2.** se brancher sur (un programme).

branchpoint, 1. embranchement *m*; **2.** point *m* de connexion (*ou* de branchement).

breadboard, montage expérimental.

break, control b., rupture *f* de contrôle; **string b.,** rupture *f* de monotonie.

break (to), interrompre (*un circuit*), couper (*un circuit*).

breakdown, 1. panne *f*; **2.** interruption *f*.

breaker, disjoncteur *m*.

break-make, b.-m. ratio, rapport *m* d'impulsions.

breakpoint, point *m* d'arrêt (*dans un programme*), point *m* d'interruption (*ou* de rupture); **b. instruction,** instruction *f* de point d'interruption; **b. switch,** inverseur *m* de point d'interruption; **b. symbol,** symbole *m* de renvoi sur point d'interruption.

breakthrough, discontinuité *f* d'encrage (*OCR*).

B register, registre *m* d'index.

bridge, b. duplex system, système *m* duplex à pont.

brightness, réflectivité moyenne (*OCR*).

bring in (to), alimenter (un programme).

broadband, bande *f* large.

broadcast, diffusion *f*.

browse (to), passer en revue, balayer.

brush, balai *m* (de lecture); **b. assembly,** ensemble *m* porte-balais; **b. compare check,** contrôle *m* entre brosses de lecture; **b. station,** poste *m* de lecture (par balais).

BS (=backspace character), caractère *m* espace arrière.

B store, registre *m* d'index.

B.T.A.M. (=basic telecommunication access method), méthode *f* d'accès de base en télétraitement.

bucket, emplacement *m* de rangement (en mémoire); **overflow b.,** emplacement de débordement (en mémoire).

budgetary, b. control, contrôle *m* budgétaire.

buffer, tampon *m*; **card punch b.,** tampon de perforateur de cartes; **input b.,** tampon d'entrée; **input/output b.,** tampon d'entrée-sortie; **output b.,** tampon de sortie; **peripheral b.,** tampon de périphérique; **storage b.,** mémoire *f* tampon; **b. amplifier,** amplificateur *m* tampon, amplificateur *m* intermédiaire; **b. drum,** tambour *m* tampon; **b. store** (*or* **storage**), mémoire *f* tampon.

buffered, b. computer, calculateur *m* à mémoire(s) tampon(s); **b. input/output,** entrée-sortie *f* à tampon; **b. peripheral,** périphérique *m* à mémoire-tampon.

buffering, double b., utilisation *f* de double tampon; **exchange b.,** utilisation *f* de tampons par méthode d'échange; **simple b.,** utilisation *f* de tampon unique.

bug, 1. erreur *f*; **2.** mauvais fonctionnement; **program b.,** erreur dans un programme.

built-in, incorporé *adj.*; **b.-i. automatic check,** contrôle *m* automatique; **b.-i. check,** contrôle *m* automatique.

bump, mémoire *f* annexe.

bureau, service b., service *m* de travaux à façon, façonnier *m*.

buried, b. cable, câble souterrain, câble enterré.

burst, error b., paquet *m* d'erreurs, groupe *m* d'erreurs; **b. mode,** mode *m* de transfert par paquets, mode continu.

burst (to), éclater.

burster, rupteur *m* (d'imprimés), rupteuse *f*, éclateuse *f*.

bus, 1. voie principale, canal *m*; **2.** câblage *m*; **3.** circuit *m* d'alimentation; **check b.,** voie de contrôle; **digit transfer b.,** voie de transfert de chiffres; **ground b.,** câble *m* de mise à la terre; **laminar b.,** distributeur *m* laminaire.

business, b. data processing, informatique *f* de gestion, traitement *m* de l'information en gestion; **b. machine,** machine *f* de gestion.

busy, occupé *adj.*; **b. hour,** heure *f* de pointe; **b. test** (*Am.*), test *m* d'occupation.

button, initiate b., interrupteur *m* de mise en route; **panic b.,** interrupteur *m* de secours; **start b.,** interrupteur *m* de mise en route.

by-product, sous-produit *m*; **b.-p. circuit,** circuit superposé.

byte, multiplet *m*, groupe *m* de bits consécutifs; **eight-bit b.,** octet *m*; **five-bit b.,** quintet *m*; **four-bit b.,** quartet *m*; **seven-bit b.,** septet *m*; **six-bit b.,** sextet *m*; **three-bit b.,** triplet *m*.

C

cabinet, armoire *f*, coffret *m*.

cable, câble *m*; **aerial c.,** câble (*ou* fil *m*) aérien; **branch c.,** câble de dérivation; **buried c.,** câble souterrain, câble enterré; **coaxial c.,** câble coaxial; **coaxial pair telephone c.,** câble téléphonique à paires coaxiales; **combination c.,** câble à paires et quartes mixtes; **composite c.,** câble mixte; **distribution c.,** câble de distribution; **feeder c.,** feeder *m*; **flat c.,** câble ruban; **paired c.,** câble à paires; **quadded c.,** câble à quartes; **quad-pair c.,** câble à paires câblées en étoile; **tape c.,** câble ruban.

cache, antémémoire *f*.

calculated, c. address, adresse calculée.

calculating, calcul *m*; **card programmed c.**, calcul par cartes-programme; **c. punch**, calculateur *m* perforateur.

calculation, calcul(s) *m*; **fixed-point c.**, calcul(s) à virgule fixe; **floating-point c.**, calcul(s) à virgule flottante.

calculator, calculateur *m*; **automatic sequence-controlled c.**, calculateur automatique à séquence contrôlée; **hand-held c.**, calculatrice *f* de poche; **network c.**, simulateur *m* (d'étude) de réseaux; **relay c.**, calculateur à relais; **remote c.**, calculateur de télégestion, calculateur à distance; **sequence-controlled c.**, calculateur automatique à séquence contrôlée.

calculus, calcul *m*.

calibrating, **c. tape**, bande *f* d'étalonnage.

call, **1.** communication *f*; **2.** appel *m*; **chargeable c.**, communication taxable; **duplex telex c.**, communication télex en duplex; **exchange c.**, appel urbain; **local c.**, communication locale, communication urbaine; **operator-connected c.**, communication établie par l'opérateur (-trice); **subroutine c.**, appel d'un sous-programme; **telex c.**, communication télex; **toll c.** (*Am.*), communication interurbaine; **trunk c.**, communication interurbaine; **c. channel**, voie *f* d'appel; **c. charge**, taxe *f* téléphonique; **c. confirmation signal**, signal *m* de confirmation d'appel; **c.-connected signal**, signal *m* de connexion; **c. in**, appel (*de sous-programme*); **c. indicator**, indicateur lumineux d'appel; **c. instruction**, instruction *f* d'appel; **c. number**, numéro *m* d'appel; **c. rates**, tarification *f* des communications; **c. relay**, relais *m* d'appel; **c. sign**, indicatif *m* d'appel; **c. switch**, commutateur *m* d'appel; **c. word**, mot *m* d'appel (*de sous-programme*).

call (to), appeler.

called, appelé; **c. exchange**, central demandé; **c. line**, ligne appelée; **c. party**, demandé *m*; **c. station**, station appelée.

calling, appel *m*; **selective c.**, appel sélectif; **c. band**, bande *f* d'appel; **c. channel**, voie *f* d'appel; **c. circuit**, circuit *m* d'appel; **c. exchange**, central demandeur; **c. frequency**, fréquence *f* d'appel; **c. line**, ligne appelante; **c. office**, bureau demandeur; **c. party**, demandeur *m*; **c. relay**, relais *m* d'appel; **c. sequence**, séquence *f* d'appel; **c.**

set, poste appelant; **c. signal**, signal *m* d'appel; **c. station**, station appelante; **c. subscriber**, abonné demandeur.

camp-on, mise *f* en attente.

can, capsule *f*.

CAN (=**cancel character**), caractère *m* (d')annulation, caractère *m* de rejet.

cancel, **c. character**, caractère *m* (d')annulation, caractère *m* de rejet.

cancel (to), **1.** (re)mettre à zéro, garnir de zéros; **2.** annuler.

capacitance, capacité *f* (*p. ex. d'un condensateur*); **c.-coupled flip-flop**, bascule *f* à couplage alternatif (*ou* capacitif).

capacitor, condensateur *m*; **ceramic chip c.**, condensateur (*ou* capacité *f*) intégré(e) sur microplaquette; **c. store (or storage)**, mémoire *f* à condensateurs.

capacity, capacité *f*; **channel c.**, capacité de voie; **circuit c.**, capacité en nombre de canaux; **memory c.**, capacité de mémoire; **register c.**, capacité de registre; **storage c.**, **1.** capacité de stockage; **2.** capacité de mémoire; **store c.**, capacité de mémoire; **traffic c.**, capacité d'écoulement de trafic.

capstan, cabestan *m*.

capture, **data c.**, saisie *f* de données, collecte *f* de données, rassemblement *m* de données.

carbon, carbone *m*; **c. paper**, papier-carbone *m*; **c. ribbon**, ruban-carbone *m*.

card, carte *f*; **aperture c.**, carte à fenêtre; **binary c.**, carte binaire; **blank c.**, carte vierge; **border-punched c.**, carte à perforations marginales; **column binary c.**, carte binaire par colonne; **control c.**, carte paramètre, ordre *m* de gestion; **detail c.**, carte détail; **edge-notched c.**, carte à encoches marginales; **edge-perforated c.**, carte à perforations marginales; **edge-punched c.**, carte à perforations marginales; **eighty column c.**, carte à quatre-vingts colonnes; **end of job c.**, carte fin de travail; **header c.**, carte (d')en-tête; **heading c.**, carte (d')en-tête; **laced c.**, carte-grille *f*; **ledger c.**, carte de compte, extrait *m* de compte; **magnetic c.**, carte magnétique; **margin-notched c.**, carte à encoches marginales; **margin-perforated c.**, carte à perforations marginales; **margin-punched c.**, carte à perforations marginales; **master c.**, carte maîtresse; **ninety column c.**, carte à quatre-vingt-dix colonnes; **parameter c.,** carte paramètre; **pilot c.,** carte-pilote *f*; **printed circuit c.,** (plaque(tte) *f* à) circuit imprimé; **program c.,** carte (de) programme; **punch(ed) c.,** carte perforée; **row binary c.,** carte binaire par rangée; **search c.,** carte chercheuse; **stub c.,** carte à volet; **summary c.,** carte récapitulative; **transfer c.,** carte de lancement (de programme); **transfer-of-control c.,** carte de lancement (de programme); **transition c.,** carte de lancement (de programme); **verge-perforated c.,** carte à perforations marginales; **verge-punched c.,** carte à perforations marginales; **c. back,** verso *m* d'une carte, dos *m* d'une carte; **c. bed,** chemin *m* de cartes; **c. code,** code *m* carte; **c. column,** colonne *f* de carte; **c. deck,** paquet *m* de cartes; **c. drive,** (dispositif *m* d')entraînement *m* de cartes; **c. face,** face *f* d'une carte, recto *m* d'une carte; **c. feed,** alimentation *f* de cartes; **c. field,** zone *f* de carte; **c. format,** dessin *m* de cartes; **c. hopper,** magasin *m* d'alimentation (de cartes); **c. image,** image *f* de carte; **c. input,** entrée *f* par cartes; **c. jam,** bourrage *m* de cartes; **c. leading edge,** bord *m* avant de carte; **c. loader,** (programme *m*) chargeur *m* de cartes-programme; **c. mode,** mode *m* (d'exploitation) cartes; **c. programmed calculating,** calcul *m* par cartes-programme; **c. punch,** perforateur *m* de cartes; **c. punch buffer,** tampon *m* de perforateur de cartes; **c. punching,** perforation *f* de cartes; **c. punch unit,** perforateur *m* de cartes; **c. reader,** lecteur *m* de cartes; **c. reader punch,** lecteur-perforateur *m* de cartes; **c. reader unit,** lecteur *m* de cartes; **c. reproducer,** reproductrice *f* de cartes; **c. row,** ligne *f* (sur une carte); **c. stacker,** case *f* de réception de cartes; **c. systems,** systèmes *m* à cartes; **c. throat,** filière *f*; **c.-to-disk conversion,** conversion *f* cartes (à) disque; **c.-to-magnetic tape converter,** convertisseur *m* cartes (à) bande magnétique; **c.-to-tape conversion,** conversion *f* cartes (à) bande; **c.-to-tape converter,** convertisseur *m* cartes (à) bande; **c. track,** chemin *m* de cartes; **c. trailing edge,** bord *m* arrière de carte; **c. transceiver,** émetteur-récepteur *m* à cartes perforées; **c. verifier,** vérificatrice *f* de cartes; **c. verifying,** vérification *f* des (perforations de) cartes; **c. weight,** presse-cartes *m*; **c. wreck,** bourrage *m* de cartes.

card-to-card, carte-à-carte *adj. ou m.*
card-to-tape, carte-à-bande *adj. ou m.*
caret, 1. caret *m*; 2. signe *m* d'omission.
carriage, chariot *m*; **automatic c.,** chariot automatique; **dual feed tape c.,** chariot à double saut de papier; **tape-controlled c.,** chariot automatique; **c. control tape,** bande *f* pilote; **c. return,** retour *m* de chariot; **c. return character (CR),** caractère *m* retour de chariot; **c. return signal,** signal *m* de retour du chariot; **c. tape,** bande *f* pilote.
carrier, onde porteuse, courant porteur; **data c.,** support *m* de données; **majority c.,** porteur *m* majoritaire; **minority c.,** porteur *m* minoritaire; **c. current,** courant porteur; **c. (current) telegraphy,** télégraphie *f* par courants porteurs; **c. frequency,** fréquence porteuse; **c. noise level,** niveau *m* de bruit de porteuse; **c. shift,** déplacement *m* de la porteuse; **c. system,** système *m* à courants porteurs; **c.-to-noise ratio,** écart *m* entre porteuse et bruit; **c. wave,** onde porteuse.
carry, report *m*; **addition without c.,** exclusion *f* réciproque, opération *f* de non-équivalence; **cascaded c.,** report en cascade; **complete c.,** report total; **end-around c.,** report en boucle; **high-speed c.,** report rapide; **partial c.,** report partiel; **ripple-through c.,** report rapide; **simultaneous c.,** report simultané; **standing-on-nines c.,** report bloqué sur neuf; **c.-complete signal,** signal *m* de fin de report; **c. register,** registre *m* de report; **c. time,** temps *m* de report.
carry (to), reporter.
cartridge, 1. cartouche *f*; 2. chargeur *m*.
cascade, connection in c., montage *m* en cascade; **c. control,** contrôle *m* en cascade.
cascaded, c. carry, report *m* en cascade.
case, test c., jeu *m* d'essai; **c. shift,** inversion *f*.
cassette, cassette *f*.
casting out, c.o. nines, preuve *f* par neuf.
catalog(ue), catalogue *m*; **dictionary c.,** catalogue groupé; **split c.,** catalogue éclaté.
catalog(ue) (to), cataloguer.
catalogued, c. data set, ensemble *m* de(s) données cataloguées; **c. procedure,** procédure cataloguée.

category, catégorie *f*; **display c.,** catégorie de données affichable.
catenate (to), enchaîner.
catenation, enchaînement *m*.
cathode, cathode *f*; **c. follower,** cathode-suiveuse *f*; **c. ray oscilloscope,** oscilloscope *m* à rayons cathodiques; **c. ray storage,** mémoire *f* à tube cathodique; **c. ray tube (CRT),** tube *m* à rayons cathodiques, tube *m* cathodique; **c. ray tube display,** unité *f* de visualisation à tube (*ou* à rayons) cathodique(s); **c. ray tube store,** mémoire *f* à tube cathodique; **c. screen,** écran *m* cathodique.
ceiling, plafond *m*; **false c.,** faux plafond.
cell, 1. unité *f* (*ou* élément *m*) de stockage (en mémoire); **2.** cellule *f*; **binary c.,** élément binaire; **disturbed c.,** élément perturbé; **magnetic c.,** unité de stockage magnétique; **partially switched c.,** élément perturbé; **photovoltaic c.,** cellule photovoltaïque; **selected c.,** élément sélectionné; **static magnetic c.,** unité de stockage magnétique; **storage c.,** élément de mémoire; **c. area,** surface *f* élémentaire d'analyse (*OCR*).
central, central *adj.*; **c. computer,** calculateur central; **c. control unit,** unité centrale de commande; **c. office** (*Am.*), centre *m* (*ou* central *m*) téléphonique; **c. processing unit (C.P.U.),** unité centrale de traitement; **c. processor,** unité centrale de traitement; **c. terminal,** concentrateur *m*; **c. unit,** unité centrale.
centralized, c. data processing, traitement centralisé de l'information.
centre (*Am.* **center**), centre *m*; **automatic data switching c.,** centre de prise en charge automatique de données; **automatic message switching c.,** centre automatique de commutation de messages; **automatic switching c.,** centre de commutation automatique; **computer c.,** centre de calcul; **data c.,** centre de traitement de l'information (C.T.I.); **data processing c.,** centre de traitement de l'information; **exchange c.,** central *m*; **intermediate c.,** centre intermédiaire; **message switching c.,** centre de commutation de messages; **regional c.,** centre régional; **relay c.,** centre-relais *m*; **semi-automatic message switching c.,** centre semi-automatique de commutation de messages; **switching c.,**

centre de commutation; **telegraph c.,** centre télégraphique; **torn tape switching c.,** centre de commutation par bande perforée, centre de commutation à bandes coupées.
centreline, stroke c., ligne médiane d'un segment.
ceramic, c. chip capacitor, condensateur *m* (*ou* capacité *f*) intégré(e) sur microplaquette.
chad, confetti *m*; **c. type perforation,** perforation complète.
chadded, c. paper tape, bande perforée à confettis détachés.
chadless, c. paper tape, bande perforée à confettis semi-attachés; **c. perforation,** perforation partielle.
chain, chaîne *f*; **Markov c.,** chaîne de Markov; **print c.,** chaîne d'impression; **c. code,** code *m* en chaîne; **c. printer,** imprimante *f* à chaîne; **c. search,** recherche *f* en chaîne.
chained, c. file, fichier chaîné; **c. list,** liste chaînée; **c. record,** enregistrement chaîné.
chaining, enchaînement *m*; **c. search,** recherche *f* en chaîne.
change, changement *m*, modification *f*; **comparing control c.,** rupture *f* de contrôle par comparaison (de zones); **(group) control c.,** rupture *f* de contrôle, rupture de niveau, changement de groupe; **intermediate control c.,** rupture *f* de contrôle de niveau intermédiaire; **key c.,** changement d'indicatif; **major control c.,** rupture *f* de contrôle de premier niveau; **minor control c.,** rupture *f* de contrôle de troisième niveau; **mode c.,** changement de mode; **step c.,** variation discrète; **c. dump,** vidage *m* des zones (de mémoire) mouvementées; **c. file,** fichier *m* (des) mouvements, fichier *m* de détail; **c. of control,** rupture *f* de contrôle, rupture *f* de niveau, changement de groupe; **c. record,** enregistrement *m* (de) mouvement, enregistrement (de) détail; **c. tape,** bande *f* (des) mouvements.
changeable, c. storage, mémoire *f* interchangeable.
change-over, c.-o. switch, commutateur *m*.
changer, sign c., inverseur *m* de signe.
channel, voie *f*, canal *m*; **adjacent c.,** voie adjacente; **analog c.,** voie analogique; **backward c.,** voie de retour; **block mul-**

tiplexor c., canal multiple par blocs; **call c.**, voie d'appel; **calling c.**, voie d'appel; **communication c.**, voie de communication; **data c.**, canal d'échange de données; **dedicated c.**, voie particulière; **duplex c.**, voie duplex (*ou* duplexée); **duplex telephone c.**, voie téléphonique duplex; **engaged c.**, voie occupée; **forward c.**, voie d'aller; **four-wire c.**, voie à quatre fils; **frequency-derived c.**, voie dérivée en fréquence; **half-duplex c.**, voie semi-duplex; **information c.**, voie de transfert des informations; **input c.**, canal d'entrée, voie d'entrée; **input/output c.**, canal d'entrée-sortie, voie d'entrée-sortie; **local c.**, voie locale; **multiple telephone c.**, voie téléphonique multiple; **multiplex c.**, voie multiplex; **multiplexor c.**, canal multiplexeur; **output c.**, canal de sortie, voie de sortie; **peripheral interface c.**, canal d'interface avec périphériques; **pilot c.**, voie d'onde (porteuse) pilote; **routing c.**, voie d'acheminement; **selector c.**, canal de sélection; **simplex c.**, voie simplex; **supervisory c.**, voie de surveillance, voie de supervision; **telegraph c.**, voie de communication télégraphique, voie (de transmission) télégraphique; **telemetering c.**, voie de télémesure; **telephone c.**, voie téléphonique; **teleprinter c.**, voie de téléimprimeur; **teletypewriter c.**, voie de téléimprimeur; **telex c.**, voie télex; **time-derived c.**, voie dérivée en temps, sous-voie *f*; **transmission c.**, voie de transmission; **two-wire c.**, voie à deux fils; **voice c.**, voie téléphonique; **voice grade c.**, voie à fréquence vocale; **c. address word**, mot *m* d'adresse de canal; **c. capacity**, capacité *f* de voie; **c. control word**, mot *m* de commande de canal; **c. program translation**, traduction *f* du programme canal; **c. status table**, table *f* d'état des canaux; **c. status word**, mot *m* d'état de canal; **c. trap**, déroutement *m* par canal.

chapter, chapitre *m*.

character, caractère *m*; **accuracy control c.**, caractère de contrôle de précision; **acknowledge c. (ACK)**, (caractère) accusé *m* de réception (positif); **additional c.**, caractère spécial; **backspace c.**, caractère espace arrière; **bell c.**, caractère sonnerie, caractère appel; **binary c.**, caractère binaire; **binary coded c.**, caractère codé (en) binaire; **blank c.**, caractère espace; **block cancel c.**, caractère de rejet de bloc, caractère d'annulation de bloc; **block ignore c.**, caractère de rejet de bloc, caractère d'annulation de bloc; **cancel c.**, caractère (d')annulation, caractère de rejet; **carriage return c. (CR)**, caractère retour de chariot; **check c.**, caractère de contrôle, caractère de vérification; **coded c.**, caractère codé; **code-directing c.**, caractère d'acheminement (de message); **code extension c.**, caractère de changement de code; **command c.**, caractère de commande; **communication control c.**, caractère de commande de transmission; **control c.**, caractère de commande; **data link escape c. (DLE)**, caractère d'échappement transmission; **delete c. (DEL)**, caractère d'oblitération; **device control c.**, caractère de commande d'appareil; **drifting c.**, caractère mobile; **end of medium c. (EM)**, caractère (de) fin de support; **end of message c.**, caractère (de) fin de message; **end of text c. (ETX)**, caractère (de) fin de texte; **end of transmission block c. (ETB)**, (caractère) fin de bloc de transmission; **end of transmission c.**, caractère fin de transmission; **enquiry c. (ENQ)**, demande *f* (de renseignements); **erase c.**, caractère d'oblitération; **error c.**, caractère d'annulation, caractère de rejet; **error control c.**, caractère de contrôle de précision; **escape c. (ESC)**, caractère d'échappement; **face change c.**, caractère de changement de jeu; **file separator c.**, caractère de séparation de fichiers; **floating c.**, caractère flottant; **font change c.**, caractère de changement de jeu (*de caractères*); **forbidden c.**, caractère invalide; **form feed c. (FF)**, caractère de présentation de feuille; **functional c.**, caractère de commande; **gap c.**, caractère de remplissage; **graphic c.**, caractère graphique; **group separator c.**, caractère de séparation de groupes; **horizontal skip c.**, caractère d'espacement horizontal; **horizontal tabulation c.**, caractère de tabulation horizontale; **ignore c.**, caractère d'annulation, caractère de rejet; **illegal c.**, caractère invalide; **improper c.**, caractère invalide; **inquiry c.**, demande *f* (de renseignements); **instruction c.**, caractère de commande; **layout c.**, caractère de mise en page, caractère de présentation; **least significant c.**, caractère le moins significatif; **line feed c. (LF)**, caractère interligne; **locking shift c.**, caractère de maintien (d'un changement de code); **longitudinal redundancy check c.**, caractère de contrôle (de parité) longitudinal; **magnetized ink c.**, caractère magnétique codé; **most significant c.**, caractère le plus significatif; **negative acknowledge c. (NAK)**, (caractère) accusé *m* de réception négatif; **new line c. (NL)**, (caractère) retour *m* à la ligne; **non-locking shift c.**, caractère sans maintien (d'un changement de code); **null c. (NUL)**, caractère nul, caractère de remplissage (d'espace *ou* de temps); **numeric(al) c.**, caractère numérique, chiffre *m*; **operational c.**, caractère de commande; **pad c.**, caractère de remplissage (de temps); **paper throw c.**, caractère de saut de papier; **print control c.**, caractère de contrôle d'impression; **protection c.**, caractère de substitution; **record separator c.**, caractère de séparation d'enregistrements; **redundant c.**, caractère de complément, caractère de garnissage; **rub-out c.**, caractère d'oblitération; **separating c.**, caractère séparateur (d'informations); **shift-in c. (SI)**, caractère en code, caractère de commande de code normal; **shift-out c.**, caractère hors code, caractère de commande de code spécial; **sign c.**, caractère de signe; **slew c.**, caractère de saut; **space c. (SP)**, caractère espace; **special c.**, caractère spécial; **start of heading c. (SOH)**, caractère début d'entête; **start of text c. (STX)**, caractère début de texte; **substitute c. (SUB)**, caractère substitut; **synchronization c.**, caractère de synchronisation; **synchronous idle c. (SYN)**, caractère de synchronisation; **tabulation c.**, caractère de tabulation; **throw-away c.**, caractère nul, caractère de remplissage (d'espace *ou* de temps); **transmission control c.**, caractère de commande de transmission; **unit separator c.**, caractère de séparation de blocs; **vertical tabulation c. (VT)**, caractère de tabulation verticale; **c.-at-a-time printer**, imprimante *f* caractère par caractère; **c. boundary**, limite *f* de caractère; **c. check**, contrôle *m* par

caractère; **c. density**, densité *f* en (nombre de) caractères; **c. design**, dessin *m* de caractère; **c. edge**, bord *m* de caractère; **c. emitter**, émetteur *m* d'impulsions; **c. error rate**, taux *m* d'erreurs sur les caractères; **c.-oriented computer**, ordinateur *m* à caractères; **c. outline**, contour *m* d'un caractère; **c. pitch**, entraxe *m* de caractères; **c. printer**, imprimante *f* caractère par caractère; **c. reader**, lecteur *m* de caractères; **c. recognition**, reconnaissance *f* de caractères; **c. repertoire**, répertoire *m* de caractères; **c. set**, jeu *m* de caractères, répertoire *m* de caractères; **c. signal**, signal *m* de caractère; **c. spacing reference line**, axe *m* de référence d'espacement; **c. string**, chaîne *f* de caractères; **c. stroke**, segment *m* de caractère; **c. subset**, jeu partiel de caractères, sous-ensemble *m* de caractères; **c. wheel**, roue *f* d'impression.

character fill (to), garnir (*une zone*) à un même caractère.

characteristic, caractéristique *adj.*; **c. distortion**, distorsion *f* caractéristique; **c. impedance**, impédance *f* caractéristique; **c. overflow**, dépassement *m* de capacité de la caractéristique; **c. underflow**, dépassement négatif de la caractéristique.

charge, taxe *f*; **call c.**, taxe téléphonique; **telephone c.**, taxe téléphonique; **telex c.**, taxe télex.

chargeable, taxable *adj.*; **c. call**, communication *f* taxable.

charging, **c. period**, période *f* de taxation.

chart, 1. diagramme *m*; 2. schéma *m*; 3. relevé *m*; **function c.**, diagramme de fonction; **logic c.**, organigramme *m* logique; **plugboard c.**, schéma de connexions, relevé de connexions; **plugging c.**, schéma de connexions, relevé de connexions; **process c.**, organigramme *m* (de traitement de l'information), ordinogramme *m*; **run c.**, organigramme *m* d'exploitation; **Veitch c.**, diagramme de Veitch.

check, contrôle *m*, vérification *f*; **arithmetic c.**, contrôle arithmétique; **automatic c.**, contrôle automatique; **Batten c.**, contrôle visuel; **bias c.**, contrôle par marges, test *m* de marges; **block c.**, contrôle par bloc; **brush compare c.**, contrôle entre brosses de lecture; **built-in (automatic) c.**, contrôle automatique; **character c.**, contrôle par caractère; **coding c.,** vérification de codage (de programmes); **copy c.,** contrôle de transfert; **Cordonnier c.,** contrôle visuel; **diagnostic c.,** test *m* de diagnostic; **dump c.,** contrôle de vidage; **duplication c.,** contrôle par duplication; **dynamic c.,** contrôle dynamique; **echo c.,** contrôle par écho; **even-odd c.,** contrôle de parité; **even parity c.,** contrôle de parité (paire); **false code c.,** contrôle de caractère invalide; **forbidden combination c.,** contrôle de caractère invalide; **forbidden digit c.,** contrôle de caractère invalide; **hardware c.,** contrôle automatique; **illegal command c.,** contrôle de caractère invalide; **improper command c.,** contrôle de caractère invalide; **longitudinal c.,** contrôle longitudinal; **longitudinal redundancy c.,** contrôle longitudinal; **loop c.,** contrôle par retour de l'information; **marginal c.,** contrôle par marges, test *m* de marges; **mathematical c.,** contrôle arithmétique; **modulo N c.,** contrôle sur reste; **non-existent code c.,** contrôle de caractère invalide; **odd-even c.,** contrôle de parité; **odd parity c.,** contrôle d'imparité (*ou* de parité impaire); **parity c.,** contrôle de parité; **peek-a-boo c.,** contrôle visuel; **programmed c.,** contrôle par programme, contrôle programmé; **programmed marginal c.,** contrôle par marges programmé; **read-back c.,** contrôle par écho; **read/write c.,** contrôle de lecture/écriture; **redundancy c.,** contrôle par redondance; **redundant c.,** contrôle par redondance; **residue c.,** contrôle sur reste; **routine c.,** contrôle par programme, contrôle programmé; **selection c.,** contrôle de sélection; **sequence c.,** contrôle de séquence; **sight c.,** contrôle visuel; **static c.,** contrôle statique; **sum c.,** contrôle par totalisation (*ou* addition); **summation c.,** contrôle par totalisation (*ou* addition); **system c.,** contrôle de système; **transfer c.,** contrôle de transfert (par répétition); **transverse c.,** contrôle transversal; **twin c.,** double contrôle; **validity c.,** contrôle de validité; **c. bit,** bit *m* de contrôle; **c. bus,** voie *f* de contrôle; **c. character,** caractère *m* de contrôle, caractère *m* de vérification; **c. digit,** chiffre *m* de contrôle; **c. field,** 1. zone auto-contrôlée; 2. zone *f* de contrôle; 3. zone *f* de contrôle de marquage (*OCR*);

c. indicator, indicateur *m* de contrôle; **c. number,** nombre *m* de contrôle; **c. problem,** problème *m* de contrôle, problème-test *m*; **c. register,** registre *m* de contrôle, registre *m* de vérification; **c. row,** rangée *f* de contrôle; **c. sum,** total *m* de contrôle; **c. symbol,** symbole *m* de contrôle; **c. total,** total *m* de vérification; **c. trunk,** voie *f* de contrôle; **c. word,** mot *m* de contrôle.

check (to), vérifier, contrôler; **code c. (to),** vérifier le codage (d'un programme).

checking, contrôle *m*, vérification *f*; **desk c.,** contrôle de programmation sur papier; **echo c.,** contrôle par écho; **loop c.,** contrôle par retour de l'information; **c. feature,** dispositif *m* d'auto-contrôle; **c. program,** programme *m* de contrôle; **c. routine,** programme *m* de contrôle.

checkout, contrôle *m*, vérification *f*; **program c.,** mise *f* au point de programme; **c. routine,** programme *m* de mise au point.

checkpoint, point *m* de contrôle, point *m* de reprise.

Chinese, C. binary, binaire par colonne.

chip, 1. confetti *m*; 2. microplaquette *f*, puce *f*, pastille *f*; 3. micro-image *f* optique (*Recherche documentaire*); **video-c.,** micro-image magnétique; **c. tray,** bac *m* à confettis, tiroir *m* à confettis.

chirps, keying c., parasites *m* de transmission.

chop, multiplex *m* par partage de temps; **binary c.,** recherche *f* dichotomique.

chopper, c.-stabilized amplifier, amplificateur *m* à découpage.

circuit, circuit *m*; **addition c.,** circuit d'addition; **amplifier c.,** circuit amplificateur; **AND c.,** circuit ET; **anticoincidence c.,** circuit de non-équivalence; **balanced c.,** circuit équilibré, circuit symétrique; **bistable (trigger) c.,** bascule *f*; **blocking c.,** circuit de blocage; **both-way c.,** circuit exploité dans les deux sens; **by-product c.,** circuit superposé; **calling c.,** circuit d'appel; **clamping c.,** circuit de limitation; **clipping c.,** circuit écrêteur; **coincidence c.,** dispositif *m* d'équivalence; **complementing c.,** circuit à complément; **control c.,** circuit de commande; **controlling c.,** circuit directeur; **dedicated c.,** voie particulière; **differentiating c.,** montage *m* différentiateur; **direct (telegraph) c.,** circuit (télégraphique) direct; **direct telex c.,** circuit télex direct; **duplex c.,** ligne duplex (*ou* duplexée); **earth return c.,** circuit à retour par la terre; **Eccles-Jordan c.,** montage *m* Eccles-Jordan; **equality c.,** élément *m* d'égalité, comparateur *m* d'égalité; **equivalent c.,** circuit équivalent; **etched c.,** circuit gravé; **external load c.,** circuit de charge; **faulty c.,** circuit en dérangement; **feeding c.,** circuit d'alimentation; **four-wire c.,** circuit à quatre fils; **frame grounding c.,** circuit de mise à la masse; **ground return c.** (*Am.*), circuit à retour par la terre; **half-duplex c.,** circuit semi-duplex; **holding c.,** circuit de maintien; **hybrid integrated c.,** circuit intégré hybride, circuit semi-intégré; **incoming c.,** circuit d'arrivée; **inhibiting c.,** circuit inhibiteur; **input c.,** circuit d'entrée; **integrated c.,** circuit intégré; **integrating c.,** montage intégrateur; **isolating c.,** circuit d'isolement; **leased c.,** circuit en location; **loaded c.,** circuit chargé; **logical c.,** circuit logique; **longitudinal c.,** circuit longitudinal; **monolithic integrated c.,** circuit intégré monolithique; **monostable (trigger) c.,** circuit monostable; **multipoint c.,** circuit multipoint; **multi-tone c.,** circuit multivoie; **non-equivalence c.,** circuit de non-équivalence; **NOR c.,** circuit NON-OU; **NOT c.,** circuit NON; **OR c.,** circuit OU; **outgoing c.,** circuit de départ; **output c.,** circuit de sortie; **passive c.,** circuit passif; **phantom c.,** circuit fantôme; **plated c.,** circuit imprimé; **prewired c.,** circuit précâblé; **printed c.,** circuit imprimé; **pulse c.,** circuit d'impulsions; **pulse selection c.,** circuit de sélection à impulsions; **push-pull c.,** montage *m* symétrique, montage *m* push-pull; **record c.,** ligne *f* d'annotatrice; **reserve c.,** circuit de secours; **see-saw c.,** inverseur *m* de polarité; **shaping c.,** circuit de mise en forme; **side c.,** circuit combinant; **simplex c.,** communication *f* simplex; **superposed c.,** circuit superposé; **switching c.,** circuit de commutation; **tank c.,** circuit oscillant, circuit bouchon; **telegraph c.,** circuit télégraphique; **telemetering c.,** circuit de télémesure; **telephone c.,** circuit téléphonique; **telephone-telegraph c.,** liaison *f* téléphonique-télégraphique; **teleprinter c.,** liaison *f* par téléimprimeurs; **telex c.,** circuit télex; **toll c.** (*Am.*), circuit in-terurbain; **tributary c.,** circuit tributaire; **trunk c.,** circuit interurbain; **two-wire c.,** circuit à deux fils; **video c.,** circuit vidéo; **wideband c.,** circuit à large bande; **c. capacity,** capacité *f* en nombre de canaux; **c. grade,** type *m* de circuit; **c. module,** élément *m* de circuit; **c. noise level,** niveau relatif de bruit de circuit; **c. switching,** commutation *f* de circuit(s).

circuitry, 1. ensemble *m* de circuits; 2. montage *m*.

circular, circulaire *adj.*; **c. shift,** décalage *m* circulaire.

circulating, circulant *adj.*; **c. memory,** mémoire *f* cyclique; **c. register,** registre *m* de décalage cyclique; **c. store (*or* storage),** mémoire circulante, mémoire *f* cyclique.

clamping, c. circuit, circuit *m* de limitation.

clamp-on, mise *f* en attente.

class, classe *f*, catégorie *f*.

classification, classification *f*; **concept c.,** classification par concept; **facetted c.,** classification à facettes (*Recherche documentaire*).

classify (to), classifier, ranger par classe, classer.

clause, clause *f*.

clear, c. area, zone *f* à ne pas marquer; **c.-back signal,** signal *m* de raccrochage; **c. band,** zone *f* à ne pas marquer; **c.-forward signal,** signal *m* de fin (de communication).

clear (to), effacer, remettre à zéro.

cleared, c. condition, état initial, état de référence.

clearing, c. signal, signal *m* de libération.

clipper, circuit écrêteur.

clipping, c. circuit, circuit écrêteur.

clock, 1. horloge *f*; 2. base *f* de temps; 3. générateur *m* de rythme; **digital c.,** horloge à signaux numériques; **master c.,** horloge; **real-time c.,** horloge à signaux horaires; **c. frequency,** fréquence *f* d'horloge, fréquence de base (de temps); **c. pulse,** impulsion *f* de synchronisation, impulsion d'horloge; **c. pulse generator,** générateur de rythme; **c. rate,** fréquence *f* d'horloge, fréquence de base; **c. signal,** signal *m* d'horloge; **c. signal generator,** générateur de rythme, horloge; **c. track,** piste *f* de référence, piste *f* de base de temps.

closed, 1. fermé *adj.*; 2. en boucle; **c.-circuit**

working, transmission *f* par interruption de courant; **c. core,** noyau fermé; **c. loop, 1.** boucle fermée (*de programme*); **2.** circuit fermé; **c. routine,** programme fermé, programme en boucle; **c. shop operation,** exploitation *f* en salle fermée; **c. subroutine,** sous-programme fermé.

cluster, tape c., groupe *m* de dérouleurs.

clutch, embrayage *m*.

coalesce (to), fusionner, interclasser.

coating, revêtement *m*, couche *f*.

coaxial, coaxial *adj.*; **c. cable,** câble coaxial; **c. pair telephone cable,** câble *m* téléphonique à paires coaxiales.

COBOL (=**Common Business Oriented Language**), COBOL.

code, code *m*; **absolute c.,** code réel (*en langage machine*); rt3actual c., code réel (*en langage machine*); **address c.,** code d'adresse; **alphabetic(al) c.,** code alphabétique; **alphabetic data c.,** code alphabétique; **alphameric c.,** code alphanumérique; **alphanumeric (data) c.,** code alphanumérique; **answerback c.,** indicatif *m*; **automatic c.,** code automatique; **basic c.,** code réel (*en langage machine*); **Baudot c.,** code Baudot; **binary c.,** code binaire; **biquinary c.,** code biquinaire; **card c.,** code carte; **chain c.,** code en chaîne; **command c.,** code de commande; **computer c.,** code machine; **computer instruction c.,** code machine; **constant ratio c.,** code à rapport constant; **continuous progression c.,** code à signaux à espacement unitaire; **continuous progressive c.,** code à signaux à espacement unitaire; **conversion c.,** code; **cyclic c.,** code Gray, code binaire réfléchi; **cyclic permuted c.,** code à signaux à espacement unitaire; **data c.,** code de données; **dense binary c.,** code binaire saturé; **dialling c.,** code de sélection (*ou* de numérotation); **dictionary c.,** code dictionnaire; **direct c.,** code réel (*en langage machine*); **eight-level c.,** code à huit moments (*ou* éléments); **equal-length c.,** code à moments; **error c.,** code d'erreur; **error-checking c.,** code de contrôle d'erreurs; **error-correcting c.,** code correcteur d'erreurs; **error-detecting c.,** code détecteur d'erreurs; **excess-fifty c.,** représentation majorée de cinquante; **excess-three c.,** code plus trois; **false c.,**

caractère *m* invalide; **five-level c.,** code à cinq moments (*ou* éléments); **five-unit c.,** code à cinq moments, code à cinq éléments; **fixed-ratio c.,** code à rapport fixe; **forbidden c.,** code interdit, code prohibé; **four-address c.,** instruction *f* à quatre adresses; **function c.,** code de fonction; **Gray c.,** code Gray, code binaire réfléchi; **Hamming c.,** code auto-rectifiable; **Hollerith c.,** code Hollerith; **identifying c.,** code d'identification; **illegal c.,** code interdit, code prohibé; **improper c.,** code interdit, code prohibé; **input instruction c.,** code d'instruction d'entrée; **instruction c.,** code d'instruction; **interpretive c.,** pseudo-code *m*; **invalid c.,** code invalide; **line feed c.,** code de changement de ligne; **machine c.,** code machine; **machine instruction c.,** code machine; **machine language c.,** code machine; **macro c.,** macro-code *m*; **micro c.,** micro-code *m*; **minimum access c.,** code à (temps d')accès minimum; **minimum distance c.,** code à distance minimum; **minimum latency c.,** code à (temps d')accès minimum; **mnemonic c.,** code mnémonique; **mnemonic operation c.,** code d'opération mnémonique; **modulation c.,** code de modulation; **M out of N c.,** code N dont M; **multiple-address c.,** code à adresses multiples; **non-existent c.,** caractère *m* invalide; **non-print c.,** code de non-impression; **non-reproducing c.,** code de non-reproduction; **numeric(al) c.,** code numérique; **numerical data c.,** code numérique; **object c.,** code objet; **octal c.,** code octal; **one-address c.,** instruction *f* à une adresse; **one-level c.,** code réel (*en langage machine*); **operation c.,** code d'opération; **optimum c.,** code optimum; **order c.,** code de commande; **paper tape c.,** code de bande perforée; **print restore c.,** code de reprise d'impression; **program indicator c.,** code d'identification de programme; **pseudo-c.,** pseudo-code *m*; **punch(ed) tape c.,** code de bande perforée; **quibinary c.,** code quibinaire; **redundant c.,** code redondant; **reflected binary c.,** code binaire réfléchi; **relative c.,** code relatif; **reproduction c.,** code de reproduction; **return c.,** code de retour (sur programme); **routing c.,** indicatif *m*; **self-checking c.,** code détecteur d'erreurs; **self-demarcating** c., code auto-délimité; **single-address c.,** code à une adresse; **skeletal c.,** code paramétrable; **skip c.,** code de saut (de papier); **source c.,** code source; **space c.,** code (de commande) d'espace; **specific c.,** code réel (en langage machine); **start-stop c.,** code arythmique; **stop c.,** code d'arrêt; **symbolic c.,** code symbolique; **systematic error checking c.,** code de contrôle systématique d'erreurs; **telegraph c.,** code télégraphique; **thirty-nine feature c.,** code spécial 0–39 (par colonne); **three-address c.,** code à trois adresses; **transmitter start c.,** code de lancement de transmission; **twenty-nine feature c.,** code spécial 0–29 (par colonne); **two-address c.,** code à deux adresses; **two-out-of-five c.,** code deux parmi cinq, code quinaire; **unit distance c.,** code à signaux à espacement unitaire; **U.S.A. Standard C. for Information Interchange,** code standard américain pour l'échange d'information; **c. checking time,** temps m de mise au point; **c. conversion,** conversion f de codes; **c. directing character,** caractère m d'acheminement (de message); **c. distance,** distance f inter-signaux; **c. element,** combinaison f de code, élément m de code; **c. element unit,** unité f d'éléments de code; **c. extension character,** caractère m de changement de code; **c. hole,** perforation f, perforation siposition, emplacement m de perforation (bande); **c. set,** jeu m de représentations, jeu m d'éléments de code; **c. track,** voie f d'information; **c. translator,** convertisseur m de codes; **c. value,** combinaison f de code, élément m de code; **c. wheel,** disque m codeur.

code (to), coder, programmer.

code check (to), vérifier le codage (d'un programme).

coded, codé adj.; **c. character,** caractère codé; **c. character set,** jeu m de caractères codés; **c. decimal,** décimal codé; **c. decimal notation,** notation (ou numération) décimale codée; **c. decimal number,** nombre décimal codé; **c. program,** programme codé, programme enregistré; **c. representation,** combinaison f de code, élément m de code; **c. stop,** arrêt codé, arrêt programmé.

coder, codeur m; **pulse c.,** générateur m d'impulsions codées; **telemetering c.,** appareil m de codage des télémesures.

codification, codification f.

coding, 1. codage m; 2. programmation f; **absolute c.,** codage absolu; **actual c.,** codage absolu; **automatic c.,** codage automatique; **basic c.,** codage de base; **binary c.,** codage binaire; **direct c.,** programmation en langage machine; **inline c.,** séquence f de la partie principale du programme; **macro c.,** programmation à macro-instructions; **micro c.,** micro-programmation f; **minimal latency c.,** codage à temps d'accès minimum, programmation à temps d'exécution minimum; **minimum access c.,** codage à accès minimum; **minimum delay c.,** codage à temps d'accès minimum, programmation à temps d'exécution minimum; **numerical c.,** codage numérique; **optimum c.,** codage optimum; **out of line c.,** séquence extérieure au programme principal; **own c.,** séquence f (complémentaire) d'utilisateur; **relative c.,** codage relatif; **single column duodecimal c.,** codage duodécimal sur une colonne; **skeletal c.,** codage à instruction paramétrable; **specific c.,** codage absolu; **straight-line c.,** codage en succession; **symbolic c.,** programmation symbolique; **c. check,** vérification f de codage (de programmes); **c. form,** feuille f de programmation, imprimé m de programmation; **c. scheme,** codification f, code m; **c. sheet,** feuille f de programmation.

coefficient, 1. coefficient m; 2. mantisse f (représentation à virgule flottante); **attenuation c.,** constante f d'affaiblissement, affaiblissement m linéique; **coupling c.,** coefficient de couplage; **matrix c.,** coefficient matriciel; **reflection c.,** coefficient de réflexion; **scale c.,** échelle f, facteur m de multiplication (ou de division).

cognition, machine c., perception artificielle.

coherence, cohérence f; **modulation c.,** cohérence d'une modulation.

coil, bobine f, bobinage m; **blank c.,** bobine de bande non perforée; **blank paper tape c.,** bobine de bande non perforée; **hybrid c.,** transformateur différentiel; **induction c.,** bobine d'induction; **repeating c.,** translateur m; **side circuit loading c.,** bobine de charge de circuit combinant; **virgin c.,** bobine de bande vierge; **virgin**

paper tape c., bobine (*de bande perforée*) vierge.

coincidence, coïncidence *f*; **c. circuit,** dispositif *m* d'équivalence; **c. element,** élément *m* d'équivalence; **c. error,** erreur *f* de coïncidence, erreur *f* de simultanéité; **c. gate,** circuit *m* ET; **c. unit,** dispositif *m* d'équivalence.

coincident-current, c.-c. selection, sélection *f* par courants simultanés.

collate (to), interclasser, fusionner.

collating, interclassement *m*; **c. sequence,** séquence *f* (*ou* ordre *m*) d'interclassement.

collation, interclassement *m*; **c. operation,** opération *f* d'interclassement; **c. sequence,** séquence *f* (*ou* ordre *m*) d'interclassement.

collator, interclasseuse *f*.

collection, 1. collecte *f*; **2.** rassemblement *m*; **data c.,** collecte de données, rassemblement de données, saisie *f* de données.

collector, collecteur *m*.

colour, couleur *f*; **c.-bleeding resistance,** résistance *f* au déteintage.

column, colonne *f*; **binary c.,** colonne (en) binaire; **blank c.,** colonne vierge; **card c.,** colonne de carte; **vacuum c.,** puits *m* à vide; **c. binary,** binaire par colonne; **c. binary card,** carte *f* binaire par colonne; **c. 1 leading,** colonne 1 en tête; **c. split,** séparation *f* de colonne.

C.O.M. (=**computer output microfilm**), microfilm *m* de sortie d'ordinateur, sortie *f* d'ordinateur sur microfilm.

combination, forbidden c., code interdit, code prohibé; **c. cable,** câble *m* à paires et quartes mixtes.

combinational, c. logic element, élément *m* de logique combinatoire.

combined, combiné *adj.*; **c. (read/write) head,** tête *f* de lecture/écriture.

command, 1. instruction *f*; **2.** commande *f*; **3.** ordre *m*; **operator c.,** directive *f* (d')opérateur, message *m* (d')opérateur; **c. character,** caractère *m* de commande; **c. code,** code *m* de commande; **c. language,** langage *m* de commandes; **c. signal,** signal *m* de commande.

comment, commentaire *m*.

commercial, c. data processing, informatique *f* de gestion.

common, commun *adj.*; **c. area,** zone commune; **c.-base connection,** montage *m* en base commune; **c. business oriented language (COBOL),** langage adapté aux problèmes de gestion; **c.-collector connection,** montage *m* en collecteur commun; **c.-emitter connection,** montage *m* en émetteur commun; **c. field,** zone commune, zone partagée, zone normalisée; **c. language,** langage commun; **c. machine language,** langage machine commun; **c. storage area,** zone commune de mémoire; **c. trunk,** ligne commune.

communication, communication *f*, transmission *f*; **data c.,** transmission de données; **radio c.,** radiocommunication *f*; **c. channel,** voie *f* de communication; **c. control character,** caractère *m* de commande de transmission; **c. link,** liaison *f*.

communications, communications *f*; **electrical c.,** communications électriques; **telex c.,** communications télex.

commutator, distributeur *m*; **c. pulse,** impulsion *f* de contrôle.

compact (to), tasser.

compaction, data c., condensation *f* de données.

compandor, compresseur-extenseur *m*.

comparator, comparateur *m*; **analog c.,** comparateur analogique; **digital c.,** comparateur numérique; **tape c.,** comparateur de bandes (perforées).

compare (to), comparer.

comparing, c. control change, rupture *f* de contrôle par comparaison (de zones); **c. unit,** comparateur *m*.

comparison, comparaison *f*; **logical c.,** comparaison logique.

compartment, compartiment *m*.

compatibility, compatibilité *f*; **equipment c.,** compatibilité entre équipements; **program c.,** compatibilité des programmes; **c. test,** essai *m* de compatibilité.

compatible, compatible *adj.*; **computer-c.,** compatible avec plusieurs (types de) calculateurs, utilisable sur plusieurs types de calculateurs; **plug-to-plug c.,** à connexion *f* compatible, directement connectable.

compendium, résumé succinct.

compensating, c. network, circuit compensateur.

compensator, compensateur *m*; **level c.,** compensateur de niveau.

compilation, compilation *f*; **c. time,** durée *f* de compilation.

compile (to), compiler.

compiler, compilateur *m*, programme *m* de compilation; **conversational c.,** compilateur conversationnel; **program c.,** compilateur, programme de compilation.

compiling, compilation *f*; **c. computer,** calculateur *m* de compilation; **c. duration,** durée *f* de compilation; **c. phase,** phase *f* de compilation; **c. program,** compilateur *m*, programme *m* de compilation; **c. routine,** compilateur *m*, programme *m* de compilation.

complement, complément *m*; **diminished radix c.,** complément à la base moins un, complément restreint; **nines c.,** complément à neuf; **noughts c.,** complément à zéro, complément à la base; **ones c.,** complément à un; **radix c.,** complément à la base, complément à zéro; **radix-minus-one c.,** complément à la base moins un, complément restreint; **tens c.,** complément à dix; **true c.,** complément à la base, complément à zéro; **twos c.,** complément à deux; **zero c.,** complément à zéro, complément à la base; **c. base,** base *f* du complément; **c. on nine,** complément à neuf; **c. on one,** complément à un; **c. on ten,** complément à dix.

complementary, complémentaire *adj*; **c. operation,** opération *f* complémentaire; **c. operator,** opérateur *m* complémentaire.

complementation, Boolean c., opération *f* NON.

complementing, c. circuit, circuit *m* à complément.

complete, complet (-ète) *adj*.; **c. carry,** report total; **c. instruction,** instruction complète; **c. operation,** opération complète; **c. routine,** programme figé.

component, composant *m*; **solid-state c.,** composant transistorisé, composant à semi-conducteur(s); **c. error,** erreur due au(x) composant(s).

composite, c. cable, câble *m* mixte.

compound, c. modulation, modulation *f* multiple.

compression, data c., condensation *f* de données; **digit c.,** condensation *f* de chiffres.

computation, calcul *m*; **address c.,** calcul d'adresse.

compute, c.-limited, subordonné au (*ou* limité par le) temps de calcul; **c. mode,** état *m* de fonctionnement.

compute (to), calculer.

computer, ordinateur *m*, calculateur *m*; **absolute value c.,** calculateur à valeurs réelles; **all-purpose c.,** calculateur universel, calculateur polyvalent; **analog c.,** calculateur analogique; **arbitrary sequence c.,** calculateur séquentiel à enchaînement arbitraire; **arithmetic c.,** calculateur arithmétique; **asynchronous c.,** calculateur asynchrone, calculateur arythmique; **automatic c.,** calculateur automatique; **buffered c.,** calculateur à mémoire(s) tampon(s); **central c.,** calculateur central; **character-oriented c.,** ordinateur à caractères; **compiling c.,** calculateur de compilation; **consecutive c.,** calculateur séquentiel, calculateur (en) série; **consecutive sequence c.,** calculateur séquentiel à enchaînement fixe; **control c.,** calculateur (*ou* ordinateur) de contrôle de processus (industriels); **digital c.,** calculateur numérique, calculateur numéral; **first-generation c.,** calculateur de première génération; **fixed-point c.,** ordinateur à virgule fixe; **fixed program c.,** calculateur à programme fixe; **floating-point c.,** ordinateur à virgule flottante; **general purpose c.,** calculateur universel, calculateur polyvalent; **host c.,** ordinateur central, ordinateur principal; **hybrid c.,** calculateur hybride; **incremental c.,** calculateur par accroissements; **keyboard c.,** ordinateur de bureau; **logic-controlled sequential c.,** ordinateur à séquence contrôlée par logique; **object c.,** calculateur objet, calculateur d'exécution; **parallel c.,** calculateur simultané; **pneumatic c.,** ordinateur à fluides; **process control c.,** calculateur de contrôle de processus industriels; **program-controlled sequential c.,** ordinateur à séquence contrôlée par programme; **scientific c.,** ordinateur scientifique; **second-generation c.,** calculateur de deuxième génération; **sequential c.,** calculateur séquentiel, calculateur (en) série; **serial c.,** calculateur séquentiel, calculateur (en) série; **simultaneous c.,** calculateur simultané; **slave c.,** ordinateur asservi, ordinateur satellite; **solid-state c.,**

calculateur transistorisé; **special purpose c.,** calculateur spécialisé; **stored-program c.,** calculateur à programme enregistré; **synchronous c.,** calculateur synchrone; **target c.,** calculateur objet, calculateur d'exécution; **third-generation c.,** calculateur de troisième génération; **time-sharing c.,** calculateur en partage de temps; **visible record c. (VRC),** machine *f* électro-comptable, ordinateur de bureau; **wired program c.,** calculateur à programme câblé; **word-oriented c.,** ordinateur à mots; **c. aided design,** conception (*ou* étude) automatisée (*ou* assistée par ordinateur); **c. application,** application *f* de l'ordinateur; **c. assisted management,** gestion automatisée; **c. centre,** centre *m* de calcul; **c. code,** code *m* machine; **c.-compatible,** compatible avec plusieurs (types de) calculateurs; utilisable sur plusieurs types de calculateurs; **c. configuration,** configuration *f* d'ordinateur; **c. control,** unité *f* de commande (de calculateur); **c.-controlled machine tool,** machine-outil commandée par calculateur; **c.-dependent language,** langage *m* propre au (type de) calculateur; **c.-independent language,** langage indépendant du (type de) calculateur; **c. instruction,** instruction *f* de programme, instruction machine; **c. instruction code,** code *m* machine; **c. instruction set,** répertoire *m* d'instructions de calculateur; **c. language,** langage *m* machine; **c.-limited,** subordonné au (*ou* limité par le) temps de calcul; **c. network,** réseau *m* de calculateurs; **c. operation,** opération *f* machine; **c.-oriented language,** langage orienté vers le calculateur; **c. output microfilm (C.O.M.),** microfilm *m* de sortie d'ordinateur, sortie *f* d'ordinateur sur microfilm; **c. professional,** informaticien (-enne); **c. program,** programme *m* de calculateur; **c. run,** passage *m* (en) ordinateur, passage (en) machine; **c.-sensitive language,** langage *m* propre au (type de) calculateur; **c. store,** mémoire *f* interne; **c. system,** système *m* de traitement de l'information, système informatique, système de calcul; **c. time,** temps *m* machine; **c. word,** mot *m* machine.

computerize (to), automatiser, informatiser, prendre en charge sur calculateur (*ou* ordinateur).

computerized, c. typesetting, composition automatisée (*ou* assistée par ordinateur).

computing, c. amplifier, amplificateur calculateur; **c. machinery,** matériel *m* de calcul.

concatenate (to), enchaîner.

concatenated, c. data set, ensemble *m* de données enchaînées.

concatenation, concaténation *f*, enchaînement *m*.

concentration, line c., concentration *f* de lignes.

concentrator, concentrateur *m*.

concept, concept *m*; **c. classification,** classification *f* par concept.

concordance, concordance *f*.

concurrent, simultané *adj.*; **c. conversion,** conversion *f* en simultanéité; **c. operation,** opération simultanée, fonctionnement *m* en parallèle; **c. working,** fonctionnement simultané.

condensed, condensé *adj.*; **c. (instruction) deck,** paquet *m* de cartes-programme sous forme condensée.

condenser, condensateur *m*; **c. storage,** mémoire *f* à condensateurs.

condensing, condensation *f*; **c. routine,** programme *m* de condensation (des programmes).

condition, 1. condition *f*; 2. état *m*; **cleared c.,** état initial, état de référence; **cyclically magnetized c.,** état de magnétisation cyclique (*ou* périodique); **entry c.,** condition d'entrée; **initial c.,** condition initiale; **one c.,** état «un»; **page wait c.,** attente *f* de page; **paper low c.,** indication *f* de fin de papier; **ready c.,** état de disponibilité; **symmetrical cyclically magnetized c.,** magnétisation *f* cyclique symétrique; **wait c.,** état d'attente; **zero c.,** état «zéro»; **c. name,** nom *m* de condition.

conditional, conditionnel (-elle) *adj.*; **c. branch,** branchement conditionnel, saut conditionnel; **c. breakpoint instruction,** instruction conditionnelle de point d'interruption; **c. (control) transfer,** branchement conditionnel, saut conditionnel; **c. (control) transfer instruction,** instruction *f* de branchement (*ou* saut) conditionnel; **c. implication operation,** 1. inclusion *f*; 2. implication *f*; **c. jump,** branchement conditionnel, saut conditionnel; **c. jump, instruction,** instruction *f* de branchement (*ou* saut) conditionnel; **c. statement,** instruction conditionnelle; **c. stop,** arrêt conditionnel; **c. stop instruction,** instruction *f* d'arrêt conditionnel; **c. transfer of control,** branchement conditionnel, saut conditionnel.

conditioning, air c., conditionnement *m* d'air, climatisation *f*; **signal c.,** conditionnement *m* de signaux.

conductive, conducteur (-trice) *adj.*; **c. ink,** encre conductrice; **c. pencil,** crayon *m* à mine conductrice.

conductor, conducteur *m*; **ground c.,** fil *m* de terre.

confetti, confetti *m*.

configuration, configuration *f*; **bit c.,** configuration binaire; **computer c.,** configuration d'ordinateur; **object c.,** configuration objet; **target c.,** configuration objet.

conflict, access c., conflit *m* d'accès.

conjunction, conjonction *f*, affirmation *f* connexe, opération *f* ET, intersection *f*; **c. gate,** circuit *m* ET.

conjunctive, c. search, recherche *f* par groupe de mots-clés (*Recherche documentaire*).

connect (to), connecter, relier, raccorder.

connected, c. graph, graphe *m* connexe

connecting, c. lead, conducteur *m* de raccordement, fil *m* de connexion; **c. line,** ligne *f* de raccordement; **c. strip,** barrette *f*; **c. wire,** fil *m* de connexion, fil de liaison, fil de raccordement.

connection, 1. connexion *f*; **2.** montage *m*; **common-base c.,** montage en base commune; **common-collector c.,** montage en collecteur commun; **common-emitter c.,** montage en émetteur commun; **faulty c.,** connexion défectueuse; **ground c.,** retour *m* (*ou* connexion) à la masse, prise *f* de terre; **permanent c.,** connexion permanente; **telegraph c.,** commnication *f* télégraphique, liaison *f* télégraphique; **telephone c.,** communication *f* téléphonique, liaison *f* téléphonique; **teleprinter c.,** liaison *f* par téléimprimeurs; **telex c.,** liaison *f* télex, raccordement *m* télex; **temporary c.,** connexion temporaire; **c. box, 1.** boîte *f* de connexion; **2.** boîte *f* de jonction; **c. in cascade,** montage en

cascade; **c. diagram,** schéma *m* de montage, schéma *m* de câblage; **c. time,** heure *f* d'établissement (d'une communication).

connective, opérateur *m* logique, opérateur booléen; **Boolean c.,** opérateur booléen; **logical c.,** opérateur logique.

connector, 1. connecteur *m*; **2.** renvoi *m* d'organigramme; **edge c.,** connecteur latéral; **external c.,** connecteur de raccordement; **flowchart c.,** renvoi d'organigramme; **multiple c.,** connecteur multiple; **variable c.,** renvoi multiple.

connexion = connection.

consecutive, consécutif (-ive) *adj.*; **c. computer,** calculateur séquentiel, calculateur *m* (en) série; **c. sequence computer,** calculateur séquentiel à enchaînement fixe.

consistent, c. unit, élément cohérent.

console, pupitre *m* (de commande), console *f*; **control c.,** pupitre de commande; **data station c.,** console de terminal; **display c.,** console de visualisation; **duplex c.,** console commune à deux ordinateurs; **remote c.,** console de télétraitement; **c. display register,** registre *m* d'unité de visualisation; **c. typewriter,** machine *f* à écrire de pupitre.

constant, constante *f ou adj.*; **address c.,** adresse *f* de base, adresse *f* origine; **figurative c.,** constante figurative; **time c.,** constante de temps; **c. area,** zone *f* de constantes; **c. ratio code,** code *m* à rapport constant; **c. storage,** zone *f* de constantes.

constraint, contrainte *f*.

consultant, ingénieur-conseil *m*, expert-conseil *m*.

contact, contact *m*; **in c.,** au contact (de), en contact (avec); **n-c c.,** contact normalement fermé; **n-o c.,** contact normalement ouvert; **out of c.,** hors contact, hors de contact (avec); **pin c.,** contact à broche; **c. alignment,** alignement *m* de contacts.

content, c.-addressed store (*or* storage), mémoire associative.

content(s), contenu *m*.

contention, encombrement *m*, engorgement *m*.

context, contexte *m*; **key word in c. (KWIC),** mot-clé *m* dans son contexte (*Recherche documentaire*); **key word out of c. (KWOC),** mot-clé *m* hors de son contexte (*Recherche documentaire*).

contiguous, contigu (-uë) *adj.*; adjacent *adj.*

continuation, c. line, ligne *f* de prolongation, ligne suite.

continuous, continu *adj.*; **c. form,** imprimé *m* (en) continu; **c. progression code,** code *m* à signaux à espacement unitaire; **c. progressive code,** code *m* à signaux à espacement unitaire; **c. stationery,** papier *m* en continu; **c. stationery reader,** lecteur *m* de documents en continu (*OCR*).

contour, contour *m*; **c. analysis,** suivi *m* des contours.

contrast, contraste *m*.

control, 1. commande *f*; **2.** contrôle *m*; **3.** régulation *f*; **automatic c.,** commande automatique, contrôle automatique, régulation automatique; **budgetary c.,** contrôle budgétaire; **cascade c.,** contrôle en cascade; **change of c.,** rupture *f* de contrôle, rupture de niveau, changement *m* de groupe; **computer c.,** unité *f* de commande (de calculateur); **conditional transfer of c.,** branchement conditionnel, saut conditionnel; **data c.,** contrôle des données; **device c.,** commande d'appareil; **direct c.,** commande directe; **display c.,** contrôleur *m* d'unité(s) de visualisation; **distant c.,** commande à distance, télécommande *f*; **electronic c.,** commande électronique; **feedback c.,** régulation par réaction; **format c.,** contrôle de format (des données); **indirect c.,** commande indirecte; **input/output c.,** contrôleur *m* d'entrée-sortie; **instruction c.,** (unité *f* de) contrôle des instructions; **inventory c.,** contrôle des stocks; **job flow c.,** contrôle du déroulement des travaux; **manual c.,** contrôle manuel; **margin c.,** contrôle des marges; **numerical c.,** commande numérique; commande symbolique; **operation c.,** (unité *f* de) contrôle des opérations arithmétiques; **process c.,** contrôle de processus industriels; **production c.,** contrôle de production; **program c.,** commande par calculateur; **proportional c.,** commande proportionnelle; **real-time c.,** commande en temps réel; **remote c.,** commande à distance, télécommande *f*; **selection c.,** (unité *f* de) contrôle de sélection (d'instructions); **sequential c.,** mode séquentiel; **sequential-stacked job c.,** contrôle de séquence des travaux; **supervisory c.,** commande de surveillance; **transfer of c.,** branchement *m*,

saut *m*; **c. block,** zone *f* de contrôle (*p. ex.* du système d'exploitation); **c. break,** rupture *f* de contrôle; **c. card,** carte *f* paramètre, ordre *m* de gestion; **c. change,** rupture *f* de contrôle, rupture *f* de niveau, changement *m* de groupe; **c. character,** caractère *m* de commande; **c. circuit,** circuit *m* de commande; **c. computer,** calculateur *m* (*ou* ordinateur *m*) de contrôle de processus (industriels); **c. console,** pupitre *m* de commande; **c. counter,** registre *m* (d'adresse) d'instruction; **c. cycle, 1.** cycle *m* de commande; **2.** cycle *m* opératoire; **3.** intercycle *m*; **c. data,** données *f* de contrôle; **c. desk,** pupitre *m* (de commande); **c. field,** zone *f* de contrôle; **c. function,** fonction *f*; **c. grid, 1.** grille *f* de contrôle (de cartes); **2.** grille *f* de commande; **c. hole,** perforation *f* de contrôle; **c. knob,** bouton *m* de commande; **c. light,** lampe-témoin *f*, voyant (lumineux); **c. line,** ligne *f* de commande; **c. loop,** bande *f* pilote; **c. mode,** mode *m* de contrôle; **c. operation,** fonction *f*; **c. panel,** tableau *m* de commande; **c. program,** programme *m* de contrôle, programme *m* de commande; **c. punching,** perforation *f* de contrôle; **c. record,** enregistrement *m* de gestion, ordre *m* de gestion; **c. register,** registre *m* (d'adresse) d'instruction; **c. relationship,** interdépendance *f*; **c. routine,** programme superviseur, programme directeur; **c. section,** section *f* de contrôle; **c. sequence,** séquence *f* (d'exécution) des instructions; **c. signal,** signal *m* de commande; **c. station,** station *f* de commande; **c. switch,** commutateur *m* de commande, commutateur *m* de contrôle; **c. tape,** bande *f* pilote; **c. total,** total *m* de contrôle; **c. transfer,** branchement *m*, saut *m*; **c. transfer instruction,** instruction *f* de branchement, instruction de saut; **c. unit,** unité de commande; **c. word (of subroutine),** mot *m* de commande.

control (to), 1. commander; **2.** contrôler; **3.** superviser.

controlled, c. variable, variable contrôlée.

controller, élément *m* de commande, contrôleur *m*, régulateur *m*; **automatic c.,** unité *f* de commande (*ou* de contrôle *ou* de régulation) automatique; **program c.,** contrôleur d'exécution de programme.

controlling, c. circuit, circuit directeur; c. exchange, centre directeur; c. position, position directrice.

conventional, c. telegraph word, mot télégraphique conventionnel.

convergence, convergence f.

conversational, de dialogue, conversationnel (-elle) adj.; c. compiler, compilateur conversationnel; c. data processing, traitement m de l'information (en mode) conversationnel; c. mode, mode conversationnel, mode dialogué; c. terminal, terminal conversationnel, terminal m de dialogue; c. time-sharing, partage m de temps conversationnel.

conversion, conversion f; address c., calcul m d'adresses (réelles); binary to decimal c., conversion binaire (à) décimal; card-to-disk c., conversion cartes (à) disque; card-to-tape c., conversion cartes (à) bande; code c., conversion de codes; concurrent c., conversion en simultanéité; data c., conversion de données; decimal to binary c., conversion décimal (à) binaire; c. code, code m; c. device, dispositif m de conversion; c. equipment, matériel m de conversion; c. program, programme m de conversion; c. routine, programme m de conversion.

convert (to), convertir.

converter, convertisseur m; analog to digital c., convertisseur analogique-numérique; card-to-magnetic tape c., convertisseur cartes (à) bande magnétique; card-to-tape c., convertisseur cartes (à) bande; digital to analog c., convertisseur numérique-analogique; parallel to series c., convertisseur parallèle-série; regrouping c., convertisseur de regroupement; tape-to-card c., convertisseur bande (à) cartes; ticket c., convertisseur de tickets.

co-ordinate, c. indexing, indexation précoordonnée (Recherche documentaire); c. paper, papier quadrillé; c. store, mémoire (à sélection) matricielle.

copy, copie f; hard c., copie sur (support) papier, copie en clair; c. check, contrôle m de transfert.

copy (to), copier, reproduire.

cordless, c. plug, cavalier m.

Cordonnier, C. check, contrôle visuel.

core, 1. tore m (magnétique); 2. noyau m;

closed c., noyau fermé; dust c., noyau à poudre de fer; ferrite c., tore de ferrite; magnetic c., tore magnétique; multiple-aperture c., tore à plusieurs trous; powdered iron c., noyau à poudre de fer; storage c., tore; switch c., tore de commutation; tape c., tore enroulé; tape wound c., tore enroulé; c. array, matrice f de tores; c. bank, bloc m de mémoire (à tores); c. dump, vidage m (de) mémoire; c. memory, mémoire f à tores (magnétiques); c. memory resident, résidant en mémoire; c. stack, bloc m de mémoire; c. store (or storage), mémoire f à tores (magnétiques).

corner, c. cut, à coin coupé.

corporate, c. data base, base f de données de l'entreprise.

correcting, c. signal, signal m de correction.

correction, correction f; automatic error c., correction d'erreurs automatique; c. from signals, correction sans courants spéciaux.

corrective, correctif (-ive) adj.; c. maintenance, entretien correctif, entretien m de dépannage, dépannage m; c. maintenance time, durée f de dépannage.

correlation, corrélation f.

correlative, c. indexing, indexation précoordonnée (Recherche documentaire).

correspondence, telex c., message m télex.

count, cycle c., nombre m de cycles; record c., nombre m d'enregistrements.

countdown, compte m à rebours.

counter, compteur m, registre m; binary c., compteur binaire; control c., registre (d'adresse) d'instruction; cycle (index) c., compteur de cycles, compteur d'itérations; decade c., compteur à décades; delay c., compteur à retard; electromechanical c., compteur électromécanique; instruction c., registre (d'adresse) d'instruction; location c., registre (d'adresse) d'instruction; program c., registre (d'adresse) d'instruction; program address c., registre (d'adresse) d'instruction; pulse c., compteur d'impulsions; reversible c., compteur réversible, compteur-décompteur m; sequence c., registre (d'adresse) d'instruction; step c., compteur des phases d'une opération; subsequence c., compteur auxiliaire.

coupling, couplage *m*; **acoustic c.,** couplage acoustique; **c. coefficient,** coefficient *m* de couplage.

C.P.M. (=**critical path method**), méthode *f* de chemin critique.

C.P.U. (=**central processing unit**), unité centrale de traitement.

C R (=**carriage return character**), caractère *m* retour de chariot.

crippled, **c.-leapfrog test,** test saute-mouton partiel; **c. mode operation,** fonctionnement *m* en mode dégradé.

criterion, **cycle c.,** 1. nombre *m* d'itérations; 2. compteur *m* d'itérations; **decision c.,** critère *m* de décision.

critical, critique *adj.*; **c. path analysis,** analyse *f* de chemin critique; **c. path method (C.P.M.),** méthode *f* de chemin critique.

C.R.O. (=**cathode ray oscilloscope**), oscilloscope *m* à rayons cathodiques.

cross, **c. modulation,** intermodulation *f*, transmodulation *f*.

crossbar, crossbar *adj.*; **c. switch,** commutateur *m* crossbar; **c. system,** système *m* crossbar.

crosscheck, double contrôle *m*, recoupement *m*.

crossfire (*Am.*), courant *m* perturbateur; **receiving-end c.,** courant perturbateur côté réception.

crossfoot, addition horizontale.

crosstalk, diaphonie *f*; **far-end c.,** télédiaphonie *f*; **near-end c.,** paradiaphonie *f*; **c. attenuation,** affaiblissement *m* diaphonique.

crowd (to), 1. condenser; 2. grouper.

C R T (=**cathode ray tube**), tube *m* à rayons cathodiques, tube *m* cathodique; **CRT terminal,** terminal *m* (à écran) cathodique.

cryogenic, cryogénique *adj.*; **c. element,** élément *m* cryogénique; **c. store (or storage),** mémoire *f* cryogénique.

cryogenics, cryogénie *f*.

cryosar, cryosar *m*.

cryostat, cryostat *m*.

cryotron, cryotron *m*.

crystal, cristal *m*; **liquid c.,** cristal liquide; **single c.,** monocristal *m*; **c. diode,** diode *f* à cristal; **c. puller,** four *m* d'étirage de cristaux; **c. pulling,** tirage *m* d'un monocristal.

cumulative, **c. indexing,** indexation *f* multiple.

current, courant *m*, intensité *f*; **alternating c. (a.c.),** courant alternatif; **carrier c.,** courant porteur; **direct c. (d.c.),** courant continu; **erasure c.,** courant d'effacement; **parasitic c.,** courant parasite; **peak c.,** courant de crête, courant de pointe; **r.m.s. c.,** intensité efficace; **telephone c.,** courant téléphonique; **c. instruction register,** registre *m* d'instruction en cours.

curtate, portion horizontale (*d'une carte*); **lower c.,** portion des rangées inférieures (*d'une carte*); **upper c.,** portion des rangées supérieures (*d'une carte*).

curve, courbe *f*; **B-H c.,** courbe de magnétisation; **magnetization c.,** courbe de magnétisation; **c. follower,** lecteur *m* de courbes.

customer, client *m*.

cut, **corner c.,** à coin coupé.

cut-in, 1. mise *f* en circuit; 2. déblocage *m*.

cut-off, 1. coupure *f*; 2. blocage *m*; **c.-o. relay,** relais *m* de coupure.

cut-out, disjoncteur *m*; **c.-o. switch,** coupe-circuit *m*, interrupteur *m*.

cybernetics, cybernétique *f*.

cycle, cycle *m*; **access c.,** cycle d'accès; **control c.,** 1. cycle de commande; 2. cycle opératoire; 3. intercycle *m*; **dot c.,** fréquence *f* de points; **execute c.,** phase *f* d'exécution; **execution c.,** phase *f* d'exécution; **grandfather c.,** cycle de conservation (de bandes) sur trois générations; **instruction c.,** cycle de réalisation d'une instruction; **machine c.,** cycle machine; **major c.,** cycle majeur; **memory c.,** cycle (de) mémoire; **minor c.,** cycle mineur; **operation c.,** cycle d'exécution (d'une instruction); **reset c.,** cycle de remise à l'état initial (*ou* antérieur); **search c.,** cycle de recherche; **store c.,** cycle (de) mémoire; **c. counter,** compteur *m* de cycles, compteur d'itérations; **c. criterion,** 1. nombre *m* d'itérations; 2. compteur *m* d'itérations; **c. index,** compteur *m* de cycles; **c. index counter,** compteur *m* de cycles, compteur *m* d'itérations; **c. per second,** hertz *m* (Hz); **c. reset,** réinitialisation *f* du compteur de cycles; **c. time,** durée *f* de cycle.

cycle-stealing, **c.-s. mode,** mode *m* d'exploitation en vol de cycles.

cyclic, c. code, code *m* Gray, code binaire
réfléchi; c. feeding, alimentation *f* cyclique;
c. permuted code, code *m* à signaux à espacement unitaire; c. shift, décalage *m* circulaire; c. store (*or* storage), mémoire circulante, mémoire *f* cyclique.
cyclically, c. magnetized condition, état *m*
de magnétisation cyclique (*ou* périodique).
cylinder, cylindre *m*.

D

dagger, d. operation, opération *f* NON-OU
(*ou* NI), négation *f* connexe.
damping, amortissement *m*.
DAT (=dynamic address translation),
traduction *f* dynamique d'adresse.
data, 1. données *f*; 2. information *f*;
alphanumeric d., données
alphanumériques; analog d., données
analogiques; auxiliary d., données
auxiliaires; control d., données de contrôle;
digital d., données numériques (*ou*
numérales); discrete d., données discrètes;
input d., données d'entrée (*ou* en entrée);
machine-readable d., données exploitables
sur machine; master d., données de base;
mechanized d., données exploitables sur
machine; numeric(al) d., données
numériques; output d., données de sortie;
raw d., données brutes (*ou* non traitées);
source d., données de base; test d., données
d'essai; transaction d., données variables
(*ou* de mouvement); d. acquisition, collecte
f de données, rassemblement *m* de
données, saisie *f* de données; d. adapter unit, adaptateur *m* de ligne(s); d. array,
arrangement *m* de données; d. bank,
banque *f* de données; d. base, base *f* de
données; d. capture, saisie *f* de données,
collecte *f* de données, rassemblement *m* de
données; d. carrier, support *m* de données;
d. carrier store, mémoire *f* à support
amovible; d. centre, centre *m* de traitement
de l'information (C.T.I.); d. channel, canal
m d'échange de données; d. code, code *m*
de données; d. collection, collecte *f* de
données, rassemblement *m* de données,
saisie *f* de données; d. communication,
transmission *f* de données; d. com-

munications network, réseau *m* informatique; d. communication terminal, terminal *m* de transmission de données; d.
compaction, condensation *f* de données; d.
compression, condensation *f* de données;
d. control, contrôle *m* de données; d. control block, zone *f* de contrôle (de transfert
de données); d. conversion, conversion *f* de
données; d. delay, retard dû aux données;
d. description, description *f* de données; d.
description language (DDL), langage *m* de
description de données; d. display unit,
unité *f* d'affichage de données; d. division,
division *f* des données (*COBOL*); d. element, rubrique *f*; d. encoder, enregistreur
m; d. error, erreur *f* de données; d. evaluation, évaluation *f* des données; d. field, zone
f de données; d. flowchart, organigramme
m des données; d. flow diagram,
organigramme *m* des données; d. format,
format *m* des données, disposition *f* des
données; d. gathering, collecte *f* de
données, rassemblement *m* de données,
saisie *f* de données; d. handling, maniement
m (*ou* manipulation *f*) de données; d.
hierarchy, hiérarchie *f* des données; d.
item, article *m*; d. layout, format *m*; d. level,
niveau *m*; d. link, liaison *f* (*ou* voie *f*) de
transmission de données; d. link escape
character (DLE), caractère *m* d'échappement transmission; d. logging, enregistrement *m* de données; d. management, gestion *f* de(s) données; d. manipulation
language (DML), langage *m* de manipulation de données; d. medium, support *m*
d'information, support de données; d.
name, nom *m* de données; d. organization,
organisation *f* des données; d. plotter,
traceur *m* de courbes; d. preparation, saisie
f de données; d. preparation equipment,
matériel *m* de saisie de données; d.
processing, informatique *f*, traitement *m* de
l'information, traitement des données; d.
processing centre, centre *m* de traitement
de l'information (C.T.I.); d. processing
machine, machine *f* de traitement de l'information, ordinateur *m*, calculateur *m*; d.
processing system, système *m* de traitement de l'information, système *m* informatique; d. processor, machine *f* de traitement de l'information, ordinateur *m*,
calculateur *m*; d. purification, validation *f*

des données; **d. receiver,** récepteur *m* de données; **d. record,** enregistrement *m* (de données); **d. recorder,** enregistreur *m* de données; **d. reduction,** réduction *f* de données; **d. reliability,** fiabilité *f* des données; **d. representation,** représentation *f* de données; **d. retrieval,** recherche *f* de données; **d. set,** 1. ensemble *m* de données; 2. unité *f* de transmission; **d. set label,** étiquette *f* d'ensemble de données; **d. signal,** signal *m* de données; **d. signalling rate,** vitesse *f* de transmission de données; **d. sink,** collecteur *m* de données; **d. source,** source *f* de données; **d. station console,** console *f* de terminal; **d. storage,** stockage *m* de données; **d. terminal equipment,** équipement terminal de données; **d. transfer rate,** taux *m* de transfert de données; **d. transfer system,** système *m* de transmission des données; **d. transmission,** transmission *f* de données; **d. transmission equipment,** matériel *m* de transmission de données; **d. transmission trap,** déroutement *m* en transmission de données; **d. transmitter,** transmetteur *m* de données; **d. use identifier,** identificateur *m*; **d. validity,** validité *f* des données; **d. word,** mot *m* de données.

date, date *f*; **delivery d.,** date de livraison; **installation d.,** date d'installation; **purge d.,** date de péremption; **void d.,** date de péremption.

dating, d. subroutine, sous-programme *m* dateur.

dB (=decibel), décibel *m*.

d.c. (=direct current), courant continu; **d.c. coupled flip-flop,** bascule *f* à couplage continu (*ou* résistif); **d.c. dump,** coupure *f* de courant continu; **d.c. erasing,** effacement *m* par courant continu.

DCTL (=direct-coupled transistor logic), logique *f* à transistors couplés directement.

d.d.a. (=digital differential analyser), analyseur différentiel numérique, calculateur numérique différentiel.

DDL (=data description language), langage *m* de description de données.

dead, d. file, fichier mort; **d. halt,** arrêt immédiat; **d. time,** temps mort.

de-allocation, libération *f*, désaffectation *f*.

debatable, d. time, temps *m* non imputable.

deblocking, dégroupage *m*.

debug (to), 1. mettre au point (*un programme*); 2. dépanner (*un matériel*).

debugging, 1. mise *f* au point; 2. dépannage *m*; **remote d.,** mise au point à distance; **d. aid routine,** programme *m* d'aide à la mise au point.

decade, décade *f*; **d. counter,** compteur *m* à décades.

decay, d. time, période *f* d'extinction.

deceleration, décélération *f*; **d. time,** temps *m* de décélération.

decibel (dB), décibel *m*.

decimal, 1. décimale *f*; 2. décimal *adj.*; **binary coded d.,** décimal codé binaire; **coded d.,** décimal codé; **packed d.,** décimal condensé; **d. coded digit,** chiffre codé décimal; **d. digit,** chiffre décimal; **d. notation,** notation décimale; **d. number,** nombre décimal; **d. numbering system,** système *m* de numération décimale; **d. numeral,** nombre décimal; **d. numeration,** numération décimale; **d. point,** virgule décimale, signe décimal; **d. representation,** représentation décimale; **d. to binary conversion,** conversion *f* binaire (à) décimal.

decipher (to), décoder.

decipherer, décodeur *m*.

decision, décision *f*; **logical d.,** décision logique; **d. box,** aiguillage *m*; **d. criterion,** critère *m* de décision; **d. feedback system,** système détecteur d'erreurs avec demande de répétition; **d. instruction,** instruction *f* de branchement; **d.-making games,** jeux *m* d'entreprise; **d. mechanism,** organe *m* de décision (*OCR*); **d. table,** table *f* de décision.

deck, paquet *m* (de cartes), jeu *m* (de cartes); **assembled card d.,** paquet de cartes-programme en langage machine; **binary d.,** jeu de cartes en binaire; **card d.,** paquet de cartes; **condensed (instruction) d.,** paquet de cartes-programme sous forme condensée; **instruction d.,** jeu de cartes-programme; **magnetic tape d.,** unité *f* de bande magnétique, dérouleur *m* de bande magnétique; **source d.,** paquet de cartes en langage source; **symbolic d.,** jeu de cartes-programme en langage symbolique (*ou* en langage source); **tape d.,** unité *f* de bande magnétique, dérouleur *m* de bande magnétique.

declaration, déclaration *f.*

declarative, d. statement, instruction *f* de déclaration (*en COBOL*).

decode (to), décoder.

decoded, d. operation, opération décodée.

decoder, décodeur *m*; **operation d.,** décodeur (du type) d'opération.

decoding, décodage *m.*

decollate (to), 1. déliasser; 2. déclasser.

decollator, déliasseuse *f.*

decrement, décrément *m*; **logarithmic d.,** décrément logarithmique; **d. field,** zone *f* de modification d'adresse.

decryption, décryptage *m,* décodage *m.*

dedicated, d. channel, voie particulière; **d. circuit,** voie particulière; **d. leased line,** ligne louée spécialisée; **d. storage,** mémoire réservée.

default, d. attribute, attribut *m* par défaut.

defect, défaut *m,* défectuosité *f.*

defective, défectueux (-euse) *adj.*; **d. modulation,** modulation incorrecte.

deferred, différé *adj.*; **d. addressing,** adressage indirect à plusieurs niveaux; **d. entry,** entrée différée; **d. exit,** sortie différée.

definition, définition *f*; **problem d.,** définition de problème.

deflection, d. sensitivity, sensibilité *f* de déviation.

degenerative, d. feedback, contre-réaction *f.*

degradation, graceful d., fonctionnement *m* en mode dégradé.

degree, degré *m*; **vertex d.,** degré d'un sommet; **d. of inherent distortion,** degré de distorsion propre.

DEL (=delete character), caractère *m* d'oblitération.

delay, retard *m*; **data d.,** retard dû aux données; **differential d.,** retard différentiel; **d. counter,** compteur *m* à retard; **d. distortion,** distorsion *f* de phase; **d. element,** élément *m* à retard; **d. equalizer,** compensateur *m* de phase; **d. line,** ligne *f* à retard; **d. line register,** registre *m* à ligne à retard; **d. line store (*or* storage),** mémoire *f* à ligne à retard.

delayed, d.-output equipment, matériel *m* à sortie différée.

delays, retards *m*; **external d.,** retards extérieurs; **operating d.,** retards d'exploitation, retards dus aux opérateurs.

deleave (to), déliasser.

delete, 1. effacement *m*; 2. élimination *f,* suppression *f*; **d. character (DEL),** caractère *m* d'oblitération.

delete (to), 1. effacer; 2. éliminer, supprimer.

deleted, d. representation, oblitération *f.*

deleter, blank d., suppresseur *m* d'espaces.

deletion, d. record, enregistrement *m* d'annulation.

delimit (to), délimiter, borner.

delimiter, délimiteur *m,* borne *f.*

delivery, livraison *f*; **d. date,** date *f* de livraison.

demand, d. paging, pagination *f* sur demande; **d. processing,** traitement immédiat, traitement *m* à la demande; **d. reading,** lecture *f* à la demande; **d. writing,** écriture *f* à la demande.

demodulation, démodulation *f*; **analog d.,** démodulation analogique.

demodulator, démodulateur *m*; **telegraph d.,** démodulateur télégraphique.

denary, décimal *adj.*

denial, alternative d., opération *f* NON-ET; **joint d.,** opération *f* NON-OU (*ou* NI); négation *f* connexe.

dense, condensé *adj.*; dense *adj.*; **d. binary code,** code binaire saturé.

density, densité *f*; **bit d.,** densité en (nombre de) bits; **character d.,** densité en (nombre de) caractères; **packing d.,** densité d'enregistrement; **recording d.,** densité d'enregistrement; **track d.,** densité en (nombre de) pistes.

dependent, d. variable, variable dépendante.

deposit (to), mettre en réserve.

descending, décroissant *adj.*; **d. order,** ordre décroissant.

description, description *f*; **data d.,** description de données; **problem d.,** dossier *m* d'application.

descriptive, d. abstract, résumé descriptif.

descriptor, descripteur *m* (*Recherche documentaire*).

design, 1. conception *f*; 2. dessin *m,* modèle *m*; 3. étude *f*; **character d.,** dessin de caractère; **computer aided d.,** conception (*ou* étude) automatisée (*ou* assistée par ordinateur); **functional d.,** conception fonctionnelle; **item d.,** dessin d'article; **logic(al)**

d., conception logique; **program d.,** analyse *f* organique; **systems d.,** conception de systèmes, analyse fonctionnelle; **d. automation,** automatisation *f* d'étude.

designation, désignation *f*; **frequency spectrum d.,** désignation du spectre de fréquences; **d. hole,** perforation *f* de contrôle; **d. punching,** perforation *f* de contrôle.

designator, indicateur *m*; **register d.,** indicateur de registre.

desk, 1. bureau *m*; **2.** pupitre *m*; **control d.,** pupitre de commande; **d. calculating machine,** machine *f* à calculer de bureau; **d. checking,** contrôle *m* de programmation sur papier.

deskew, correction *f* de défaut d'alignement, correction *f* de mise en travers.

destructive, destructif (-ive) *adj.*; **d. addition,** addition *f* avec effacement; **d. read(ing),** lecture destructive, lecture *f* avec effacement; **d. read-out,** lecture destructive, lecture *f* avec effacement; **d. storage,** mémoire *f* à lecture destructive; **d. test,** essai *m* destructeur.

detachable, amovible *adj.*; **d. plugboard,** tableau *m* de connexions amovible.

detail, détail *m*; **d. card,** carte *f* détail; **d. file,** fichier *m* de détail, fichier (des) mouvements.

detection, détection *f*; **automatic error d.,** détection d'erreurs automatique; **linear d.,** détection linéaire; **mark d.,** lecture *f* de marques *(OCR)*; **square-law d.,** détection parabolique; **d. system,** système *m* de détection.

detector, détecteur *m*; **AM d.,** détecteur AM *(ou* MA*)*; **blank column d.,** détecteur de colonnes vierges; **property d.,** système *m* de reconnaissance *(OCR)*.

development, 1. développement *m*; **2.** mise *f* au point; **d. time,** temps *m* de mise au point.

deviation, déviation *f*; **frequency d.,** déviation de fréquence, excursion *f* de fréquence; **d. ratio,** rapport *m* de déviation.

device, 1. dispositif *m*; **2.** appareil *m*; **analog d.,** dispositif analogique; **asynchronous d.,** dispositif asynchrone; **attention d.,** dispositif d'appel d'attention; **conversion d.,** dispositif de conversion; **direct access d.,** dispositif à accès direct; **film optical scan-**ning d., dispositif de lecture optique de film; **input d.,** appareil d'entrée; **input/output d.,** appareil d'entrée-sortie; **mass storage d.,** mémoire *f* de masse; **memory protect d.,** dispositif de protection de mémoire; **multiplex d.,** dispositif multiplex; **network analog d.,** réseau *m* d'étude analogique; **optional d.,** dispositif en option, dispositif facultatif; **output d.,** appareil de sortie; **random access d.,** appareil à accès direct, appareil à accès sélectif; **sensing d., 1.** dispositif de lecture; **2.** détecteur *m*, capteur *m*, palpeur *m*; **solid-state d.,** dispositif à semi-conducteurs, dispositif transistorisé; **special d.,** dispositif spécial; **storage d.,** dispositif de mémorisation, mémoire *f*; **stylus input d.,** crayon lumineux, marqueur lumineux, stylet lumineux, luminostyle *m*; **system output d.,** appareil de sortie du système; **terminal d.,** terminal *m*; **transmitting d.,** appareil de transmission; **voice-operated d.,** dispositif à commande par fréquence vocale; **d. control,** commande *f* d'appareil; **d. control character,** caractère *m* de commande d'appareil.

diagnosis, diagnostic *m*.

diagnostic, diagnostique *adj.*

diagnostic, diagnostic *m*; **error d.,** diagnostic d'erreurs; **d. check,** test *m* de diagnostic; **d. program,** programme *m* de diagnostic; **d. routine,** programme *m* de diagnostic; **d. test,** test *m* de diagnostic.

diagnotor, programme *m* de diagnostic.

diagram, diagramme *m*, schéma *m*; **block d.,** schéma fonctionnel, schéma synoptique; **connection d.,** schéma de montage, schéma de câblage; **data flow d.,** organigramme *m* des données; **dynamic flow d.,** organigramme *m* dynamique; **energy level d.,** diagramme énergétique; **flow d.,** organigramme *m* (de traitement de l'information), ordinogramme *m*; **flow-process d.,** organigramme *m* de système(s); **functional d.,** schéma fonctionnel; **level d.,** hypsogramme *m*; **logic(al) d.,** organigramme *m* *(ou* schéma*)* logique, logigramme *m*; **programming flow d.,** organigramme *m* de programmation; **run d.,** organigramme *m* d'exploitation; **set-up d.,** schéma d'implantation, schéma d'installation, schéma de montage; **timing d.,** diagramme de temps; **Veitch d.,**

diagramme de Veitch; **Venn d.**, diagramme de Venn; **wiring d.**, schéma de câblage.

dial, cadran *m*; **rotary d.**, cadran rotatif; **d. exchange**, central *m* automatique; **d. operation**, appel *m* (*ou* sélection *f*) au cadran; **d. pulse**, impulsion *f* de cadran.

dial (to), composer au cadran, sélectionner.

dialling, appel *m* au cadran, sélection *f* au cadran; **push-down d.**, appel par boutons-poussoirs; **tone d.**, appel par boutons-poussoirs; **d. code**, code *m* de sélection (*ou* de numérotation); **d. number**, numéro *m* de sélection; **d. signal**, signal *m* de sélection.

dial-up, appel *m* au cadran, sélection *f* au cadran.

dibit, dibit *m*, groupe *m* de deux bits.

dichotomizing, dichotomique *adj.*; **d. search**, recherche *f* dichotomique.

dichotomy, dichotomie *f*.

dicing, découpage *m* en dés.

dictionary, dictionnaire *m*; **automatic d.**, dictionnaire automatique; **dual d.**, index croisé (*Recherche documentaire*); **external symbol d.**, liste *f* des références symboliques externes; **relocation d.**, liste *f* des adresses relogeables (*ou* translatables); **d. catalog(ue)**, catalogue groupé; **d. code**, code *m* dictionnaire.

die, punch d., matrice *f* de perforation.

difference, différence *f*; **logical d.**, différence logique; **symmetric d.**, exclusion *f* réciproque, opération *f* de non-équivalence.

differential, différentiel (-elle) *adj.*; **d. amplifier**, amplificateur différentiel; **d. analyser**, analyseur différentiel, calculateur analogique différentiel; **d. delay**, retard différentiel; **d. equation**, équation différentielle; **d. gear**, mécanisme *m* additionneur-soustracteur; **d. modulation**, modulation différentielle; **d. preamplifier**, préamplificateur différentiel.

differentiating, d. amplifier, amplificateur différentiateur; **d. circuit**, montage différentiateur; **d. network** (*Am.*), montage différentiateur.

differentiator, 1. différentiateur *m*; 2. montage différentiateur.

diffusion, diffusion *f*.

digit, chiffre *m*; **binary d.**, chiffre binaire, poids *m* binaire, bit *m*; **check d.**, chiffre de contrôle; **decimal d.**, chiffre décimal;

decimal coded d., chiffre codé décimal; **forbidden d.**, caractère *m* invalide; **gap d.**, chiffre (*ou* caractère *m*) de service; **high-order d.**, chiffre d'ordre plus élevé; **least significant d.**, chiffre le moins significatif; **low-order d.**, chiffre d'ordre moins élevé; **most significant d.**, chiffre le plus significatif; **n-ary d.**, chiffre n-aire; **octal d.**, chiffre octal; **sign d.**, chiffre de signe; **significant d.**, chiffre significatif; **sum-check d.**, chiffre de contrôle de totalisation; **zone d.**, perforation *f* hors-texte; **d. compression**, condensation *f* de chiffres; **d. delay element**, élément retardateur d'un chiffre; **d. emitter**, émetteur *m* de signaux, distributeur *m*; **d. filter**, sélecteur *m* de perforation; **d. period**, durée *f* d'impulsion; **d. place**, emplacement *m* de chiffre, rang *m* (d-'un chiffre); **d. plane**, plan *m* de mémoire; **d. position**, emplacement *m* de chiffre, rang *m* (d'un chiffre); **d. selector**, sélecteur *m* de perforation; **d. time**, temps *m* élémentaire; **d. transfer bus**, voie *f* de transfert de chiffres; **d. transfer trunk**, voie *f* de transfert de chiffres.

digital, numérique *adj.*; numéral *adj.*; **d. adder**, additionneur *m* numérique; **d. clock**, horloge *f* à signaux numériques; **d. comparator**, comparateur *m* numérique; **d. computer**, calculateur *m* numérique, calculateur numéral; **d. data**, données numériques (*ou* numérales); **d. differential analyser (d.d.a.)**, analyseur différentiel numérique, calculateur numérique différentiel; **d. display**, affichage *m* de valeurs numériques; **d. divider**, diviseur *m* numérique; **d. incremental plotter**, traceur *m* de courbes incrémental; **d. integrator**, intégrateur *m* numérique; **d. multiplier**, multiplicateur *m* numérique; **d. representation**, représentation numérique (*ou* numérale); **d. sort**, tri *m* numérique; **d. subset**, 1. ensemble *m* de données; 2. unité *f* de transmission; **d. subtracter**, soustracteur *m* numérique; **d. tabulator**, tabulatrice *f* numérique; **d. to analog converter**, convertisseur *m* numérique-analogique.

digitize (to), 1. convertir en numérique; 2. chiffrer, codifier (*ou* exprimer) en numérique.

digitizer, convertisseur *m* analogique-numérique.

digits, equivalent binary d., équivalent *m* binaire d'une combinaison alphabétique; **function d.,** partie *f* «type d'opération»; **gap d.,** chiffres *m* de remplissage; **significant d.,** 1. chiffres significatifs; 2. mantisse *f* (*en représentation à virgule flottante*).

diminished, d. radix complement, complément *m* à la base moins un, complément restreint.

diode, diode *f*; **crystal d.,** diode à cristal; **germanium d.,** diode au germanium; **light-emitting d. (LED),** diode électroluminescente; **tunnel d.,** diode tunnel; **d.-capacity memory,** mémoire *f* à diodes/condensateurs; **d. function generator,** générateur *m* de fonctions à diodes; **d. logic (DL),** logique *f* à diodes; **d.-transistor logic (DTL),** logique *f* à diodes et transistors.

diplex, diplex *adj.*

direct, direct *adj.*; **d. access,** accès direct, accès sélectif; **d. access device,** dispositif *m* à accès direct; **d. access store (*or* storage),** mémoire *f* à accès direct, mémoire à accès sélectif; **d. address,** adresse directe, adresse réelle; **d. addressing,** adressage direct; **d. allocation,** allocation *f* fixe; **d. code,** code réel (*en langage machine*); **d. coding,** programmation *f* en langage machine; **d. control,** commande directe; **d.-coupled flip-flop,** bascule *f* à couplage continu (*ou* résistif); **d.-coupled transistor logic (DCTL),** logique *f* à transistors couplés directement; **d. current (d.c.),** courant continu; **d. display,** affichage direct; **d. insert subroutine,** sous-programme *m* relogeable; **d. instruction,** instruction *f* à opérande incorporé; **d. output,** sortie directe; **d. route,** voie directe; **d. (telegraph) circuit,** circuit (télégraphique) direct; **d. telex circuit,** circuit télex direct.

direct current, courant continu; **d.c. amplifier,** amplificateur *m* à couplage direct; **d.c. restorer,** régénérateur *m* de composante continue; **d.c. transmission,** transmission *f* par courant continu.

direction, flow d., sens *m* de liaison (*sur un organigramme*).

directive, pseudo-instruction *f*.

directly, d. coupled amplifier, amplificateur *m* à couplage direct.

directory, répertoire *m*.

disable (to), 1. mettre hors service; 2. refuser, interdire; 3. invalider.

disaster, d. dump, vidage *m* sur incident grave.

disconnect, d. signal (*Am.*), signal *m* de fin (de communication).

disconnect (to), déconnecter.

discontinuous, discontinu *adj.*; **d. function,** fonction discontinue.

discrete, discret (-ète) *adj.*; **d. data,** données discrètes; **d. representation,** représentation discrète.

discrimination, frequency d., sélection *f* d'une fréquence; **d. instruction,** instruction *f* de branchement (*ou* saut) conditionnel.

disjunction, disjonction *f*, réunion *f*, opération *f* OU; **d. gate,** circuit *m* OU.

disjunctive, d. search, recherche *f* par mot-clé unique (*Recherche documentaire*).

disk, disque *m*; **floppy d.,** disque souple, disquette *f*; **magnetic d.,** disque magnétique; **system d.,** disque de système; **d. drive,** unité *f* de disques; **d. drive unit,** unité *f* de disques; **d. file,** fichier *m* (sur) disque; **d. operating system (D.O.S.),** système *m* d'exploitation sur disques; **d. pack,** chargeur *m* de disques amovible; **d. storage,** mémoire *f* à disques.

diskette, minidisque *m*.

dispatcher, distributeur *m*, répartiteur *m*; **task d.,** distributeur de tâches.

dispatching, d. priority, priorité *f* de prise en charge.

disperse (to), ventiler.

dispersion, 1. ventilation *f*; 2. opération *f* NON-ET; **d. gate,** circuit *m* NON-ET.

displacement, déplacement *m*.

display, 1. affichage *m*, visualisation *f*; 2. console *f* de visualisation, visuel *m*; **cathode ray tube d.,** unité *f* de visualisation à tube (*ou* à rayons) cathodique(s); **digital d.,** affichage de valeurs numériques; **direct d.,** affichage direct; **forced d.,** affichage systématique; **point mode d.,** affichage par points; **d. category,** catégorie *f* de données affichable; **d. console,** console *f* de visualisation; **d. control,** contrôleur *m* d'unité(s) de visualisation; **d. tube,** tube-écran *m*, tube *m* d'affichage; **d. unit,** unité *f* d'affichage, unité de visualisation.

display (to), visualiser, afficher.

dissector, dissecteur *m*; **image d.,** dissecteur optique, analyseur *m* optique.

distance, distance *f*; **code d.**, distance inter-signaux; **Hamming d.**, distance inter-signaux; **signal d.**, distance inter-signaux; **d. gate**, circuit OU exclusif.

distant, distant *adj.*; **d. control**, commande *f* à distance, télécommande *f*.

distortion, distorsion *f*; **amplitude d.**, distorsion d'amplitude; **asymmetrical d.**, distorsion dissymétrique; **attenuation d.**, distorsion d'affaiblissement; **bias d.**, distorsion dissymétrique; **characteristic d.**, distorsion caractéristique; **degree of inherent d.**, degré *m* de distorsion propre; **delay d.**, distorsion de phase; **fortuitous d.**, distorsion fortuite; **frequency d.**, distorsion de fréquence; **harmonic d.**, distorsion harmonique; **non-linearity d.**, distorsion de non-linéarité; **phase d.**, distorsion de phase; **quantization d.**, distorsion de quantification; **telegraph d.**, distorsion télégraphique.

distribution, **d. cable**, câble *m* de distribution; **d. frame**, répartiteur *m*.

distributor, distributeur *m*; **time-pulse d.**, distributeur de rythmes, distributeur d'impulsions d'horloge; **transmitter d.**, distributeur transmetteur.

disturbed, perturbé *adj.*; **d. cell**, élément perturbé; **d. one-output signal**, signal *m* de sortie «un» avec perturbation; **d. response signal**, signal *m* de sortie avec perturbation; **d. response voltage**, signal *m* de sortie avec perturbation; **d. zero-output signal**, signal *m* de sortie «zéro» avec perturbation.

diversity, diversité *f*; **frequency d.**, diversité de fréquence; **space d.**, diversité dans l'espace; **d. gate**, circuit OU exclusif; **d. reception**, réception *f* en diversité.

dividend, dividende *m*.

divider, diviseur *m*; **analog d.**, diviseur analogique; **digital d.**, diviseur numérique; **inductive potential d. (IPOT)**, potentiomètre bobiné.

division, division *f*; **data d.**, division des données (*COBOL*); **environment d.**, division «environnement» (*COBOL*); **identification d.**, division «identification» (*COBOL*); **procedure d.**, division «traitement» (*COBOL*); **d. subroutine**, sous-programme *m* de division.

divisor, diviseur *m*.

D L (=**diode logic**), logique *f* à diodes.

D L E (=**data link escape character**), caractère *m* d'échappement transmission.

D M L (=**data manipulation language**), langage *m* de manipulation de données.

document, document *m*; **original d.**, document de base; **source d.**, document de base; **turn around d.**, document circulant (*ou* tournant); **d. alignment**, alignement *m* de documents; **d. gauge**, calibre *m* de cadrage; **d. handler**, lecteur *m* de documents; **d. leading edge**, bord *m* avant de document; **d. reference edge**, bord *m* de référence d'un document; **d. retrieval**, recherche *f* documentaire; **d. sorter**, trieuse *f* de documents; **d. transportation**, alimentation *f* de documents.

documentation, documentation *f*; **program d.**, dossier *m* de programmation; **system d.**, dossier *m* d'application.

docuterm, docuterme *m* (*Recherche documentaire*).

donor, donneur *m*.

do-nothing, **d.-n. instruction**, instruction *f* factice, instruction *f* de remplissage.

don't care, **d. c. gate**, circuit indifférent.

dormant, **d. state**, état *m* d'inactivité.

D.O.S. (=**disk operating system**), système *m* d'exploitation sur disques.

dot, **d. cycle**, fréquence *f* de points; **d. printer**, imprimante *f* par points.

double, double *adj.*; **d. buffering**, utilisation *f* de double tampon; **d.-current transmission**, transmission *f* par double courant; **d. error**, erreur *f* double; **d. modulation**, double modulation *f*; **d. pulse recording**, enregistrement *m* par double impulsion; **d. punch(ing)**, double perforation *f*; **d.-sideband transmission**, émission *f* sur double bande latérale.

double-ended, à deux extrémités *f*; **d.-e. amplifier**, amplificateur *m* push-pull, amplificateur *m* symétrique.

double-length, à longueur *f* double; **d.-l. number**, nombre *m* en longueur double; **d.-l. numeral**, nombre *m* en longueur double; **d.-l. working**, fonctionnement *m* en longueur double.

double-precision, en (*ou* à) double précision *f*; **d.-p. arithmetic**, arithmétique *f* en double précision; **d.-p. number**, nombre *m* en double précision; **d.-p. numeral**, nombre *m* en double précision; **d.-p. quantity,** quantité *f* en double précision.

double-pulse, d.-p. reading, lecture *f* par double impulsion.

doublet, doublet *m*.

down, d. time, temps *m* de panne.

drift, dérive *f*; **d. corrected amplifier,** amplificateur *m* à compensation de dérive; **d. error,** erreur *f* de dérive.

drifting, d. character, caractère *m* mobile.

drive, dispositif *m* d'entraînement; **card d.,** (dispositif d')entraînement *m* de cartes; **disk d.,** unité *f* de disques; **multi-spindle disk d.,** unité *f* de disques multibroches; **paper d.,** entraînement *m* de papier; **tape d.,** (dispositif d')entraînement *m* de bande magnétique; **d. belt,** courroie *f* d'entraînement, courroie *f* de transmission; **d. pulse,** impulsion *f* de commande; **d. winding,** fil *m* de commande; **d. wire,** fil *m* de commande.

drop, false d., bruit *m* (*Recherche documentaire*); **d. dead halt,** arrêt immédiat.

drop-in, (lecture *f* de) signal *m* parasite.

drop-out, défaut *m* d'enregistrement.

drum, tambour *m*; **buffer d.,** tambour tampon; **magnetic d.,** tambour magnétique; **program d.,** tambour (de) programme; **type d.,** tambour d'impression; **d. mark,** marque *f* de tambour; **d. memory,** tambour magnétique; **d. storage,** mémoire *f* à tambour magnétique.

dry, d. running, contrôle *m* de programmation sur papier.

D T L (=**diode-transistor logic**), logique *f* à diodes et transistors.

dual, double *adj.*; **d. dictionary,** index croisé (*Recherche documentaire*); **d. feed tape carriage,** chariot *m* à double saut de papier; **d. operation,** opération inverse (booléenne).

ducol, système *m* de perforation double par colonne; **d. (punched card) system,** système de perforation double par colonne.

dummy, factice *adj.*; **d. instruction,** instruction *f* factice, instruction de remplissage.

dump, 1. vidage *m*; **2.** mise *f* en réserve; **a.c. d.,** coupure *f* de courant alternatif; **binary d.,** vidage (en) binaire; **change d.,** vidage des zones (de mémoire) mouvementées; **core d.,** vidage (de) mémoire; **d.c. d.,** coupure *f* de courant continu; **disaster d.,** vidage sur incident grave; **dynamic d.,**

vidage dynamique; **memory d.,** vidage (de) mémoire; **post-mortem d.,** vidage post-mortem; **power d.,** coupure *f* d'alimentation électrique; **programmed d.,** vidage programmé; **rescue d.,** vidage de sauvegarde; **selective d.,** vidage sélectif; **snapshot d.,** vidage dynamique sélectif; **static d.,** vidage (de) mémoire à l'arrêt; **store d.,** vidage (de) mémoire; **d. check,** contrôle *m* de vidage; **d. point,** point *m* de contrôle, point *m* de reprise.

dump (to), 1. vider; **2.** mettre en réserve.

dumping, vidage *m*.

duodecimal, duodécimal *adj.*; **d. number,** nombre duodécimal.

duplex, duplex *m ou adj.*, bidirectionnel (-elle) *adj.*, bilatéral *adj.*; **full-d.,** duplex, bidirectionnel, bilatéral; **half-d.,** semi-duplex; **incremental d.,** duplex par accroissements; **d. apparatus,** appareil *m* duplex; **d. channel,** voie duplex (*ou* duplexée); **d. circuit,** ligne duplex (*ou* duplexée); **d. computer system,** système *m* à ordinateurs en double; **d. console,** console commune à deux ordinateurs; **d. line,** ligne *f* duplex; **d. operation,** exploitation *f* en duplex; **d. system,** système *m* duplex; **d. telephone channel,** voie *f* téléphonique duplex; **d. telex call,** communication *f* télex en duplex.

duplexed, duplexé *adj.*; **d. line,** ligne duplexée; **d. system,** système duplexé.

duplexer, duplexeur *m*.

duplexing, duplexage *m*.

duplicate, double *m ou adj.*; **d. record,** enregistrement *m* en double, enregistrement redondant.

duplicate (to), reproduire, copier.

duplicated, d. record, enregistrement dupliqué.

duplicating, duplication *f*; **d. card punch,** perforateur duplicateur de cartes.

duplication, duplication *f*; **d. check,** contrôle *m* par duplication.

duration, durée *f*; **compiling d.,** durée de compilation; **pulse d.,** durée d'impulsion; **response d.,** temps *m* de réponse; **run d.,** durée d'exécution (*d'un passage en machine*).

dust, d. core, noyau *m* à poudre de fer.

dyadic, d. Boolean operation, opération booléenne diadique; **d. operation,** opération *f* binaire à deux opérandes.

dynamic, dynamique *adj.*; **d. address translation (DAT),** traduction *f* dynamique d'adresse; **d. allocation,** allocation *f* dynamique, affectation *f* dynamique; **d. area,** zone *f* dynamique; **d. check,** contrôle *m* dynamique; **d. dump,** vidage *m* dynamique; **d. error,** erreur *f* dynamique; **d. flow diagram,** organigramme *m* dynamique; **d. memory,** mémoire *f* dynamique; **d. memory relocation,** réallocation *f* dynamique de mémoire; **d. print-out,** impression *f* dynamique; **d. program loading, chargement** *m* dynamique de programmes; **d. programming,** programmation *f* dynamique; **d. range,** portée *f* dynamique; **d. stop,** arrêt *m* sur boucle (*de programme*); **d. storage,** mémoire *f* cyclique, mémoire dynamique; **d. store (***or* **storage) allocation,** allocation *f* dynamique de mémoire; **d. subroutine,** sous-programme *m* paramétrable; **d. test,** contrôle *m* dynamique.

dynamicizer, convertisseur *m* parallèle-série.

E

E.A.M. (=electrical accounting machine), machine *f* comptable électrique.

earth, terre *f*, masse *f*; **e. return circuit,** circuit *m* à retour par la terre.

earth (to), raccorder à la masse, raccorder à la terre.

EBR (=electron beam recording), enregistrement *m* électronique sur microfilm.

Eccles-Jordan, E.-J. circuit, montage *m* Eccles-Jordan.

echo, écho *m*; **e. attenuation,** atténuation *f* d'échos, affaiblissement *m* des courants d'échos; **e. check(ing),** contrôle *m* par écho; **e. mode,** mode *m* écho; **e. suppressor,** suppresseur *m* d'écho, éliminateur *m* d'écho; **e. testing,** contrôle *m* par écho.

ECL (=emitter-coupled logic), logique *f* à couplage par l'émetteur.

EC mode (=extended control mode), mode étendu, mode *m* EC, mode 370.

econometrics, économétrie *f*.

edge, bord *m*; **card leading e.,** bord avant de

carte; **card trailing e.,** bord arrière de carte; **character e.,** bord de caractère; **document leading e.,** bord avant de document; **document reference e.,** bord de référence d'un document; **guide e.,** bord de référence (de bande perforée); **leading e.,** bord avant; **reference e.,** bord de référence; **stroke e.,** bord de segment; **trailing e.,** bord arrière; **e. connector,** connecteur latéral; **e.-notched card,** carte *f* à encoches marginales; **e.-perforated card,** carte *f* à perforations marginales; **e.-punched card,** carte *f* à perforations marginales.

edit, e. routine, (programme *m*) éditeur *m*.

edit (to), mettre en forme.

editing, text e., édition *f* de texte; **e. subroutine,** sous-programme *m* éditeur.

editor, (programme *m*) éditeur *m*; **linkage e.,** programme assembleur, programme éditeur de liens.

E.D.P. (=electronic data processing), traitement *m* électronique de l'information (*ou* des données).

effect, effet *m*; **electrostrictive e.,** effet d'électrostriction; **magnetostrictive e.,** effet de magnétostriction; **parasitic e.,** effet parasite; **piezoelectric e.,** effet piézoélectrique.

effective, 1. effectif (-ive) *adj.*; **2.** réel (-elle) *adj.*; **e. address,** adresse effective; **e. data-transfer rate,** vitesse effective de transfert de données, débit effectif; **e. instruction,** instruction effective; **e. speed,** vitesse effective; **e. time,** temps *m* d'utilisation effective; **e. transmission rate,** vitesse effective de transfert de données, débit effectif; **e. transmission speed,** vitesse effective de transmission.

effector, effecteur *m*; **format e. (FE),** caractère *m* de mise en page, caractère *m* de présentation.

efficiency, efficacité *f*, rendement *m*.

eight, huit; **e.-bit byte,** octet *m*; **e. level code,** code *m* à huit moments (*ou* éléments).

eighty, quatre-vingts; **e. column card,** carte *f* à quatre-vingts colonnes.

either-OR, e.-OR operation, disjonction *f*.

eject (to), éjecter.

ejection, éjection *f*; **e. track,** piste *f* d'éjection.

electric, électrique *adj.*; **e. delay line,** ligne *f* à retard électrique.

electrical, électrique *adj.*; e. accounting machine (E.A.M.), machine *f* comptable électrique; e. communications, communications *f* électriques.

electrode, électrode *f*.

electromagnet, électro-aimant *m*.

electromagnetic, électromagnétique *adj.*; e. delay line, ligne *f* à retard électromagnétique.

electromechanical, électromécanique *adj.*; e. counter, compteur *m* électromécanique; e. recorder, enregistreur *m* électromécanique.

electron, électron *m*; e. beam, faisceau *m* électronique; e. beam recording (EBR), enregistrement *m* électronique sur microfilm.

electronic, électronique *adj.*; e. calculating punch, calculateur *m* perforateur électronique; e. control, commande *f* électronique; e. data processing (E.D.P.), traitement *m* électronique de l'information (*ou* des données); e. data processing equipment, matériel *m* de traitement électronique des données (*ou* de l'information); e. data processing machine, calculateur *m* électronique; e. data processing system, système *m* électronique de traitement de l'information; e. differential analyser, analyseur différentiel électronique; e. funds transfer system, système *m* automatique de transactions bancaires; e. relay, relais *m* électronique; e. switch, commutateur *m* électronique.

electronics, électronique *f*.

electrostatic, électrostatique *adj.*; e. printer, imprimante *f* électrostatique; e. store (*or* storage), mémoire *f* électrostatique; e. storage tube, tube *m* d'accumulation électrostatique.

electrostrictive, e. effect, effet *m* d'électrostriction.

element, élément *m*; active e., élément actif; AND e., élément ET, intersecteur *m*; anticoincidence e., élément de non-équivalence, élément OU exclusif; binary e., élément binaire, binon *m*; code e., combinaison *f* de code, élément de code; coincidence e., élément d'équivalence; combinational logic e., élément de logique combinatoire; cryogenic e., élément cryogénique; data e., rubrique *f*; delay e.,

élément à retard; digit delay e., élément retardateur d'un chiffre; equivalence e., élément d'équivalence; equivalent-to e., élément d'équivalence; exclusive-OR e., élément OU exclusif; identity e., élément d'identité; logic e., élément logique; majority e., élément de majorité; majority decision e., circuit *m* de majorité; modulation e., élément de modulation; NAND e., élément NON-ET; negation e., élément d'inversion; non-equivalence e., élément de non-équivalence, élément OU exclusif; non-equivalent(-to) e., élément de non-équivalence, élément OU exclusif; NOR e., élément NON-OU (*ou* NI), mélangeur-inverseur *m*; NOT e., élément NON, inverseur *m*; NOT-AND e., élément NON-ET, conditionneur-inverseur *m*; OR e., élément OU, mélangeur *m*; passive e., élément passif; sequential (logic) e., élément logique séquentiel; signal e., 1. élément de signal; 2. (*Am.*) intervalle *m* unitaire; start e., élément de départ; stop e., élément d'arrêt; telegraph signal e., élément de signal télégraphique; threshold e., élément seuil à entrées pondérées; unit e., élément unitaire; e. error rate, taux *m* d'erreurs sur les éléments.

elementary, e. item, article *m* élémentaire.

eleven punch, perforation *f* «onze».

elimination, zero e., élimination *f* des zéros.

EM (=end of medium character), caractère *m* (de) fin de support.

embossment, foulage *m*.

emergency, e. maintenance, entretien correctif, entretien *m* de dépannage, dépannage *m*; e. route, voie *f* de secours; e. switch, interrupteur *m* de secours.

emitter, émetteur *m*; character e., émetteur d'impulsions; (selective) digit e., émetteur de signaux, distributeur *m*; e.-coupled logic (ECL), logique *f* à couplage par l'émetteur; e. pulse, impulsion *f* de distributeur.

emitter-follower, émetteur-suiveur *m*.

empirical, empirique *adj.*

empty, vierge *adj.*, vide *adj.*; e. medium, support *m* vierge.

emulate (to), émuler.

emulation, e. mode, mode *m* d'émulation.

emulator, émulateur *m*; integrated e., émulateur intégré.

enable, e. pulse, impulsion *f* complémentaire (de validation).
enabling, e. signal, signal *m* de validation.
encipher (to), 1. chiffrer; 2. coder.
encipherer, codeur *m*.
encode (to), coder.
encoded, codé *adj.*; **e. question,** question codée.
encoder, 1. codeur *m*; 2. enregistreur *m*, encodeur *m*; **data e.,** enregistreur; **magnetic tape e.,** enregistreur sur bande magnétique; **shaft position e.,** codeur de position angulaire.
encoding, encodage *m*; **e. station,** poste *m* d'encodage.
end, extrémité *f* (*d'une bande*), fin *f*; **leading e.,** début *m* de bande, amorce *f* de bande; **logical leading e.,** extrémité logique (sur bande); **trailing e.,** fin (de bande); **e.-around carry,** report *m* en boucle; **e.-around shift,** décalage *m* circulaire; **e. instrument,** appareil terminal; **e. mark,** marque *f* de fin, marque terminale; **e. of block signal,** signal *m* de fin de bloc; **e. of call signal,** signal *m* de fin de conversation; **e. of data marker,** marque *f* de fin de données; **e. of disk mark,** marque *f* de fin de disque; **e. of file (E.O.F.),** fin de fichier; **e. of file indicator,** indicateur *m* de fin de fichier; **e. of file mark,** marque *f* de fin de fichier; **e. of file routine,** programme *m* de traitement de fin de fichier; **e. of job card,** carte *f* fin de travail; **e. of medium character (EM),** caractère *m* (de) fin de support; **e. of message (E.O.M.),** fin de message; **e. of message character,** caractère *m* de fin de message; **e. of message signal,** signal *m* de fin de message; **e. of record word,** mot *m* de fin d'article; **e. of reel,** fin de bobine; **e. of run,** fin d'exécution; **e. of run routine,** programme *m* de fin d'exécution; **e. of tape mark(er),** marque *f* de fin de bande; **e. of tape routine,** programme *m* de traitement de fin de bande; **e. of text character (ETX),** caractère *m* (de) fin de texte; **e. of transmission (E.O.T.),** fin de transmission; **e. of transmission block character (ETB),** (caractère *m*) fin de bloc de transmission; **e. of transmission character,** caractère *m* fin de transmission; **e. printing,** impression *f* en bout de carte; **e. value,** valeur *f* limite.
endorser, endosseur *m*.

endwise, e. feed, alimentation *f* colonne par colonne.
energy, énergie *f*; **e. level diagram,** diagramme *m* énergétique.
engaged, occupé *adj.*; **e. channel,** voie occupée; **e. signal,** signal *m* d'occupation; **e. test,** test *m* d'occupation.
engineering, automatic control e., automatique *f*; **e. time,** temps *m* de maintenance.
ENQ (=enquiry character), demande *f* (de renseignements).
enquiry, e. character (ENQ), demande *f* (de renseignements).
entry, 1. entrée *f*; 2. rubrique *f*, article *m*; **deferred e.,** entrée différée; **index e.,** rubrique d'index (*Recherche documentaire*); **keyboard e.,** entrée (effectuée) au clavier; **page e.,** renvoi *m* d'organigramme en entrée; **remote batch e.,** soumission *f* de travaux à distance par lots; **remote job e. (RJE),** soumission *f* de travaux à distance; **e. condition,** condition *f* d'entrée; **e. instruction,** instruction *f* d'entrée (dans un programme); **e. point,** point *m* d'entrée.
environment, environnement *m*; **virtual e.,** contexte virtuel; **e. division,** division *f* «environnement» (*COBOL*).
E.O.F. (=end of file), fin *f* de fichier.
E.O.M. (=end of message), fin *f* de message.
E.O.T. (=end of transmission), fin *f* de transmission.
epitome, abrégé *m*, résumé *m*.
equal, égal *adj.*; **e.-length code,** code *m* à moments.
equality, égalité *f*; **e. circuit,** élément *m* d'égalité, comparateur *m* d'égalité; **e. gate,** circuit NI exclusif; **e. unit,** élément *m* d'égalité, comparateur *m* d'égalité.
equalization, compensation *f*, égalisation *f*.
equalizer, compensateur *m*; **attenuation e.,** compensateur d'affaiblissement; **delay e.,** compensateur de phase; **phase e.,** compensateur de phase.
equate (to), égaliser.
equation, équation *f*; **differential e.,** équation différentielle; **exponential e.,** équation exponentielle; **matrix e.,** équation matricielle.
equipment, 1. équipement *m*; 2. matériel *m*; **ancillary e.,** matériel auxiliaire;

automatic data processing e., matériel de traitement automatique des données (*ou* de l'information); **automatic switching e.,** matériel de commutation automatique; **auxiliary e.,** matériel auxiliaire; **conversion e.,** matériel de conversion; **data preparation e.,** matériel de saisie de données; **data terminal e.,** équipement terminal de données; **data transmission e.,** matériel de transmission de données; **delayed-output e.,** matériel à sortie différée; **electronic data processing e.,** matériel de traitement électronique des données (*ou* de l'information); **high performance e.,** matériel à haute(s) performance(s); **input e.,** matériel d'entrée, matériel d'introduction; **intermediate e.,** équipement intermédiaire; **offline e.,** matériel autonome, matériel non connecté, matériel indépendant; **online e.,** matériel connecté; **output e.,** matériel de sortie, matériel d'extraction; **pence conversion e.,** dispositif *m* de conversion de pence; **peripheral e.,** unité *f* périphérique; **printing e.,** matériel d'impression; **remote control e.,** matériel commandé à distance, matériel télécommandé; **signal-conversion e.,** équipement de conversion de signaux; **standby e.,** matériel de secours, matériel en réserve; **tabulating e.,** matériel classique, tabulatrice *f*; **terminal e.,** (équipement) terminal *m*; **unit record e.** (*Am.*), matériel classique; **word processing e.,** matériel de traitement de texte; **e. compatibility,** compatibilité *f* entre équipements; **e. failure,** panne *f* machine.

equivalence, 1. équivalence *f*; **2.** implication *f* réciproque; **e. element,** élément *m* d'équivalence; **e. gate,** circuit NI exclusif; **e. operation,** opération *f* d'équivalence.

equivalent, équivalent *adj. ou m*; **binary e.,** équivalent binaire d'une combinaison alphabétique; **e. binary digits,** équivalent binaire d'une combinaison alphabétique; **e. circuit,** circuit équivalent; **e. network,** réseau équivalent; **e.-to element,** élément *m* d'équivalence.

erasable, effaçable *adj.*; **e. store** (*or* **storage**), mémoire *f* effaçable.

erase, effacement *m*; **e. character,** caractère *m* d'oblitération; **e. head,** tête *f* d'effacement; **e. key,** touche *f* d'effacement.

erase (to), effacer.

erasing, effacement *m*; **d.c. e.,** effacement par courant continu; **e. field,** champ *m* (magnétique) d'effacement.

erasure, effacement *m*; **e. current,** courant *m* d'effacement.

ergonomics, ergonomie *f*.

erroneous, erroné *adj.*; **e. bit,** bit erroné; **e. block,** bloc erroné.

error, erreur *f*; **absolute e.,** erreur absolue; **ambiguity e.,** erreur d'ambiguïté; **balance e.,** erreur d'équilibrage; **coincidence e.,** erreur de coïncidence, erreur de simultanéité; **component e.,** erreur due au(x) composant(s); **data e.,** erreur de données; **double e.,** erreur double; **drift e.,** erreur de dérive; **dynamic e.,** erreur dynamique; **inherent e.,** erreur inhérente; **linearity e.,** erreur de linéarité; **loading e.,** erreur de charge; **machine e.,** erreur machine; **matching e.,** erreur d'adaptation; **parity e.,** erreur de parité; **program e.,** erreur de programme; **program-sensitive e.,** erreur due au programme; **propagated e.,** erreur répercutée; **read e.,** erreur de lecture; **relative e.,** erreur relative; **residual e.,** erreur résiduelle; **resolution e.,** erreur de résolution; **rounding e.,** erreur d'arrondi; **round-off e.,** erreur d'arrondi; **semantic e.,** erreur sémantique; **sequence e.,** erreur de séquence; **single e.,** erreur simple; **static e.,** erreur statique; **triple e.,** erreur triple; **truncation e.,** erreur de troncature; **e. burst,** paquet *m* d'erreurs, groupe *m* d'erreurs; **e. character,** caractère *m* d'annulation, caractère *m* de rejet; **e. checking code,** code *m* de contrôle d'erreurs; **e. code,** code *m* d'erreur; **e.-control character,** caractère *m* de contrôle de précision; **e.-correcting code,** code correcteur d'erreurs; **e.-correcting routine,** programme *m* de correction d'erreurs; **e.-correcting system,** système correcteur d'erreurs; **e.-correction routine,** programme *m* de correction d'erreurs; **e.-detecting and feedback system,** système détecteur d'erreurs avec demande de répétition; **e.-detecting code,** code détecteur d'erreurs; **e.-detecting system,** système détecteur d'erreurs (sans répétition); **e.-detection routine,** programme *m* de détection d'erreurs; **e. diagnostic,** diagnostic *m* d'erreurs; **e. list,** liste *f* d'erreurs; **e. message,** message *m* d'erreur; **e. range,** plage *f* d'erreurs; **e. rate,** taux *m* d'erreurs; **e. rate of keying,** taux *m* d'erreur d'une manipulation; **e. rate of a translation,** taux *m* d'erreur d'une traduction; **e. ratio,** taux *m* d'erreurs; **e. report,** liste *f* d'erreurs; **e. routine,** programme *m* de traitement en cas d'erreur; **e. signal,** signal *m* d'erreur.

ESC (=escape character), caractère *m* d'échappement.

escape, échappement *m*; **locking e.,** échappement avec maintien; **non-locking e.,** échappement sans maintien; **e. character (ESC),** caractère *m* d'échappement.

ETB (=end of transmission block character), (caractère *m*) fin *f* de bloc de transmission.

etched, e. circuit, circuit gravé.

ETX (=end of text character), caractère *m* (de) fin de texte.

evaluation, évaluation *f*; **data e.,** évaluation des données; **performance e.,** évaluation de(s) performance(s).

even, pair *adj.*; **e.-odd check,** contrôle *m* de parité; **e. parity,** parité paire; **e. parity check,** contrôle *m* de parité (paire).

event, événement *m*.

except, e. gate, circuit *m* SAUF, circuit OU exclusif.

exception, e. principle system, système *m* de traitement par exception.

excess-fifty, majoré de cinquante; **e.-f. code,** représentation majorée de cinquante; **e.-f. representation,** représentation majorée de cinquante.

excess-three, e.-t. code, code *m* plus trois.

exchange, 1. central *m*, centre *m*; 2. standard *m*; 3. échange *m*; **automatic e.,** central automatique, centre automatique; **automatic telex e.,** central télex automatique; **called e.,** central demandé; **calling e.,** central demandeur; **controlling e.,** centre directeur; **dial e.,** central automatique; **local e.,** central urbain; **manual e.,** central manuel; **private automatic branch e. (P.A.B.X.),** installation privée automatique; **private automatic e. (P.A.X.),** bureau privé automatique; **private branch e. (P.B.X.),** installation *f* d'abonné avec postes supplémentaires; **private e. (P.X.),** central privé; **storage e.,** échange (de données) en mémoire; **tandem**

e., central tandem; **telephone e.,** centre (*ou* central) téléphonique; **telex e.,** centre (*ou* central) télex; **trunk e.,** central interurbain; **e. buffering,** utilisation *f* de tampons par méthode d'échange; **e. call,** appel urbain; **e. centre,** central; **e. register,** registre *m* de mémoire.

exchangeable, e. disk store, mémoire *f* à disques amovibles.

exclusion, exclusion *f*.

exclusive, exclusif (-ive) *adj.*; **e. segments,** segments *m* (secondaires) à implantation exclusive.

exclusive-NOR, NI exclusif; **e.-NOR gate,** circuit NI exclusif.

exclusive-OR, OU exclusif, exclusion *f* réciproque; **e.-OR element,** élément OU exclusif; **e.-OR gate,** circuit OU exclusif; **e.-OR operation,** exclusion réciproque, opération *f* de non-équivalence; **e.-OR operator,** opérateur OU exclusif.

execute, e. cycle, phase *f* d'exécution; **e. phase,** phase *f* d'exécution; **e. statement,** instruction *f* d'exécution.

execute (to), exécuter.

execution, exécution *f*; **e. cycle,** phase *f* d'exécution; **e. time,** temps *m* d'exécution.

executive, e. instruction, instruction *f* de contrôle d'exécution; **e. program,** programme *m* superviseur, programme directeur; **e. routine,** programme *m* superviseur, programme directeur; **e. system,** système *m* d'exploitation.

exit, sortie *f*; **abnormal e.,** sortie anormale; **deferred e.,** sortie différée; **page e.,** renvoi *m* d'organigramme en sortie.

exjunction, exclusion *f* réciproque, opération *f* de non-équivalence; **e. gate,** circuit OU exclusif.

expander (*Am.* expandor), extenseur *m*, expanseur *m*.

explicit, explicite *adj.*; **e. address,** adresse *f* explicite; **e. function,** fonction *f* explicite.

explode (to), dégrouper, ventiler.

exponent, exposant *m*.

exponential, exponentiel (-elle) *adj.*; **e. equation,** équation exponentielle; **e. function,** fonction exponentielle.

expression, expression *f*; **logical e.,** expression logique.

extended, e. control (EC) mode, mode étendu, mode EC, mode 370.

exterior, e. label, étiquette extérieure (de bande).

external, externe *adj.*; extérieur *adj.*; **e. arithmetic,** fonction *f* de calcul externe; **e. connector,** connecteur *m* de raccordement; **e. delays,** retards extérieurs; **e. load circuit,** circuit *m* de charge; **e. memory,** mémoire *f* externe; **e. page address,** adresse *f* externe de page; **e. page storage,** mémoire *f* auxiliaire de pages; **e. page table (XPT),** table *f* des pages externes; **e. reference,** référence *f* symbolique externe; **e. store (** *or* **storage),** mémoire *f* externe; **e. symbol,** symbole *m* externe; **e. symbol dictionary,** liste *f* des références symboliques externes.

externally, e. stored program, programme *m* sur support externe.

extract, extrait *m*; **e. instruction,** instruction *f* de rassemblement.

extract (to), extraire, isoler.

extractor, masque *m*.

extraneous, e. ink, encre *f* excédentaire.

extrapolate (to), extrapoler.

F

fabricated, f. language, langage artificiel.

face, face *f*, recto *m*; **card f.,** face d'une carte, recto d'une carte; **inner f.,** côté intérieur (*d'une bande*); **outer f.,** côté extérieur (*d'une bande*); **type f.,** œil *m* (du caractère) (*OCR*); **f. change character,** caractère *m* de changement de jeu; **f.-down feed,** alimentation *f* (de cartes) face au-dessous; **f.-up feed,** alimentation *f* (de cartes) face au-dessus.

facet, facette *f* (*Recherche documentaire*).

facetted, f. classification, classification *f* à facettes (*Recherche documentaire*).

facilities, automatic telex f., service *m* automatique télex.

facility, hold f., possibilité *f* d'interruption; **lock/unlock f.,** verrouillage/déverrouillage *m*.

facsimile, f. posting, report *m*; **f. receiver,** récepteur *m* de fac-similé; **f. telegraphy,** télégraphie *f* fac-similé.

factor, facteur *m*; **amplification f.,** facteur d'amplification; **blocking f.,** facteur de groupage; **modulation f.,** taux *m* de modulation; **multiplier f.,** multiplicateur *m*; **noise f.,** bruit *m* (*Recherche documentaire*); **omission f.,** silence *m* (*Recherche documentaire*); **pertinency f.,** pertinence *f* (*Recherche documentaire*); **recall f.,** taux *m* de succès (*Recherche documentaire*); **scale f.,** échelle *f*, facteur de multiplication (*ou* de division); **scaling f.,** échelle *f*, facteur de multiplication (*ou* de division); **time scale f.,** échelle *f* des temps; **weighting f.,** facteur de pondération.

fading, fading *m*, évanouissement *m*; **selective f.,** fading sélectif, évanouissement sélectif.

failure, panne *f*, défaillance *f*; **equipment f.,** panne machine; **induced f.,** panne induite; **mains f.,** panne de secteur; **mean time to f.,** temps moyen jusqu'à la panne; **minor f.,** panne mineure; **primary f.,** défaillance primaire; **random f.,** défaillance aléatoire; **secondary f.,** défaillance secondaire; **unverified f.,** défaillance non contrôlée; **verified f.,** défaillance contrôlée.

failures, mean time between f., intervalle moyen entre les pannes, temps moyen de bon fonctionnement.

false, f. add, addition *f* sans report(s); **f. ceiling,** faux plafond; **f. code,** caractère *m* invalide; **f. code check,** contrôle *m* de caractère invalide; **f. drop,** bruit *m* (*Recherche documentaire*); **f. floor,** faux plancher; **f. retrieval,** bruit *m* (*Recherche documentaire*).

fan-folded, f.-f. paper, papier *m* (en continu) à pliage paravent.

fan-in, entrance *f*.

fan-out, sortance *f*.

far-end, f.-e. crosstalk, télédiaphonie *f*.

fast, rapide *adj.*; **f. access store (** *or* **storage),** mémoire *f* à accès rapide; **f. store (** *or* **storage),** mémoire *f* rapide.

father, f. tape, bande *f* de deuxième génération.

fault, défaillance *f*, incident *m*, dérangement *m*; **intermittent f.,** incident intermittent; **pattern-sensitive f.,** incident décelable par une disposition particulière des données; **permanent f.,** panne permanente; **program-sensitive f.,** incident décelable par une séquence particulière de programme; **sporadic f.,** panne intermittente; **f. finding,** recherche *f* de panne, localisation *f* de pan-

ne; **f. time,** temps *m* de panne.
faulty, défectueux (-euse) *adj.*; **f. circuit,** circuit *m* en dérangement; **f. connection,** connexion défectueuse; **f. signal,** signal erroné.
FE (=**format effector**), caractère *m* de mise en page, caractère *m* de présentation.
feasibility, praticabilité *f*; **f. study,** étude *f* de praticabilité, étude préalable.
feature, 1. dispositif *m*; **2.** accessoire *m*; **checking f.,** dispositif d'auto-contrôle; **special f.,** dispositif spécial.
feed, 1. alimentation *f*; **2.** entraînement *m*; **card f.,** alimentation de cartes; **endwise f.,** alimentation colonne par colonne; **face-down f.,** alimentation (de cartes) face au-dessous; **face-up f.,** alimentation (de cartes) face au-dessus; **form f.,** alimentation d'imprimés; **hand f.,** alimentation manuelle; **horizontal f.,** alimentation horizontale; **parallel f.,** alimentation ligne par ligne; **pin f.,** entraînement par picots, entraînement par ergots; **serial f.,** alimentation colonne par colonne; **sideways f.,** alimentation ligne par ligne; **tape f.,** alimentation de bande; **vertical f.,** alimentation verticale; **f. hole,** perforation *f* d'entraînement; **f. knife,** couteau *m* d'alimentation (de cartes); **f. pitch,** pas *m* d'entraînement; **f. reel,** bobine *f* d'alimentation, bobine émettrice; **f. track,** piste *f* d'alimentation.
feed (to), 1. alimenter; **2.** entraîner.
feedback, 1. réaction *f*; **2.** renvoi *m*; **degenerative f.,** contre-réaction *f*; **information f.,** renvoi d'information, retour *m* d'information; **message f.,** renvoi d'information, retour *m* d'information; **negative f.,** contre-réaction *f*; **positive f.,** réaction; **regenerative f.,** réaction; **f. amplifier,** amplificateur *m* à réaction; **f. control,** régulation *f* par réaction; **f. control signal,** signal *m* de régulation par réaction; **f. impedance,** impédance *f* de réaction; **f. loop,** circuit *m* à réaction; **f. system,** système correcteur d'erreurs par retour de l'information.
feeder, f. cable, feeder *m*.
feeding, alimentation *f*; **acyclic f.,** alimentation acyclique; **cyclic f.,** alimentation cyclique; **form f.,** alimentation d'imprimés; **multicycle f.,** alimentation (de cartes) à lectures multiples; **multiread f.,** alimentation (de cartes) à lectures multiples; **sideways f.,**

alimentation ligne par ligne; **single-sheet f.,** alimentation de feuilles individuelles; **f. circuit,** circuit *m* d'alimentation.
feedout, form f., alimentation *f* d'imprimés.
ferrite, ferrite *f*; **f. bead,** tore *m* de ferrite; **f. bead memory,** mémoire *f* à tores de ferrite; **f. core,** tore *m* de ferrite; **f. rod,** bâtonnet *m* de ferrite.
ferro-electric, ferro-électrique *adj.*; **f.-e. materials,** matériaux *m* ferro-électriques.
ferromagnetic, ferromagnétique *adj.*; **f. materials,** matériaux *m* ferromagnétiques.
ferromagnetics, ferromagnétisme *m*.
FET (=**field effect transistor**), transistor *m* à effet de champ.
fetch (to), rechercher (une donnée).
FF (=**form feed character**), caractère *m* de présentation de feuille.
F format, format *m* en longueur fixe.
Fibonacci, F. search, recherche *f* (dichotomique) de Fibonacci.
fiche, fiche *f*.
field, 1. zone *f*; **2.** champ *m*; **card f.,** zone de carte; **check f., 1.** zone auto-contrôlée; **2.** zone de contrôle; **3.** zone de contrôle de marquage (*OCR*); **common f.,** zone commune, zone partagée, zone normalisée; **control f.,** zone de contrôle; **data f.,** zone de données; **decrement f.,** zone de modification d'adresse; **erasing f.,** champ (magnétique) d'effacement; **fixed f.,** zone de données fixes; **free f.,** zone banalisée; **operation code f.,** zone du code d'opération; **reference f.,** champ (magnétique) de référence; **saturating f.,** champ (magnétique) de saturation; **sign f.,** zone de signe; **signed f.,** zone algébrique; **variable f.,** champ variable; **f. effect transistor (FET),** transistor *m* à effet de champ; **f. length,** longueur *f* de zone; **f. mark,** marque *f* de zone; **f. service,** service *m* d'entretien en clientèle.
FIFO (=**first in first out**), premier entré premier sorti (*dans une liste*).
figurative, figuratif (-ive) *adj.*; **f. constant,** constante figurative.
figure, chiffre *m*.
figures, chiffres *m*; **significant f.,** chiffres significatifs; **f. shift,** inversion *f* «chiffres».
file, 1. fichier *m*; **2.** dossier *m*; **active f.,** fichier actif, fichier vivant; **amendment f.,** fichier (des) mouvements, fichier (de) détail;

chained f., fichier chaîné; change f., fichier (des) mouvements, fichier de détail; dead f., fichier mort; detail f., fichier de détail, fichier (des) mouvements; disk f., fichier (sur) disque; end of f. (E.O.F.), fin *f* de fichier; follow-up f., fichier de relance; forms f., fichier des imprimés; inactive f., fichier inactif; inverted f., fichier inversé (*Recherche documentaire*); logical f., fichier logique; main f., fichier principal, fichier maître; master f., fichier maître, fichier principal; master program f., fichier général des programmes; online central f., fichier central en liaison directe; paged f., fichier organisé (*ou* subdivisé) en pages; problem f., dossier d'exploitation; program f., fichier de programmes; shared f., fichier partagé, fichier en commun; suspense f., fichier de relance; tape f., fichier sur bande; transaction f., fichier (de) détail, fichier (des) mouvements; f. activity ratio, taux *m* d'activité d'un fichier; f. gap, espace *m* entre fichiers; f. guard ring, anneau *m* d'interdiction d'écriture; f. identification, identification *f* de fichier; f. label, label *m* de bande; f. layout, dessin *m* de fichier, disposition *f* de fichier; f. maintenance, tenue *f* de fichiers; f. mark, marque *f* de fichier; f. name, nom *m* de fichier; f. protection, protection *f* de fichiers; f. protection ring, anneau *m* de protection d'écriture; f. reel, bobine émettrice, bobine dérouleuse; f. separator character, caractère *m* de séparation de fichiers; f. store, mémoire *f* (à) fichier.

fill, storage f., garnissage *m* de mémoire.
fill (to), remplir, garnir; character f. (to), garnir (une zone) à un même caractère.
filler, zone *f* de remplissage.
film, film *m*, pellicule *f*; magnetic thin f., film mince magnétique; thin f., film mince; f. optical scanning device, dispositif *m* de lecture optique de film; f. reader, lecteur *m* de film; f. recorder, enregistreur *m* sur film.
filter, filtre *m*; band elimination f. (*Am.*), filtre à élimination de bande; band-pass f., filtre passe-bande; band rejection f., filtre à élimination de bande; band-stop f., filtre à élimination de bande; digit f., sélecteur *m* de perforation; high-pass f., filtre passe-haut; low-pass f., filtre passe-bas; matched f., filtre de correspondance (*OCR*).

final, final *adj.*
finder, line f., chercheur *m* (de ligne).
finding, fault f., recherche *f* de panne, localisation *f* de panne.
fine, f. index, index détaillé.
firmware, micrologie *f*, logique *f* à microprogrammes câblés, microprogrammation *f*.
first, premier (-ère) *adj.*; f.-generation computer, calculateur *m* de première génération; f. in f. out (FIFO), premier entré premier sorti (*dans une liste*); f.-item list, indication *f* de groupe; f.-level address, adresse directe, adresse réelle; f.-order subroutine, sous-programme *m* de premier niveau; f. remove subroutine, sous-programme *m* de premier niveau.
five, cinq; f.-level code, code *m* à cinq moments (*ou* éléments); f.-unit code, code *m* à cinq moments (*ou* éléments).
five-bit, f.-b. byte, quintet *m*.
fixed, 1. sédentaire *adj.*; fixé *adj.*; 2. fixe *adj.*; f. field, zone *f* de données fixes; f. page, page *f* sédentaire, page fixée; f. radix numeration, numération *f* à base fixe; f.-ratio code, code *m* à rapport fixe; f. routine, programme *m* fixe; f. store (*or storage*), mémoire *f* fixe, mémoire permanente; f. type bar, barre *f* d'impression fixe; f. word length, longueur *f* fixe de mot.
fixed-cycle, f.-c. operation, opération *f* à nombre de cycles fixe.
fixed-length, f.-l. record, enregistrement *m* en longueur fixe; f.-l. record system, système *m* d'articles en longueur fixe; f.-l. word, mot *m* en longueur fixe.
fixed-point, f.-p. arithmetic, arithmétique *f* à virgule fixe; f.-p. calculation, calcul(s) *m* à virgule fixe; f.-p. computer, ordinateur *m* à virgule fixe; f.-p. operation, calcul(s) *m* à virgule fixe; f.-p. part, mantisse *f*; f.-p. representation, représentation *f* à virgule fixe, numération *f* à séparation fixe.
fixed-program, f.-p. computer, calculateur *m* à programme fixe.
fixed-radix, f.-r. notation, notation *f* (*ou* numération *f*) à base fixe.
fixing, page f., fixation *f* de page.
flag, drapeau *m*, marque *f*, étiquette *f*, indicateur *m*.
flange, flasque *f*.
flat, f. cable, câble *m* ruban.

Flexowriter (*Regd. trade mark*), Flexowriter *f* (*marque déposée*).
flicker, scintillation *f*; **f.-free**, exempt de scintillation.
flip-flop, bascule *f*; **a.c. coupled f.-f.**, bascule à couplage alternatif (*ou* capacitif); **capacitance-coupled f.-f.**, bascule à couplage alternatif (*ou* capacitif); **d.c. coupled f.-f.**, bascule à couplage continu (*ou* résistif); **direct-coupled f.-f.**, bascule à couplage continu (*ou* résistif); **f.-f. register**, registre *m* à bascules; **f.-f. storage**, mémoire *f* à bascules.
floating, flottant *adj.*; **f. address**, adresse flottante; **f. character**, caractère flottant; **f. decimal arithmetic**, arithmétique *f* à virgule flottante; **f. floor**, faux plancher; **f. head**, tête flottante.
floating-point, **f.-p. arithmetic**, arithmétique *f* à virgule flottante; **f.-p. base**, base *f* de séparation flottante, base *f* (de numération) à virgule flottante; **f.-p. calculation**, calcul(s) *m* à virgule flottante; **f.-p. computer**, ordinateur *m* à virgule flottante; **f.-p. number**, nombre *m* à virgule flottante; **f.-p. operation**, calcul(s) *m* à virgule flottante; **f.-p. radix**, base *f* de séparation flottante, base *f* (de numération) à virgule flottante; **f.-p. representation**, représentation *f* à virgule flottante, numération *f* à virgule flottante; **f.-p. routine**, programme *m* à virgule flottante.
floor, plancher *m*; **false f.**, faux plancher; **floating f.**, faux plancher.
floppy, **f. disk**, disque *m* souple, disquette *f*.
flow, 1. flux *m*; 2. déroulement *m*; 3. écoulement *m*; 4. débit *m*; 5. circulation *f*; **bidirectional f.**, transfert bilatéral; **information f.**, circulation de l'information; **normal direction f.**, sens normal des liaisons (*sur un organigramme*); **parallel f.**, déroulement des travaux en parallèle; **reverse direction f.**, sens *m* inverse des liaisons (*sur un organigramme*); **serial f.**, déroulement des travaux en série; **f. diagram**, organigramme *m* (de traitement de l'information), ordinogramme *m*; **f. direction**, sens *m* de liaison (*sur un organigramme*).
flowchart, organigramme *m* (de traitement de l'information), ordinogramme *m*; **data f.**, organigramme des données; **logical f.**,

organigramme logique; **outline f.**, organigramme sommaire (*ou* général); **programming f.**, organigramme de programmation; **systems f.**, organigramme de système(s); **f. connector**, renvoi *m* d'organigramme; **f. symbol**, symbole *m* d'organigramme.
flowcharting, établissement *m* d'un organigramme.
flowline, ligne *f* de liaison (*sur un organigramme*).
flow-process, **f.-p. diagram**, organigramme *m* de système(s).
fluid, **f. logic**, logique *f* à fluides, fluidique *f*.
fluidics, fluidique *f*, logique *f* à fluides.
flux, flux *m*.
flying, **f. head**, tête flottante; **f. spot**, spot *m* mobile; **f. spot scanner**, analyseur *m* à spot mobile.
FM (=frequency modulation), modulation *f* de fréquence.
folder, **problem f.**, dossier *m* d'exploitation.
follower, **cathode f.**, cathode-suiveuse *f*; **curve f.**, lecteur *m* de courbes; **graph f.**, lecteur *m* de courbes.
follow-up, **f.-u. file**, fichier *m* de relance.
font (*Am.*) = **fount**.
forbidden, 1. interdit *adj.*; prohibé *adj.*; 2. invalide *adj.*; **f. character**, caractère *m* invalide; **f. code**, code interdit, code prohibé; **f. combination**, code interdit, code prohibé; **f. combination check**, contrôle *m* de caractère invalide; **f. digit**, caractère *m* invalide; **f. digit check**, contrôle *m* de caractère invalide.
force (**to**), forcer.
forced, **f. display**, affichage *m* systématique.
foreground, avant-plan *m*; **f. processing**, traitement *m* prioritaire.
foregrounding, traitement *m* prioritaire.
form, 1. imprimé *m*; 2. formulaire *m*; 3. formule *f*; 4. forme *f*; **account f.**, imprimé de relevé de compte; **blank f.**, imprimé vierge; **coding f.**, feuille *f* de programmation, imprimé de programmation; **continuous f.**, imprimé (en) continu; **machine processible f.**, document *m* exploitable sur machine; **normalized f.**, forme normalisée (*en représentation à virgule flottante*); **printed f.**, imprimé; **standard f.**, forme normalisée (*en représentation à virgule flottante*); **f. feed**, alimentation *f* d'imprimés; **f. feed**

character (FF), caractère *m* de présentation de feuille; **f. feeding,** alimentation ƒ d'imprimés; **f. feedout,** alimentation ƒ d'imprimés; **f. stop,** arrêt *m* (de) fin de papier.

formal, formel (-elle) *adj.*; **f. language,** langage artificiel; **f. logic,** logique formelle.

format, 1. format *m*; **2.** dessin *m* (de cartes); **3.** modèle *m*; **4.** disposition ƒ; **5.** présentation ƒ (d'état); **address f.,** format d'adresse; **addressless instruction f.,** format d'instruction sans adresse; **card f.,** dessin de cartes; **data f.,** format des données, disposition des données; **F f.,** format en longueur fixe; **instruction f.,** format d'instruction; **linked f.,** format assemblé; **n-address instruction f.,** format d'instruction à n adresses; **one-address instruction f.,** format d'instruction à une adresse; **one-plus-one address instruction f.,** format d'instruction à une adresse d'opérande et une adresse de commande; **order f.,** format d'instruction; **print f.,** format d'impression; **record f.,** disposition d'enregistrement, modèle d'enregistrement; **tag f.,** format d'étiquette; **three-address instruction f.,** format d'instruction à trois adresses; **two-address instruction f.,** format d'instruction à deux adresses; **two-plus-one address instruction f.,** format d'instruction à deux adresses d'opérande et une adresse de commande; **U f.,** format en longueur indéterminée; **V f.,** format en longueur variable; **zero address instruction f.,** format d'instruction sans adresse; **f. control,** contrôle *m* de format (des données); **f. effector (FE),** caractère *m* de mise en page, caractère *m* de présentation.

formatting, 1. mise ƒ en page (*édition*); **2.** mise ƒ en forme (*messages, enregistrements*).

forms, f. file, fichier *m* des imprimés.

formula, formule ƒ.

FORTRAN (=FORmula TRANslation), FORTRAN.

fortuitous, f. distortion, distorsion ƒ fortuite.

forward, f. channel, voie ƒ d'aller; **f. sort,** tri croissant.

fount, fonte ƒ, ensemble *m* de caractères, police ƒ; **optical type f.,** ensemble *m* de caractères à lecture optique (*OCR*); **type f.,** fonte ƒ, ensemble *m* de caractères, police ƒ;

f. change character, caractère *m* de changement de jeu (*de caractères*).

four-address, à quatre adresses; **f.-a. code,** instruction ƒ à quatre adresses; **f.-a. instruction,** instruction ƒ à quatre adresses.

four-bit, f.-b. byte, quartet *m*.

four-plus-one, f.-p.-o. address, à quatre adresses d'opérande et une adresse de commande.

four-tape, f.-t. sort, tri *m* à quatre dérouleurs.

four-wire, à quatre fils *m*; **f.-w. channel,** voie ƒ à quatre fils; **f.-w. circuit,** circuit *m* à quatre fils; **f.-w. terminating set,** termineur *m*.

fractional, f. part, mantisse ƒ (*en représentation à virgule flottante*).

fragment (to), fractionner.

fragmenting, fractionnement *m*.

frame, 1. bâti *m*; châssis *m*; **2.** colonne transversale (*d'une bande*), trame ƒ; **3.** cadre *m* de page; **distribution f.,** répartiteur *m*; **intermediate distribution f.,** répartiteur *m* intermédiaire; **main distribution f.,** répartiteur *m* d'entrée; **main f.** (*Am.*), unité centrale de traitement; **page f.,** cadre de page; **f. grounding circuit,** circuit *m* de mise à la masse; **f. table,** table ƒ des cadres de page.

framing, f. bits, bits *m* de synchronisation.

free, f. field, zone banalisée; **f.-running multivibrator,** multivibrateur *m* astable.

freeze, f. mode, 1. état *m* d'interruption; **2.** état figé.

frequency, fréquence ƒ; **audio f.,** basse fréquence (BF), fréquence acoustique, fréquence audible, audiofréquence ƒ; **calling f.,** fréquence d'appel; **carrier f.,** fréquence porteuse; **clock f.,** fréquence d'horloge, fréquence de base (de temps); **instantaneous f.,** fréquence instantanée; **modulating f.,** fréquence de modulation; **modulation f.,** fréquence de modulation; **natural f.,** fréquence naturelle; **nominal f.,** fréquence nominale; **parasitic f.,** fréquence parasite; **pulse f.,** fréquence d'impulsion; **pulse repetition (*or* recurrence) f. (p.r.f.),** fréquence de répétition des impulsions; **radio f. (RF),** haute fréquence; **telephone f.,** fréquence téléphonique; **ultra-high f. (UHF),** ultra-haute fréquence; **very high f. (VHF),** très haute fréquence; **very low f.**

(VLF), très basse fréquence; **voice f. (VF)**, fréquence vocale, fréquence téléphonique; **f. band**, bande f de fréquence; **f.-change signalling**, (formation f des signaux par) modulation f de fréquence; **f.-derived channel**, voie dérivée en fréquence; **f. deviation**, déviation f de fréquence, excursion f de fréquence; **f. discrimination**, sélection f d'une fréquence; **f. distortion**, distorsion f de fréquence; **f. diversity**, diversité f de fréquence; **f.-division multiplex**, multiplex m par partage des fréquences; **f.-exchange signalling**, modulation f par mutation des fréquences; **f. meter**, fréquencemètre m; **f. modulation (FM)**, modulation f de fréquence; **f. response**, réponse f de (*ou* en) fréquence; **f. shift**, déplacement m de fréquence; **f.-shift keying (F.S.K.)**, modulation f par déplacement de fréquence; **f.-shift signalling**, modulation f par déplacement de fréquence; **f.-shift telegraphy**, télégraphie f par déplacement de fréquence; **f. spectrum designation**, désignation f du spectre de fréquences; **f. swing**, excursion f de fréquence, déviation f de fréquence; **f. tolerance**, tolérance f de fréquence; **f. translation**, transposition f en fréquence.

front-end, **f.-e. processor**, processeur frontal, ordinateur frontal

F.S.K. (=**frequency-shift keying**), modulation f par déplacement de fréquence.

full, **f. adder**, additionneur (complet); **f. drive pulse**, impulsion f de commande (d'intensité) intégrale; **f. read pulse**, impulsion f (de commande) de lecture; **f. speed**, vitesse maximale; **f. subtracter**, soustracteur complet; **f. text**, texte intégral (*Recherche documentaire*); **f. write pulse**, impulsion f (de commande) d'écriture, impulsion f d'enregistrement.

full-duplex, duplex m *ou adj.*; bidirectionnel (-elle) *adj.*, bilatéral *adj.*; **f.-d. operation**, exploitation f en duplex; **f.-d. service**, service m duplex.

fully-perforated, **f.-p. tape**, bande perforée à confettis détachés.

function, fonction f; **algebraic f.**, fonction algébrique; **control f.**, fonction; **discontinuous f.**, fonction discontinue; **explicit f.**, fonction explicite; **exponential f.**, fonction exponentielle; **implicit f.**, fonction im-

plicite; **recursive f.**, fonction récurrente; **transfer f.**, fonction de transfert; **f. chart**, diagramme m de fonction; **f. code**, code m de fonction; **f. digits**, partie f «type d'opération»; **f. generator**, générateur m de fonctions; **f. hole**, perforation f de contrôle; **f. key**, touche f de fonction; **f. part**, partie f «type d'opération»; **f. punching**, perforation f de contrôle; **f. table**, table f de fonctions.

function (to), fonctionner.

functional, fonctionnel (-elle) *adj.*; de fonction f; **f. character**, caractère m de commande; **f. design**, conception fonctionnelle; **f. diagram**, schéma fonctionnel; **f. symbol**, symbole fonctionnel; **f. test**, essai m de fonctionnement.

functor, élément m logique.

fuse, fusible m.

G

gain, gain m; **amplifier g.**, gain d'un amplificateur; **insertion g.**, gain d'insertion; **transmission g.**, gain de transmission.

games, jeux m; **decision-making g.**, jeux d'entreprise.

gang, **g. punch**, reproduction f de constantes (*depuis une carte sur les suivantes*).

gap, espace m; **air g.**, entrefer m; **block g.**, espace inter-blocs; **file g.**, espace entre fichiers; **interblock g.**, espace inter-blocs; **inter-record g.**, espace entre enregistrements; **interword g.**, espace entre mots; **record g.**, espace entre enregistrements; **word g.**, espace entre mots; **g. character**, caractère m de remplissage; **g. digit**, chiffre m (*ou* caractère m) de service; **g. digits**, chiffres m de remplissage.

garbage, données f sans signification.

gate, 1. fonction f; 2. porte f; 3. circuit m; **add without carry g.**, circuit OU exclusif; **alternation g.**, circuit OU; **alternative denial g.**, circuit NON-ET; **AND g.**, circuit ET; **anticoincidence g.**, circuit de non-équivalence, circuit OU exclusif; **biconditional g.**, circuit NI exclusif; **coincidence g.**, circuit ET; **conjunction g.**, circuit ET; **disjunction g.**, circuit OU; **dispersion g.**, circuit NON-ET; **distance g.,** circuit OU exclusif; **diversity g.,** circuit OU exclusif; **don't-care g.,** circuit indifférent; **equality g.,** circuit NI exclusif; **equivalence g.,** circuit NI exclusif; **except g.,** circuit SAUF, circuit OU exclusif; **exclusive-NOR g.,** circuit NI exclusif; **exclusive-OR g.,** circuit OU exclusif; **exjunction g.,** circuit OU exclusif; **identity g.,** circuit d'identité; **intersection g.,** circuit ET; **join g.,** circuit NON-OU (*ou* NI); **joint denial g.,** circuit NON-OU (*ou* NI); **logic product g.,** circuit ET; **logic sum g.,** circuit OU; **majority decision g.,** circuit de majorité; **mix g.,** circuit OU; **NAND g.,** circuit NON-ET; **negation g.,** circuit NON; **non-equivalence g.,** circuit de non-équivalence, circuit OU exclusif; **NOR g.,** circuit NON-OU (*ou* NI); **NOT g.,** circuit NON; **OR g.,** circuit OU; **pocket g.,** clapet *m* (de case); **rejection g.,** circuit NON-OU (*ou* NI); **symmetric difference g.,** circuit OU exclusif; **union g.,** circuit OU; **zero-match g.,** circuit NON-OU (*ou* NI); **g. generator,** générateur *m* de rythme.

gather, g. write, écriture *f* avec regroupement.

gather (to), rassembler, regrouper.

gathering, rassemblement *m*, regroupement *m*, collecte *f*; **data g.,** collecte de données, rassemblement de données, saisie *f* de données.

gating, déclenchement *m* périodique; **g. pulse,** impulsion sélectrice, impulsion *f* de déclenchement.

gauge, document g., calibre *m* de cadrage.

GCR (=group coded recording), enregistrement *m* par groupes de caractères.

gear, differential g., mécanisme *m* additionneur-soustracteur; **integrating g.,** mécanisme intégrateur; **variable speed g.,** mécanisme intégrateur.

general, général *adj.*; **g. program,** programme général; **g. purpose computer,** calculateur universel, calculateur polyvalent; **g. purpose function generator,** générateur *m* de fonctions polyvalent; **g. routine,** programme général.

generalized, g. routine, programme polyvalent.

generate (to), générer, produire.

generated, généré *adj.*; **g. address,** adresse générée.

generating, g. program, programme générateur.

generation, génération *f*; **address g.,** génération d'adresses; **report g.,** génération (de programmes) d'édition; **system g.,** génération de système; **g. data group,** famille *f* d'ensembles de données; **g. routine,** programme générateur.

generator, 1. générateur *m*; 2. programme générateur; **analytical function g.,** générateur de fonctions analytiques; **arbitrary function g.,** générateur de fonctions polyvalent; **clock pulse g.,** générateur de rythme; **clock signal g.,** générateur de rythme, horloge *f*; **diode function g.,** générateur de fonctions à diodes; **function g.,** générateur de fonctions; **gate g.,** générateur de rythme; **general purpose function g.,** générateur de fonctions polyvalent; **macro-g.,** macro-générateur *m*; **manual word g.,** dispositif *m* d'entrée manuelle; **natural-function g.,** générateur de fonctions analytiques; **natural-law function g.,** générateur de fonctions analytiques; **noise g.,** générateur de bruit; **number g.,** générateur de nombres; **output routine g.,** générateur de programmes de sortie; **program g.,** générateur de programmes; **pulse g.,** générateur d'impulsions; **pulse-train g.,** générateur de trains d'impulsions; **random number g.,** générateur de nombres aléatoires; **report (program) g.,** générateur (de programmes) d'édition; **sort g.,** générateur de programmes de tri; **sorting routine g.,** générateur de programmes de tri; **tapped-potentiometer function g.,** générateur de fonctions à potentiomètres à prises; **variable function g.,** générateur de fonctions variables.

germanium, germanium *m*; **g. diode,** diode *f* au germanium; **g. transistor,** transistor *m* au germanium.

gibberish, g. total, total mêlé de vérification, total *m* de contrôle.

GIGO (=garbage in garbage out), à données inexactes, résultats erronés.

glassing, verrage *m*.

glossary, glossaire *m*.

graceful, g. degradation, fonctionnement *m* en mode dégradé.

grade, type *m*; **circuit g.,** type de circuit.

grandfather, g. cycle, cycle *m* de conservation (de bandes) sur trois générations; **g. tape,** bande *f* de première génération.

graph, graphe *m*; **connected g.,** graphe connexe; **non-oriented g.,** graphe non orienté; **oriented g.,** graphe orienté; **planar g.,** graphe planaire; **g. follower,** lecteur *m* de courbes.

grapheme, graphème *m*.

graphic, graphique *adj.*; **g. character,** caractère *m* graphique; **g. display unit,** unité *f* d'affichage graphique; **g. input/output,** entrée-sortie *f* graphique; **g. panel,** panneau *m* d'affichage graphique; **g. solution,** solution *f* graphique; **g. symbol,** symbole *m* graphique.

graphic, symbole *m* graphique, graphisme *m*.

graphical, g. output terminal, terminal *m* de visualisation.

Gray, G. code, code *m* Gray, code binaire réfléchi.

grid, grille *f*; **control g., 1.** grille de contrôle (de cartes); **2.** grille de commande.

gross, g. index, index général.

ground, 1. terre *f*; **2.** masse *f*; **g. bus,** câble *m* de mise à la terre; **g. conductor,** fil *m* de terre; **g. connection,** retour *m* (*ou* connexion *f*) à la masse, prise *f* de terre; **g. return circuit** (*Am.*), circuit *m* à retour par la terre.

ground (to) (*Am.*), raccorder à la masse, raccorder à la terre.

group, 1. groupe *m*; **2.** groupe *m* primaire; **generation data g.,** famille *f* d'ensembles de données; **link g.,** groupe de liaisons; **magnetic tape g.,** groupe de dérouleurs; **pulse g.,** train *m* d'impulsions; **slot g.,** groupe de cases; **tape g.,** groupe de dérouleurs; **g. addressing,** adressage *m* de groupe; **g. allocation,** répartition *f* des groupes primaires; **g. coded recording (GCR),** enregistrement *m* par groupes de caractères; **g. control change,** rupture *f* de contrôle, rupture *f* de niveau, changement *m* de groupe; **g. indicate,** indication *f* de groupe; **g. indication,** indication *f* de groupe; **g. link,** liaison *f* en groupe primaire; **g. mark(er),** marque *f* de groupe; **g. (reference) pilot,** onde *f* pilote de groupe primaire; **g. section,** section *f* de groupe primaire; **g. separator character,** caractère

m de séparation de groupes; **g. theory,** théorie *f* des groupes.

grouped, groupé *adj.*; **g. records,** articles groupés.

grouping, groupement *m*; **g. of records,** groupement d'articles.

guard, memory g., protection *f* de mémoire; **g. band,** bande *f* de garde; **g. signal,** signal *m* de garde.

guide, guide *m*; **g. edge,** bord *m* de référence (de bande perforée); **g. margin,** marge *f* de référence (sur bande perforée).

gulp, groupe *m* de multiplets.

gun, holding g., canon *m* à faisceau d'accumulation (*ou* de régénération); **light g.,** crayon lumineux, marqueur lumineux, stylet lumineux, luminostyle *m*.

H

half, demi *adj.*; **h. adder,** demi-additionneur *m*; **h. pulse,** impulsion *f* de demi-intensité; **h. subtracter,** demi-soustracteur *m*; **h. word,** demi-mot *m*.

half-adjust (to), arrondir au (chiffre le) plus proche.

half-duplex, semi-duplex *adj.*, bidirectionnel (-elle) *adj.* non simultané(e), bidirectionnel (-elle) à l'alternat; **h.-d. channel,** voie *f* semi-duplex; **h.-d. circuit,** circuit *m* semi-duplex; **h.-d. operation,** exploitation *f* (en) semi-duplex; **h.-d. service,** service *m* semi-duplex.

half-pulse, read h.-p., impulsion *f* de demi-intensité de lecture; **write h.-p.,** impulsion *f* de demi-intensité d'écriture (*ou* d'enregistrement).

halt, arrêt *m*; **dead h.,** arrêt immédiat; **drop dead h.,** arrêt immédiat; **non-programmed h.,** arrêt non programmé; **programmed h.,** arrêt programmé; **unexpected h.,** arrêt imprévu (*d'un programme*); **h. instruction,** instruction *f* d'arrêt.

hammer, marteau *m*; **print h.,** marteau d'impression.

Hamming, H. code, code *m* autorectifiable; **H. distance,** distance *f* intersignaux.

hand, h. feed, alimentation manuelle; **h.(-feed) punch,** perforatrice *f* à alimentation manuelle; **h.-held calculator,** calculatrice *f* de poche.

handler, document h., lecteur *m* de documents; **tape h.,** unité *f* de bande magnétique, dérouleur *m* de bande magnétique.

handling, data h., maniement *m* (*ou* manipulation *f*) de données.

hang-up, blocage *m* de programme (*ou* de machine), arrêt imprévu (*de programme*).

hard, h. copy, copie *f* sur (support) papier, copie en clair.

hardware, matériel *m* (de traitement de l'information), équipement *m*, «hardware» *m*; **h. check,** contrôle *m* automatique.

harmonic, h. distortion, distorsion *f* harmonique.

hash, h. total, total mêlé de vérification, total *m* de contrôle.

head, 1. tête *f*; **2.** tête *f* magnétique; **combined (read/write) h.,** tête de lecture/écriture; **erase h.,** tête d'effacement; **floating h.,** tête flottante; **flying h.,** tête flottante; **magnetic h.,** tête magnétique; **playback h.,** tête de lecture; **pre-read h.,** tête de prélecture; **read(ing) h.,** tête de lecture; **record(ing) h.,** tête d'enregistrement; **write (or writing) h.,** tête d'enregistrement, tête d'écriture; **h. stack,** groupe *m* de têtes de lecture/écriture.

header, en-tête *m*; **h. card,** carte *f* (d')entête; **h. label,** label *m* de bande; **h. record,** enregistrement *m* en-tête; **h. table,** table *f* des en-têtes.

heading, en-tête *m*; **h. card,** carte *f* (d')entête; **h. line,** ligne *f* d'en-tête.

hesitation, pause *f*.

heuristic, heuristique *adj.*; **h. approach,** méthode *f* heuristique; **h. program,** programme *m* heuristique; **h. programming,** programmation *f* heuristique; **h. routine,** programme *m* heuristique.

heuristics, heuristique *f*.

hexadecimal, hexadécimal *adj.*; **h. notation,** notation hexadécimale.

hierarchy, hiérarchie *f*; **data h.,** hiérarchie des données.

high, haut *adj.*; élevé *adj.*; **h.-gain amplifier,** amplificateur *m* à gain élevé (*ou* à grand gain); **h. level language,** langage évolué; **h.-order digit,** chiffre *m* d'ordre plus élevé; **h.-order position,** position la plus

significative; **h. performance equipment,** matériel *m* à haute(s) performance(s); **h. threshold logic (HTL),** logique *f* à seuil élevé.

higher-order, h.-o. language, langage évolué.

highest, h. significant position, position la plus significative.

high-low, h.-l. bias test, contrôle *m* par marges, test *m* de marges.

high-pass, h.-p. filter, filtre *m* passe-haut.

high-speed, rapide *adj.*; **h.-s. carry,** report *m* rapide; **h.-s. printer,** imprimante *f* rapide; **h.-s. reader,** lecteur *m* rapide; **h.-s. rewind,** rebobinage *m* rapide; **h.-s. storage,** mémoire *f* à accès rapide.

highway, voie principale, canal *m*.

hit, correspondance *f* (*Recherche documentaire*).

hit-on-the-fly, h.-o.-t.-f. printer, imprimante *f* à la volée.

hold, track h., verrouillage *m* de piste; **h. facility,** possibilité *f* d'interruption; **h. instruction,** instruction *f* de maintien; **h. mode,** état *m* d'interruption.

hold (to), conserver, maintenir.

holding, h. beam, faisceau *m* d'accumulation, faisceau *m* de régénération; **h. circuit,** circuit *m* de maintien; **h. gun,** canon *m* à faisceau d'accumulation (*ou* de régénération).

hole, 1. perforation *f*; **2.** trou *m*; **code h.,** perforation, perforation significative; **control h.,** perforation de contrôle; **designation h.,** perforation de contrôle; **feed h.,** perforation d'entraînement; **function h.,** perforation de contrôle; **sprocket h.,** perforation d'entraînement; **h. site,** emplacement *m* de perforation.

holistic, h. mask, masque *m* holistique (*OCR*).

Hollerith, H. code, code *m* Hollerith.

holographic, h. memory, mémoire *f* holographique.

home, h. record, article *m* primaire, enregistrement *m* direct.

hoot, h. stop, arrêt *m* avec signal sonore.

hopper, magasin *m* d'alimentation; **card h.,** magasin d'alimentation (de cartes).

horizontal, horizontal *adj.*; **h. feed,** alimentation horizontale; **h. skip character,** caractère *m* d'espacement horizontal; **h.**

tabulation character, caractère *m* de tabulation horizontale.

host, h. computer, ordinateur central, ordinateur principal.

hour, heure *f*; **busy h.,** heure de pointe.

housekeeping, 1. de service; **2.** auxiliaire *adj.*; **h. operation,** opération *f* de service, opération *f* auxiliaire; **h. program,** programme *m* de service, programme *m* auxiliaire; **h. routine,** programme *m* de service, programme *m* auxiliaire.

H T L (=high threshold logic), logique *f* à seuil élevé.

hub, 1. plot *m*; **2.** moyeu *m*.

hunting, 1. instabilité *f*; **2.** recherche *f* d'une ligne libre.

hybrid, hybride *adj.*; **h. coil,** transformateur différentiel; **h. computer,** calculateur *m* hybride; **h. integrated circuit,** circuit intégré hybride, circuit semi-intégré; **h. interface,** interface *m* hybride; **h. system,** système *m* (*ou* ensemble *m*) mixte.

hysteresis, hystérésis *f*; **magnetic h.,** hystérésis (magnétique); **h. loop,** boucle *f* d'hystérésis; **h. loss,** perte *f* par hystérésis.

I

identification, identification *f*; **file i.,** identification de fichier; **input/output interrupt i.,** identification de la cause d'interruption d'entrée-sortie; **i. division,** division *f* «identification» (*COBOL*).

identifier, identificateur *m*; **data use i.,** identificateur.

identify (to), identifier, reconnaître.

identifying, i. code, code *m* d'identification.

identity, i. element, élément *m* d'identité; **i. gate,** circuit *m* d'identité; **i. unit,** élément *m* d'identité, comparateur *m* d'identité.

idle, i. time, temps *m* d'attente.

I.D.P. (=integrated data processing), traitement intégré des données, traitement unifié des données.

IF-THEN, IF-THEN operation, implication *f*.

IG FET (=insulated-gate field-effect transistor), transistor *m* à effet de champ à grille isolée.

ignore, i. character, caractère *m* d'annulation, caractère de rejet; **i. instruction,** instruction *f* d'annulation, instruction de rejet.

illegal, interdit *adj.*; prohibé *adj.*; **i. character,** caractère *m* invalide; **i. code,** code interdit, code prohibé; **i. command check,** contrôle *m* de caractère invalide.

image, image *f*; **binary i.,** image binaire; **card i.,** image de carte; **i. dissector,** dissecteur *m* optique, analyseur *m* optique.

immediate, immédiat *adj.*; **i. access,** accès immédiat, accès instantané, accès direct; **i. access store (or storage),** mémoire *f* à accès immédiat; **i. address,** adresse immédiate, adresse directe; **i. addressing,** adressage immédiat, adressage direct; **i. processing,** traitement immédiat, traitement *m* à la demande.

impedance, impédance *f*; **characteristic i.,** impédance caractéristique; **feedback i.,** impédance de réaction; **input i.,** impédance d'entrée; **output i.,** impédance de sortie; **terminal i.,** impédance terminale.

implementation, mise *f* en œuvre.

implication, implication *f*, inclusion *f*.

implicit, implicite *adj.*; **i. function,** fonction *f* implicite.

implied, i. addressing, adressage *m* à progression automatique avancée.

implode (to), regrouper, condenser.

imprint, impression *f* en creux.

improper, i. character, caractère *m* invalide; **i. code,** code interdit, code prohibé; **i. command check,** contrôle *m* de caractère invalide.

impulse, impulsion *f*; **i. noise,** impulsion parasite.

impulsing, i. signal, signal *m* d'appel par impulsions.

impurity, impureté *f*; **acceptor i.,** impureté acceptrice.

in, i. contact, au contact (de), en contact (avec).

inactive, i. file, fichier inactif.

incident, incident *m*.

incidentals, i. time, temps *m* d'utilisation annexe.

inclusion, 1. inclusion *f*; **2.** implication *f*.

inclusive, inclusif (-ive) *adj.*; **i. segments,** segments *m* (secondaires) à implantation simultanée.

inclusive-OR, OU inclusif; **i.-OR operation**, disjonction f; **i.-OR operator**, opérateur m OU inclusif.

incoming, i. **circuit**, circuit m d'arrivée.

incomplete, i. **program**, programme m paramétrable; i. **routine**, programme m paramétrable.

incorrect, i. **modulation**, modulation incorrecte.

increment, accroissement m, incrément m, pas m de progression.

increment (to), augmenter, faire progresser.

incremental, i. **computer**, calculateur m par accroissements; i. **duplex**, duplex m par accroissements; i. **integrator**, intégrateur m par accroissements; i. **plotter**, traceur incrémental; i. **representation**, représentation f par accroissements.

independent, indépendant *adj.*; **machine-i.**, indépendant du type de machine; i. **operation**, opération indépendante; i. **sideband transmission**, transmission f à bandes latérales indépendantes; i. **variable**, variable indépendante.

index, 1. index m; 2. indice m; **cycle i.**, compteur m de cycles; **fine i.**, index détaillé; **gross i.**, index général; **modulation i.**, indice de modulation; **permutation i.**, index de permutation, index permuté (*Recherche documentaire*); **permuted-title i.**, index de permutation, index permuté (*Recherche documentaire*); **quality i.**, indice de qualité; **i. entry**, rubrique f d'index (*Recherche documentaire*); **i. point**, point m machine; **i. register**, registre m d'index; **i. word**, mot m d'index.

index (to), indexer.

indexed, indexé *adj.*; **i. address**, adresse indexée; **i. sequential data set**, ensemble m de données (organisé) en séquentiel indexé.

indexing, indexation f, répertoriage m (*Recherche documentaire*); **co-ordinate i.**, indexation précoordonnée (*Recherche documentaire*); **correlative i.**, indexation précoordonnée (*Recherche documentaire*); **cumulative i.**, indexation multiple; **manipulative i.**, indexation précoordonnée (*Recherche documentaire*); **multiple-aspect i.**, indexation précoordonnée (*Recherche documentaire*); **Uniterm i.**, indexation par Unitermes (*Recherche documentaire*);

word i., indexation par mot-clé (*Recherche documentaire*); **Zatocode i.**, indexation précoordonnée (*Recherche documentaire*).

indicate, group i., indication f de groupe.

indication, indication f; **group i.**, indication de groupe; **negative i.**, indication de signe négatif.

indicator, 1. indicateur m; 2. indicatif m; **call i.**, indicateur lumineux d'appel; **check i.**, indicateur de contrôle; **end of file i.**, indicateur de fin de fichier; **input/output interrupt i.**, indicateur d'interruption entrée-sortie; **overflow (check) i.**, indicateur de dépassement de capacité; **power-off i.**, indicateur de débranchement; **power-on i.**, indicateur de branchement; **priority i.**, indicatif de priorité; **read/write check i.**, indicateur de contrôle de lecture/écriture; **role i.**, indicateur de rôle (*Recherche documentaire*); **routing i.**, indicatif d'acheminement; **sign check i.**, indicateur de contrôle de signe.

indirect, indirect *adj.*; **i. address**, adresse indirecte; **i. addressing**, adressage indirect; **i. control**, commande indirecte; **i. output**, sortie indirecte, sortie différée.

individual, individuel (-elle) *adj.*; **i. line**, ligne individuelle; **i. trunk**, ligne individuelle.

induced, i. **failure**, panne induite.

induction, induction f; **magnetic i.**, induction magnétique; **i. coil**, bobine f d'induction.

inductive, i. **potential divider (IPOT)**, potentiomètre bobiné; **i. potentiometer**, potentiomètre bobiné.

industrial, i. **data processing**, informatique industrielle.

ineffective, i. **time**, temps m de non-utilisation.

inequivalence, OU exclusif, exclusion f réciproque.

infix, i. **notation**, notation infixée.

informatician (*Am.*), informaticien (-enne).

information, information f; **administrative i.**, information de gestion; **alphanumeric i.**, information alphanumérique; **loss of i.**, perte f d'information; **machine-sensible i.**, information détectable par (une) machine; **numerical i.**, information numérique; **i. bit**, bit m d'information; **i. channel,** voie *f* de transfert des informations; **i. feedback,** renvoi *m* d'information, retour *m* d'information; **i. feedback system,** système correcteur d'erreurs par retour de l'information; **i. flow,** circulation *f* de l'information; **i. flow analysis,** analyse *f* de circulation de l'information; **i. link,** liaison *f* (*ou* voie *f*) de transmission de données; **i. processing,** informatique *f*, traitement *m* de l'information; **i. retrieval,** recherche *f* de l'information, recherche *f* documentaire; **i. retrieval system,** système *m* de recherche de l'information; **i. retrieval techniques,** techniques *f* de recherche documentaire; **i. separator (IS),** caractère séparateur (d'informations); **i. system, 1.** système *m* informatique; **2.** système *m* d'informations; **i. theory,** théorie *f* de l'information; **i. transfer,** transfert *m* d'information; **i. word,** mot *m* d'information.

inherent, i. error, erreur inhérente; **i. store,** mémoire *f* interne.

inhibit, i. pulse, impulsion *f* de blocage, impulsion d'inhibition.

inhibit (to), interdire, empêcher, invalider.

inhibiting, inhibiteur (-trice) *adj.*; **i. circuit,** circuit inhibiteur; **i. input,** signal inhibiteur; **i. signal,** signal *m* d'interdiction.

in-house, interne *adj.*, intérieur *adj.*

initial, initial *adj.*; **i. condition,** condition initiale; **i. condition mode,** condition initiale; **i. instructions,** ordres initiaux (de programme); **i. orders,** ordres initiaux (de programme); **i. program loader,** procédure *f* de chargement initial; **i. program loading,** chargement initial de programmes.

initialization, initialisation *f*.

initialize (to), initialiser, mettre à la valeur initiale.

initiate, i. button, interrupteur *m* de mise en route; **i. key,** interrupteur *m* de mise en route.

initiate (to), lancer, faire démarrer, déclencher.

initiation, lancement *m*, déclenchement *m*, début *m*.

initiator/terminator, programme *m* de lancement et de terminaison (de travaux).

ink, encre *f*; **conductive i.,** encre conductrice; **extraneous i.,** encre excédentaire; **magnetic i.,** encre magnétique; **i. reflectance,** réflectance *f* de l'encre (*OCR*); **i. rib-**bon, ruban *m* encreur; **i. smudge,** bavochure *f* (*OCR*); **i. squeezeout,** écrasage *m*.

inking, encrage *m*.

inline, i. coding, séquence *f* de la partie principale du programme; **i. processing,** traitement immédiat; **i. subroutine,** sous-programme *m* relogeable.

inner, i. face, côté intérieur (*d'une bande*).

in-plant, interne *adj.*, intérieur *adj.*; **i.-p. system,** système intérieur.

input, 1. entrée *f*, introduction *f*; **2.** données *f* d'entrée (*ou* en entrée); **3.** d'entrée, entrant *adj.*; **card i.,** entrée par cartes; **inhibiting i.,** signal inhibiteur; **manual i.,** introduction manuelle; **real-time i.,** introduction en temps réel, entrée en temps réel; **tape i.,** entrée par bande; **i. area,** zone *f* d'entrée, zone d'introduction; **i. block,** zone *f* d'entrée, zone d'introduction; **i. buffer,** tampon *m* d'entrée; **i. channel,** canal *m* d'entrée, voie *f* d'entrée; **i. circuit,** circuit *m* d'entrée; **i. data,** données d'entrée (*ou* en entrée); **i. device,** appareil *m* d'entrée; **i. equipment,** matériel *m* d'entrée, matériel *m* d'introduction; **i. impedance,** impédance *f* d'entrée; **i. instruction code,** code *m* d'instruction d'entrée; **i. job stream,** flot *m* des travaux en entrée; **i. magazine,** magasin *m* d'alimentation (de cartes); **i. process,** entrée, introduction; **i. program,** (sous-)programme *m* d'introduction; **i. register,** registre *m* d'entrée; **i. routine,** programme *m* d'introduction (*ou* d'entrée); **i. section,** zone *f* d'entrée, zone d'introduction; **i. stacker,** magasin *m* d'alimentation; **i. state,** état *m* d'entrée; **i. station,** poste *m* de saisie de données; **i. storage,** zone *f* d'entrée, zone d'introduction; **i. unit,** unité *f* d'entrée, élément *m* d'introduction; **i. work queue,** file *f* d'attente d'entrée des travaux.

input (to), introduire, entrer.

input/output, entrée(s)-sortie(s) *f*; **buffered i./o.,** entrée-sortie à tampon; **graphic i./o.,** entrée-sortie graphique; **real-time i./o.,** entrée-sortie en temps réel; **simultaneous i./o.,** entrée-sortie simultanées; **voice i./o.,** entrée-sortie vocale; **i./o. area,** zone *f* d'entrée-sortie; **i./o. buffer,** tampon *m* d'entrée-sortie; **i./o. channel,** canal *m* d'entrée-sortie, voie *f* d'entrée-sortie; **i./o. control,** contrôleur *m* d'entrée-sortie; **i./o. control system (I.O.C.S.),** système *m* de contrôle des entrées-sorties; **i./o. device,** appareil *m* d'entrée-sortie; **i./o. interrupt,** interruption *f* d'entrée-sortie; **i./o. interrupt identification,** identification *f* de la cause d'interruption d'entrée-sortie; **i./o. interrupt indicator,** indicateur *m* d'interruption entrée-sortie; **i./o. library,** bibliothèque *f* de sous-programmes d'entrée-sortie; **i./o.-limited,** subordonné au temps d'entrée-sortie; **i./o. medium,** support *m* d'entrée-sortie; **i./o. process,** transfert radial, opération *f* d'entrée-sortie; **i./o. register,** registre *m* d'entrée-sortie; **i./o. storage,** zone *f* d'entrée-sortie; **i./o. switching,** commutation *f* de canaux d'entrée-sortie; **i./o. trunks,** voies *f* d'entrée-sortie; **i./o. typewriter,** machine *f* à écrire d'entrée-sortie; **i./o. unit,** élément *m* d'entrée-sortie, dispositif *m* d'entrée-sortie.

inquiry, 1. interrogation *f*; 2. demande *f* d'information; **keyboard entry and i.,** introduction *f* et interrogation au clavier; **remote i.,** interrogation à distance; **i. application,** consultation *f* (de fichier); **i. character,** demande *f* (de renseignements); **i. display terminal,** terminal *m* d'interrogation à visualisation; **i. station,** poste *m* d'interrogation, poste de consultation; **i. unit,** unité *f* d'interrogation.

insertion, insertion *f*; **switch i.,** introduction *f* par commutateur; **i. gain,** gain *m* d'insertion; **i. loss,** affaiblissement *m* d'insertion; **i. track,** piste *f* d'insertion.

installation, installation *f*; **terminal i.,** installation terminale, terminal *m*; **i. date,** date *f* d'installation; **i. tape number,** numéro *m* d'identification de bande; **i. time,** temps *m* d'installation.

instantaneous, instantané *adj.*; **i. access,** accès immédiat, accès instantané, accès direct; **i. data-transfer rate,** vitesse instantanée de transfert de données, débit instantané; **i. frequency,** fréquence instantanée; **i. storage,** mémoire *f* à accès immédiat; **i. transmission rate,** vitesse instantanée de transfert de données, débit instantané.

instants, significant i., instants significatifs.

instruction, instruction *f*; **absolute i.,** instruction réelle; **accumulator jump i.,** instruction de saut fonction de l'ac-

cumulateur; **accumulator shift i.,** instruction de décalage dans l'accumulateur; **accumulator transfer i.,** instruction de saut fonction de l'accumulateur; **actual i.,** instruction réelle; **add(ing) i.,** instruction d'addition; **alphanumeric i.,** instruction alphanumérique; **arithmetic i.,** instruction arithmétique; **blank i.,** instruction factice, instruction de remplissage; **branch i.,** instruction de branchement, instruction de saut; **breakpoint i.,** instruction de point d'interruption; **call i.,** instruction d'appel; **complete i.,** instruction complète; **computer i.,** instruction de programme, instruction machine; **conditional breakpoint i.,** instruction conditionnelle de point d'interruption; **conditional (control) transfer i.,** instruction de branchement (*ou* saut) conditionnel; **conditional jump i.,** instruction de branchement (*ou* saut) conditionnel; **conditional stop i.,** instruction d'arrêt conditionnel; **control transfer i.,** instruction de branchement, instruction de saut; **decision i.,** instruction de branchement; **direct i.,** instruction à opérande incorporé; **discrimination i.,** instruction de branchement (*ou* saut) conditionnel; **do-nothing i.,** instruction factice, instruction de remplissage; **dummy i.,** instruction factice, instruction de remplissage; **effective i.,** instruction effective; **entry i.,** instruction d'entrée (dans un programme); **executive i.,** instruction de contrôle d'exécution; **extract i.,** instruction de rassemblement; **four-address i.,** instruction à quatre adresses; **halt i.,** instruction d'arrêt; **hold i.,** instruction de maintien; **ignore i.,** instruction d'annulation, instruction de rejet; **jump i.,** instruction de branchement, instruction de saut; **logic(al) i.,** instruction logique; **machine i.,** instruction (en code) machine; **macro-i.,** macro-instruction *f*; **micro-i.,** micro-instruction *f*; **multiaddress i.,** instruction à adresses multiples; **multiple-address i.,** instruction à adresses multiples; **no address i.,** instruction sans adresse; **non-print i.,** instruction de non-impression; **no-op i.,** instruction factice, instruction de remplissage; **no-operation i.,** instruction factice, instruction de remplissage; **null i.,** instruction factice, instruction de remplissage; **one-address i.,** instruction à une adresse; **optional halt i.**, instruction d'arrêt conditionnel; **optional stop i.**, instruction d'arrêt conditionnel; **presumptive i.**, instruction sous forme initiale; **primary i.**, instruction élémentaire; **pseudo-i.**, pseudo-instruction f; **quasi-i.**, pseudo-instruction f; **repetition i.**, instruction de répétition; **return i.**, instruction de retour, instruction de raccordement (*vers le programme principal*); **single-address i.**, instruction à une adresse; **skip i.**, instruction de saut, instruction de branchement; **stop i.**, instruction d'arrêt; **supervisory i.**, instruction de contrôle d'exécution; **symbolic i.**, instruction symbolique; **table look-up i.**, instruction de consultation de table; **three-address i.**, instruction à trois adresses; **transfer i.**, instruction de branchement, instruction de saut; **two-address i.**, instruction à deux adresses; **two-plus-one address i.**, instruction à deux adresses d'opérande et une adresse de commande; **unconditional branch i.**, instruction de branchement sans condition; **unconditional (control) transfer i.**, instruction de branchement sans condition; **unconditional jump i.**, instruction de branchement sans condition; **unmodified i.**, instruction sous forme initiale; **waste i.**, instruction factice, instruction de remplissage; **zero address i.**, instruction sans adresse; **i. address**, adresse f d'instruction; **i. address register**, registre m de contrôle de séquence; **i. area**, zone f (de stockage) d'instruction(s), zone de programme; **i. character**, caractère m de commande; **i. code**, code m d'instruction; **i. control**, (unité f de) contrôle m des instructions; **i. counter**, registre m (d'adresse) d'instruction; **i. cycle**, cycle m de réalisation d'une instruction; **i. deck**, jeu m de cartes-programme; **i. format**, format m d'instruction; **i. mix**, sélection représentative d'instructions; **i. modification**, modification f d'instructions; **i. register**, registre m d'instruction; **i. repertory**, répertoire m d'instructions; **i. set**, répertoire m d'instructions; **i. storage**, zone f (de stockage) d'instruction(s), zone de programme; **i. tape**, bande f programme; **i. time**, 1. temps m de prise en charge d'instruction; 2. temps d'exécution; **i. word**, mot m d'instruction.

instructions, initial i., ordres initiaux (de programme).

instrument, end i., appareil terminal.

insulated, i.-gate field-effect transistor (IG FET), transistor m à effet de champ à grille isolée.

integer, nombre entier.

integrand, fonction f à intégrer.

integrated, intégré *adj.*; **i. circuit**, circuit intégré; **i. data processing (I.D.P.)**, traitement intégré des données, traitement unifié des données; **i. emulator**, émulateur intégré.

integrating, i. amplifier, amplificateur intégrateur; **i. circuit**, montage intégrateur; **i. gear**, mécanisme intégrateur; **i. mechanism**, mécanisme intégrateur; **i. motor**, moteur intégrateur; **i. network** (*Am.*), montage intégrateur.

integration, intégration f; **analog i.**, intégration analogique; **large scale i. (LSI)**, intégration à large échelle; **medium scale i. (MSI)**, intégration à moyenne échelle; **numerical i.**, intégration numérique; **rectangular i.**, intégration rectangulaire; **trapezoidal i.**, intégration trapézoïdale.

integrator, 1. intégrateur m; 2. montage intégrateur; **digital i.**, intégrateur numérique; **incremental i.**, intégrateur par accroissements; **limited i.**, intégrateur à limite; **pulse i.**, intégrateur d'impulsions; **saturating i.**, intégrateur par accroissements; **summing i.**, intégrateur additionneur; **wheel and disk i.**, intégrateur à disque et plateau.

intelligence, intelligence f; **artificial i.**, intelligence artificielle.

intelligent, i. terminal, terminal intelligent, terminal lourd.

intensity, intensité f; **magnetic i.**, intensité magnétique.

interactive, i. mode, mode interactif, mode m de dialogue.

interblock, i. gap, espace m inter-blocs; **i. space**, espace m inter-blocs.

intercalate (to), intercaler.

interchangeable, i. disk store, mémoire f à disques amovibles; **i. type bar**, barre f d'impression à caractères amovibles.

interconnect (to), interconnecter.

intercycle, 1. cycle m opératoire; 2. intercycle m.

interface, interface *m*, zone *f* d'échange; **hybrid i.,** interface hybride; **standard i.,** interface standard.

interference, interférence *f*; **adjacent-channel i.,** interférence adjacente.

interfering, i. signal, signal *m* parasite, signal perturbateur.

interfix, interdépendance *f*.

interior, i. label, label *m* interne.

interlace (to), imbriquer, entremêler, entrelacer.

interleave (to), imbriquer, entremêler, entrelacer.

interleaved, i. carbon set, liasse carbonée.

interleaving, imbrication *f* (de programmes); **multiprocessor i.,** allocation imbriquée de mémoire (*pour système multiprocesseur*).

interlock (to), verrouiller.

interlude, séquence *f* préliminaire de programme.

intermediate, intermédiaire *adj.*; **i. centre,** centre *m* intermédiaire; **i. control change,** rupture *f* de contrôle de niveau intermédiaire; **i. distribution frame,** répartiteur *m* intermédiaire; **i. equipment,** équipement *m* intermédiaire; **i. language,** langage *m* de niveau intermédiaire; **i. product,** produit partiel, produit *m* intermédiaire; **i. result,** résultat *m* intermédiaire; **i. storage,** mémoire *f* de manœuvre; **i. subcarrier,** sous-porteuse *f* intermédiaire; **i. total,** total *m* intermédiaire.

intermittent, intermittent *adj.*; **i. fault,** incident intermittent.

internal, interne *adj.*; **i. arithmetic,** arithmétique *f* interne; **i. memory,** mémoire *f* interne; **i. store (or storage),** mémoire *f* interne.

internally, i. stored program, programme enregistré.

international, international *adj.*; **i. algebraic language,** langage algébrique international.

interpolator, interclasseuse *f*.

interpret (to), 1. traduire (*une carte*), interpréter (*une carte*); **2.** convertir.

interpreter, 1. traductrice *f*; **2.** programme traducteur; **transfer i.,** traductrice reporteuse, reporteuse *f*; **i. routine,** programme interprétatif.

interpretive, i. code, pseudo-code *m*; **i. language,** langage interprétatif; **i. program,** programme interprétatif; **i. programming,** programmation *f* en pseudo-instructions; **i. routine,** programme interprétatif.

inter-record, i.-r. gap, espace *m* entre enregistrements.

interrogating, i. typewriter, machine *f* à écrire d'entrée-sortie.

interrupt, interruption *f*; **input/output i.,** interruption d'entrée-sortie; **processor error i.,** interruption sur erreur de parité; **i. mask,** masque *m* d'interruption; **i. mode,** état *m* d'interruption; **i. routine,** programme *m* de traitement des interruptions; **i. signal,** signal *m* d'interruption.

interrupt (to), interrompre.

interrupted, i. continuous waves, ondes modulées.

interruption, interruption *f*.

intersection, 1. intersection *f*; **2.** opération *f* ET; **i. gate,** circuit *m* ET.

interstage, i. punching, perforation intercalée.

inter-switchboard, i.-s. line, ligne privée.

interval, intervalle *m*; **minimum i.,** intervalle minimum; **significant i.,** intervalle significatif; **unit i.,** intervalle unitaire; **i. timer,** rythmeur *m*.

interword, i. gap, espace *m* entre mots; **i. space,** espace *m* entre mots.

intrinsic, i. semi-conductor, semi-conducteur *m* intrinsèque.

invalid, invalide *adj.*; **i. address,** adresse *f* invalide; **i. code,** code *m* invalide.

inventory, i. control, contrôle *m* des stocks.

inversion, inversion *f*.

invert (to), inverser.

inverted, i. file, fichier inversé (*Recherche documentaire*).

inverter, 1. convertisseur *m*; **2.** inverseur *m*.

inverting, i. amplifier, amplificateur inverseur (*ou* changeur) de signe.

I/O (=input/output), entrée(s)-sortie(s) *f*.

I.O.C.S. (=input/output control system), système *m* de contrôle des entrées-sorties.

IPOT (=inductive potential divider), potentiomètre bobiné.

irreversible, irréversible *adj.*; **i. magnetic process,** transformation *f* magnétique irréversible; **i. process,** processus *m* irréversible.

IS (=**information separator**), caractère séparateur (d'informations).

isochronous, isochrone *adj.*; **i. modulation**, modulation *f* isochrone; **i. restitution**, restitution *f* isochrone.

isolated, **i. locations**, positions (de mémoire) protégées.

isolating, **i. circuit**, circuit *m* d'isolement.

item, **1.** article *m*; **2.** rubrique *f*; **data i.**, article; **elementary i.**, article élémentaire; **i. advance**, balayage *m* d'articles (*en mémoire*); **i. design**, dessin *m* d'article; **i. size**, grandeur *f* d'article.

iterate (to), effectuer des itérations *f*.

Iteration, itération *f*.

iterative, itératif (-ive) *adj.*; **i. operation**, opération itérative; **i. process**, processus itératif; **i. routine**, programme itératif.

I.T.U. (=**International Telecommunication Union**), Union Internationale des Télécommunications (U.I.T.).

J

jack, **1.** connecteur *m*; **2.** jack *m*; **answering j.**, jack de réponse; **j. panel**, **1.** tableau *m* de connexions; **2.** tableau *m* de jacks.

jam, bourrage *m*; **card j.**, bourrage de cartes.

JES (=**job entry subsystem**), sous-système *m* de soumission des travaux.

jitter, instabilité *f* (de la base de temps).

job, travail *m*; tâche *f*, unité *f* de traitement, élément *m* de travail; **main j.**, travail principal; **j. assembly**, préparation *f* des travaux; **j. control statement**, ordre *m* de contrôle des travaux; **j. entry subsystem (JES)**, sous-système *m* de soumission des travaux; **j. flow control**, contrôle *m* du déroulement des travaux; **j. library**, bibliothèque *f* de travaux; **j. management**, supervision *f* des travaux; **j. scheduler**, programmateur *m* de travaux; **j. statement**, ordre *m* de début des travaux; **j. step**, étape *f* de travail.

job-oriented, **j.-o. terminal**, terminal spécialisé.

joggle (to), battre (les cartes).

join, **j. gate**, circuit *m* NON-OU (*ou* NI).

joint, **j. denial**, opération *f* NON-OU (*ou* NI), négation *f* connexe; **j. denial gate**, circuit *m* NON-OU (*ou* NI); **j. use**, utilisation *f* en commun.

jump, branchement *m*, saut *m*; **conditional j.**, branchement conditionnel, saut conditionnel; **unconditional j.**, branchement inconditionnel, branchement «toujours»; **j. instruction**, instruction *f* de branchement, instruction de saut; **j. operation**, opération *f* de branchement.

jumper, cavalier *m*; **j. wire**, cavalier.

junction, **1.** jonction *f*; **2.** circuit *m* (télégraphique) de jonction; **3.** ligne *f* auxiliaire; **n-p j.**, jonction n-p; **p-n j.**, jonction p-n; **trunk j.**, ligne intermédiaire.

junctor, joncteur *m*.

justification, **1.** justification *f* (*d'un texte*); **2.** cadrage *m* (*d'un nombre*).

justified, **left j.**, **1.** justifié à gauche; **2.** cadré à gauche; **right j.**, **1.** justifié à droite; **2.** cadré à droite.

justify (to), **1.** justifier; **2.** cadrer.

juxtaposition, juxtaposition *f*.

K

Karnaugh, **K. map**, tableau *m* de Karnaugh.

key, **1.** clé *f*; **2.** poussoir *m*; **3.** indicatif *m*; **4.** touche *f*; **actual k.**, adresse réelle (*en COBOL*); **erase k.**, touche d'effacement; **function k.**, touche de fonction; **initiate k.**, interrupteur *m* de mise en route; **load k.**, poussoir de chargement (de programme); **monitoring k.**, clé de surveillance; **protection k.**, indicatif de protection; **ringing k.**, clé d'appel; **search k.**, clé (*ou* indicatif) de recherche; **sort k.**, clé (*ou* indicatif) de tri; **start k.**, interrupteur *m* de mise en route; **storage k.**, indicatif de protection (de mémoire); **k. change**, changement *m* d'indicatif; **k. perforator**, perforatrice *f* à clavier; **k. pulsing** (*Am.*), envoi *m* de signaux au clavier; **k. sending**, envoi *m* de signaux au clavier; **k. word**, mot-clé *m*; **k. word in context (KWIC)**, mot-clé *m* dans son contexte (*Recherche documentaire*); **k. word in title (KWIT)**, mot-clé *m* dans le titre (*Recherche documentaire*); **k. word out of context (KWOC)**, mot-clé *m* en dehors de son contexte (*Recherche* documentaire).

keyboard, clavier *m*; **shift-lock k.**, clavier avec garde d'inversion; **storage k.**, clavier à transfert; **k. computer**, ordinateur *m* de bureau; **k. entry**, entrée (effectuée) au clavier; **k. entry and inquiry**, introduction *f* et interrogation *f* au clavier; **k. lock-out**, verrouillage *m* de clavier; **k. perforator**, perforateur *m* à clavier, clavier perforateur; **k. punch**, perforatrice *f* à clavier; **k. selection**, numérotation *f* au clavier, sélection *f* au clavier.

key-driven, commandé par clavier.

key in (to), introduire au clavier, entrer au clavier.

keying, 1. manipulation *f*; 2. modulation *f*; **error rate of k.**, taux *m* d'erreur d'une manipulation; **frequency-shift k. (F.S.K.)**, modulation par déplacement de fréquence; **two-tone k.**, télégraphie *f* à deux fréquences porteuses; **k. chirps**, parasites *m* de transmission.

keypunch, perforatrice *f*; **k. operator**, perforatrice, perforeuse *f*.

key-verify, vérificatrice *f* (de cartes) (à clavier).

key-verify (to), vérifier (les perforations de cartes).

keyword, mot-clé *m*.

killer, noise k., dispositif *m* antiparasites.

kilobaud, kilobaud *m*.

knife, feed k., couteau *m* d'alimentation (de cartes); **punch k.**, poinçon *m*.

knob, control k., bouton *m* de commande.

KWIC (=key word in context), mot-clé *m* dans son contexte (*Recherche documentaire*).

KWIT (=key word in title), mot-clé *m* dans le titre (*Recherche documentaire*).

KWOC (=key word out of context), mot-clé *m* en dehors de son contexte (*Recherche documentaire*).

L

label, étiquette *f*; article-repère *m*, label *m*; **data set l.**, étiquette d'ensemble de données; **exterior l.**, étiquette extérieure (*de bande*); **file l.**, label de bande; **header l.**, label de bande; **interior l.**, label interne; **tape l.**, label de bande; **trailer l.**, label fin (de bande).

lace (to), faire une grille (*dans une carte*).

laced, l. card, carte-grille *f*.

lag, 1. retard *m*; 2. décalage *m* de temps; **magnetic l.**, hystérésis *f*.

laminar, l. bus, distributeur *m* laminaire.

lamp, lampe *f*; **answer l.**, lampe de réponse; **warning l.**, lampe témoin.

land, dépôt conducteur; **l. pattern**, modèle *m* de circuit, dessin *m* du dépôt conducteur.

language, langage *m*; **absolute l.**, langage machine; **algebraic l.**, langage algébrique; **algorithmic l.**, langage algorithmique; **artificial l.**, langage artificiel; **assembly l.**, langage d'assemblage; **basic l.**, langage non évolué; **command l.**, langage de commandes; **common business oriented l. (COBOL)**, langage adapté aux problèmes de gestion; **common l.**, langage commun; **common machine l.**, langage machine commun; **computer-dependent l.**, langage propre au (type de) calculateur; **computer-independent l.**, langage indépendant du (type de) calculateur; **computer l.**, langage machine; **computer-oriented l.**, langage orienté vers le calculateur; **computer-sensitive l.**, langage propre au (type de) calculateur; **data description l. (DDL)**, langage de description de données; **data manipulation l. (DML)**, langage de manipulation de données; **fabricated l.**, langage artificiel; **formal l.**, langage artificiel; **higher-order l.**, langage évolué; **high level l.**, langage évolué; **intermediate l.**, langage de niveau intermédiaire; **international algebraic l.**, langage algébrique international; **interpretive l.**, langage interprétatif; **low level l.**, langage non évolué; **machine l.**, langage machine; **machine-independent l.**, langage indépendant du (type de) calculateur; **machine-oriented l.**, langage orienté vers la machine; **natural l.**, langage naturel; **object l.**, langage objet, langage généré; **original l.**, langage source; **problem-oriented l.**, langage orienté vers le problème; **procedure-oriented l.**, langage orienté vers le traitement; **programming l.**, langage de programmation; **scientific l.**, langage scientifique; **source l.**, langage source; **symbolic l.**, langage symbolique; **synthetic l.**, langage synthétique, langage artificiel; **tabular l.**, langage de traitement de tables (de décision); **target l.,** langage objet, langage généré; **l. translation,** traduction *f* de langage(s); **l. translator,** traducteur *m* de langages.

large, l. scale integration (LSI), intégration *f* à large échelle.

last, l. in first out (LIFO), dernier entré premier sorti (*dans une liste*).

latch, bascule *f.*

latency, temps *m* d'attente, attente *f,* latence *f*; **l. time,** temps d'attente.

layer, couche *f*; **barrier l.,** couche d'arrêt.

layout, 1. agencement *m,* disposition *f*; **2.** dessin *m* (*d'état ou de carte*), description *f*; **data l.,** format *m*; **file l.,** dessin de fichier, disposition de fichier; **record l.,** dessin d'enregistrement, disposition d'enregistrement; **l. character,** caractère *m* de mise en page, caractère de présentation.

lead, connecting l., conducteur *m* de raccordement, fil *m* de connexion.

leader, 1. début *m* de bande, amorce *f* de bande; **2.** article *m* en-tête; **tape l.,** début de bande, amorce de bande; **l. record,** enregistrement *m* en-tête.

leading, column 1 l., colonne *f* 1 en tête; **nine-edge l.,** ligne *f* des «9» en tête; **Y-edge l.,** ligne *f* des «Y» en tête; **l. edge,** bord *m* avant; **l. end,** début *m* de bande, amorce *f* de bande.

leapfrog, l. test, programme *m* de test sélectif, test *m* saute-mouton.

learning, machine l., apprentissage *m* automatique.

leased, l. circuit, circuit *m* en location; **l. line,** ligne *f* en location; **l.-line network,** réseau *m* à lignes privées (*ou* louées).

least significant, l.s. character, caractère le moins significatif; **l.s. digit,** chiffre le moins significatif.

LED (=light-emitting diode), diode électroluminescente.

ledger, l. card, carte *f* de compte, extrait *m* de compte.

left, l. justified, 1. justifié à gauche; **2.** cadré à gauche; **l. shift,** décalage *m* à gauche.

left-justify (to), 1. justifier à gauche; **2.** cadrer à gauche.

length, longueur *f*; **actual l.,** longueur réelle; **block l.,** longueur de bloc; **field l.,** longueur de zone; **fixed word l.,** longueur fixe de mot; **machine word l.,** longueur de mot machine;

pulse l., durée *f* d'impulsion; **record l.,** longueur d'enregistrement; **register l.,** longueur de registre; **string l.,** longueur de monotonie; **variable word l.,** longueur variable de mot; **word l.,** longueur de mot.

letter, lettre *f.*

letterpress, typographie *f.*

letters, lower case l., (lettres *f*) minuscules *f*; **upper case l.,** (lettres *f*) majuscules *f*; **l. shift,** inversion *f* «lettres».

level, 1. niveau *m*; **2.** coefficient *m*; **addressing l.,** niveau d'adressage; **average effectiveness l.,** niveau d'efficacité moyenne; **carrier noise l.,** niveau de bruit de porteuse; **circuit noise l.,** niveau relatif de bruit de circuit; **data l.,** niveau; **overload l.** (*Am.*), puissance *f* limite admissible; **reference l.,** niveau de référence; **relative l.,** niveau relatif de puissance; **signal l.,** niveau de signal de contraste (*OCR*); **transmission l.** (*Am.*), niveau relatif de puissance; **l. compensator,** compensateur *m* de niveau; **l. diagram,** hypsogramme *m.*

lever, levier *m*; **pinch l.,** levier pinceur.

lexeme, lexème *m.*

lexicon, lexique *m.*

LF (=line feed character), caractère *m* interligne.

librarian, 1. bibliothécaire *m ou f*; **2.** programme *m* bibliothécaire.

library, bibliothèque *f*; **input/output l.,** bibliothèque de sous-programmes d'entrée-sortie; **job l.,** bibliothèque de travaux; **link l.,** bibliothèque de programmes assemblés; **program l.,** bibliothèque de programmes; **routine l.,** bibliothèque de programmes; **source (program) l.,** bibliothèque de programmes source; **subroutine l.,** bibliothèque de sous-programmes; **system l.,** bibliothèque (de programmes) d'une installation; **tape l.,** magnétothèque *f,* bibliothèque de bandes magnétiques; **l. program,** programme *m* de bibliothèque; **l. routine,** programme *m* de bibliothèque; **l. subroutine,** sous-programme *m* de bibliothèque; **l. tape,** bande *f* (de) bibliothèque; **l. track,** piste *f* de référence.

LIFO (=last in first out), dernier entré premier sorti (*dans une liste*).

light, control l., lampe *f* témoin, voyant (lumineux); **l.-emitting diode (LED),** diode électro-luminescente; **l. gun (*or* pen),**

crayon lumineux, marqueur lumineux, stylet lumineux, luminostyle *m*.

limit, **operating l.**, puissance *f* limite admissible; **l. priority**, priorité *f* limite.

limited, limité *adj.*; borné *adj.*; **compute(r)-l.**, subordonné au (*ou* limité par le) temps de calcul; **input/output-l.**, subordonné au temps d'entrée-sortie; **peripheral-l.**, limité par le (*ou* subordonné au) débit des périphériques; **process-l.**, limité par la vitesse de traitement; **processor-l.**, limité par la vitesse de traitement; **tape-l.**, subordonné au débit (binaire) des dérouleurs; **l. integrator**, intégrateur *m* à limite.

limiter, limiteur *m*.

line, ligne *f*; **acoustic delay l.**, ligne à retard acoustique; **artificial l.**, ligne artificielle; **average-edge l.**, ligne de contour moyenne; **B l.**, registre *m* d'index; **balanced l.**, ligne équilibrée; **balanced transmission l.**, ligne équilibrée; **called l.**, ligne appelée; **calling l.**, ligne appelante; **character spacing reference l.**, axe *m* de référence d'espacement; **code l.**, ligne de programme; **connecting l.**, ligne de raccordement; **continuation l.**, ligne de prolongation, ligne suite; **control l.**, ligne de commande; **dedicated leased l.**, ligne louée spécialisée; **delay l.**, ligne à retard; **duplex l.**, ligne duplex; **duplexed l.**, ligne duplexée; **electric delay l.**, ligne à retard électrique; **electromagnetic delay l.**, ligne à retard électromagnétique; **heading l.**, ligne d'en-tête; **individual l.**, ligne individuelle; **interswitchboard l.**, ligne privée; **leased l.**, ligne en location; **local l.**, raccordement *m*; **magnetic delay l.**, ligne à retard magnétique; **magnetostrictive delay l.**, ligne à retard à magnétostriction; **mercury delay l.**, ligne à retard à mercure; **nickel delay l.**, ligne à retard à nickel; **open-wire l.**, ligne aérienne; **party l.**, ligne partagée; **print l.**, ligne d'impression; **private l.**, ligne privée; **private leased l.**, ligne privée; **quartz delay l.**, ligne à retard à quartz; **shared l.**, ligne partagée; **simplex l.**, ligne simplex; **sonic delay l.**, ligne à retard acoustique; **subscriber l.**, ligne d'abonné; **telephone l.**, ligne téléphonique; **teleprinter l.**, ligne de téléimprimeurs; **terminated l.**, ligne bouclée; **tie l.**, ligne privée; **transmission l.**, ligne de transmission; **l. adapter**,

adap(ta)teur *m* de ligne(s); **l.-at-a-time printer**, imprimante *f* (ligne) par ligne; **l. concentration**, concentration *f* de lignes; **l. feed character (LF)**, caractère *m* interligne; **l. feed code**, code *m* de changement de ligne; **l. finder**, chercheur *m* (de ligne); **l. link**, liaison *f* en ligne; **l. load**, charge *f* de ligne; **l. noise**, bruit *m* de circuit; **l. printer**, imprimante *f* (ligne) par ligne; **l. printing**, impression *f* (ligne) par ligne; **l. relay**, relais *m* de ligne; **l. repeater**, répéteur *m* de ligne; **l. side**, côté *m* ligne; **l. space**, interligne *m*, espacement vertical; **l. speed**, vitesse *f* de ligne; **l. switching**, commutation *f* de ligne(s).

linear, linéaire *adj.*; **l. detection**, détection *f* linéaire; **l. optimization**, programmation *f* linéaire; **l. programming (LP)**, programmation *f* linéaire; **l. unit**, élément *m* linéaire.

linearity, linéarité *f*; **l. error**, erreur *f* de linéarité.

lines, **l. per minute (LPM)**, lignes *f* par minute; **non-loaded l.**, lignes non chargées.

link, 1. liaison *f*; 2. lien *m* (de chaînage); 3. retour *m* (*depuis un sous-programme*); 4. raccord *m*; 5. fiche *f* de connexion; 6. maillon *m* (*de système crossbar*); **communication l.**, liaison; **data l.**, liaison (*ou* voie *f*) de transmission de données; **group l.**, liaison en groupe primaire; **information l.**, liaison (*ou* voie *f*) de transmission de données; **line l.**, liaison en ligne; **mastergroup l.**, liaison en groupe tertiaire; **multichannel l.**, liaison multivoie; **multidrop l.**, liaison multipoints; **multipoint l.**, liaison multipoints; **point-to-point l.**, liaison point à point; **radio l.**, liaison hertzienne; **supergroup l.**, liaison en groupe secondaire; **telephone cable l.**, liaison téléphonique par câble; **telephone l.**, liaison téléphonique; **transmission l.**, chaînon *m* de voie (de transmission *ou* de communication); **l. group**, groupe *m* de liaisons; **l. library**, bibliothèque *f* de programmes assemblés.

link (to), relier, assembler, coupler.

linkage, 1. liaison *f*; 2. couplage *m*; 3. assemblage *m* (de programmes); **basic l.**, liaison de base; **l. editor**, programme *m* assembleur, programme *m* éditeur de liens.

linked, **l. format**, format assemblé; **l. subroutine**, sous-programme fermé.

liquid, l. crystal, cristal *m* liquide.
list, liste *f*; **assembly l.,** liste d'assemblage; **audit l.,** liste de contrôle; **chained l.,** liste chaînée; **error l.,** liste d'erreurs; **first item l.,** indication *f* de groupe; **parts l.,** nomenclature *f* (de pièces); **polling l.,** liste d'appel (sélectif); **pushdown l.,** liste refoulée, liste inversée; **pushup l.,** liste directe; **l. processing,** traitement *m* de liste; **l. structure,** structure *f* de liste.
list (to), 1. imprimer; 2. établir une liste.
listing, 1. impression *f*; 2. liste *f*; **assembly l.,** impression d'assemblage; **reference l.,** liste de référence.
literal, symbole littéral.
literature, l. search, recherche *f* documentaire.
load, 1. charge *f*; 2. circuit *m* de charge; **artificial l.,** circuit de charge fictif; **line l.,** charge de ligne; **normal l.,** circuit de charge réel; **l. key,** poussoir *m* de chargement (de programme); **l. mode,** mode *m* chargement; **l. module,** module *m* (de programme) chargeable; **l. point,** point *m* de départ de lecture ou d'écriture (*d'une bande*); **l. program,** programme *m* de chargement.
load (to), charger.
load-and-go, chargement *m* et lancement *m*.
loaded, l. circuit, circuit chargé.
loader, (programme *m*) chargeur *m ou adj.*; programme *m* de chargement; **bootstrap l.,** chargeur d'instructions initiales; **card l.,** (programme) chargeur de cartes-programme; **initial program l.,** procédure *f* de chargement initial.
loading, chargement *m*; **block l.,** chargement groupé; **dynamic program l.,** chargement dynamique de programmes; **initial program l.,** chargement initial de programmes; **scatter l.,** chargement éclaté; **l. error,** erreur *f* de charge; **l. routine,** (programme *m*) chargeur *m ou adj.*; programme *m* de chargement.
local, local *adj.*; **l. call,** communication locale, communication urbaine; **l. central office** (*Am.*), central urbain; **l. channel,** voie locale; **l. exchange,** central urbain; **l. line,** raccordement *m*; **l. loop,** ligne *f* d'abonné; **l. service area,** zone *f* de taxation urbaine (*ou* locale); **l. side,** côté *m* matériel.

locate, l. mode, mode *m* localisation.
location, 1. emplacement *m*; 2. position *f*; **bit l.,** emplacement (de stockage) d'un bit; **memory l.,** position de mémoire; **protected l.,** emplacement protégé; **l. counter,** registre *m* (d'adresse) d'instruction.
locations, isolated l., positions (de mémoire) protégées.
lock, supervisor l., verrouillage *m* du superviseur.
locking, avec maintien *m*; **l. escape,** échappement *m* avec maintien; **l. shift character,** caractère *m* de maintien (d'un changement de code).
lock-out, 1. verrouillage *m*; 2. interdiction *f*; **keyboard l.-o.,** verrouillage de clavier; **write l.-o.,** verrouillage d'écriture.
lock/unlock, l./u. facility, verrouillage/déverrouillage *m*.
log, journal *m* (*de bord*).
logarithm, logarithme *m*; **napierian l.,** logarithme népérien; **natural l.,** logarithme naturel.
logarithmic, logarithmique *adj.*; **l. decrement,** décrément *m* logarithmique.
logger, enregistreur *m* (automatique).
logging, data l., enregistrement *m* de données.
logic, logique *f*; **diode l. (DL),** logique à diodes; **diode-transistor l. (DTL),** logique à diodes et transistors; **direct-coupled transistor l. (DCTL),** logique à transistors couplés directement; **emitter-coupled l. (ECL),** logique à couplage par l'émetteur; **fluid l.,** logique à fluides, fluidique *f*; **formal l.,** logique formelle; **high threshold l. (HTL),** logique à seuil élevé; **mathematical l.,** logique mathématique; **n-level l.,** logique à n niveaux; **programmed l.,** logique programmée; **resistor-capacitor-transistor l. (RCTL),** logique à résistances, condensateurs et transistors; **resistor-transistor l. (RTL),** logique à résistances et transistors; **symbolic l.,** logique symbolique; **transistor-transistor l. (TTL),** logique transistor-transistor; **tunnel diode l. (TDL),** logique à diodes tunnels; **variable l.,** logique programmée; **l. analysis,** analyse *f* logique; **l. chart,** organigramme *m* logique; **l.-controlled sequential computer,** ordinateur *m* à séquence contrôlée par logique; **l. design,** conception *f* logique; **l. diagram,**

organigramme *m* (*ou* schéma *m*) logique, logigramme *m*; **l. element,** élément *m* logique; **l. instruction,** instruction *f* logique; **l. network,** réseau *m* logique; **l. product gate,** circuit *m* ET; **l. shift,** décalage *m* logique; **l. sum gate,** circuit *m* OU; **l. symbol,** symbole *m* logique.

logical, logique *adj.*; **l. add,** réunion *f* logique, mélangeur *m*; **l. circuit,** circuit *m* logique; **l. comparison,** comparaison *f* logique; **l. connective,** opérateur *m* logique; **l. decision,** décision *f* logique; **l. design,** conception *f* logique; **l. diagram,** organigramme *m* (*ou* schéma *m*) logique, logigramme *m*; **l. difference,** différence *f* logique; **l. expression,** expression *f* logique; **l. file,** fichier *m* logique; **l. flowchart,** organigramme *m* logique; **l. instruction,** instruction *f* logique; **l. leading end,** extrémité *f* logique (sur bande); **l. multiply,** ET, conjonction *f*, affirmation *f* connexe, intersection *f* logique; **l. operation,** opération *f* logique; **l. operator,** opérateur *m* logique; **l. product,** ET, conjonction *f*, affirmation *f* connexe, intersection *f* logique; **l. record,** article *m* logique; **l. resolution,** résolution *f* d'opérations logiques; **l. shift,** décalage *m* logique; **l. sum,** disjonction *f*, réunion *f*, opération *f* OU; **l. symbol,** symbole *m* logique; **l. unit,** unité *f* logique; **l. variable,** variable *f* logique.

logician, logicien *m*.

logistics, logistique *f*.

longitudinal, longitudinal *adj.*; **l. check,** contrôle longitudinal; **l. circuit,** circuit longitudinal; **l. redundancy check,** contrôle longitudinal; **l. redundancy check character,** caractère *m* de contrôle (de parité) longitudinal.

look-up, table l.-u., consultation *f* de table, recherche *f* dans une table.

loop, boucle *f*; **closed l.,** 1. boucle fermée (*de programme*); 2. circuit fermé; **control l.,** bande *f* pilote; **feedback l.,** circuit *m* à réaction; **hysteresis l.,** boucle d'hystérésis; **local l.,** ligne *f* d'abonné; **magnetic hysteresis l.,** boucle d'hystérésis; **open l.,** circuit ouvert; **paper tape l.,** bande *f* pilote; **self-resetting l.,** boucle à auto-rétablissement; **subscriber's l.,** ligne *f* d'abonné; **l. check(ing),** contrôle *m* par retour de l'information; **l. stop,** arrêt *m* sur boucle.

loops, nesting l., boucles (de programme) emboîtées.

loss, perte *f*; **hysteresis l.,** perte par hystérésis; **insertion l.,** affaiblissement *m* d'insertion; **transmission l.,** perte de transmission; **l. of information,** perte d'information.

low, bas (-sse) *adj.*; **l. level language,** langage non évolué; **l. level modulation,** modulation *f* à faible puissance; **l. tape,** indication *f* de fin de bande (*sur un perforateur*).

lower, l. curtate, portion *f* des rangées inférieures (*d'une carte*).

lower case, l.c. letters, (lettres *f*) minuscules *f*.

low-order, l.-o. digit, chiffre *m* d'ordre moins élevé; **l.-o. position,** position la moins significative.

low-pass, l.-p. filter, filtre *m* passe-bas.

low-speed, l.-s. storage, mémoire lente.

LP (=**linear programming**), programmation *f* linéaire.

LPM (=**lines per minute**), lignes *f* par minute.

LSI (=**large scale integration**), intégration *f* à large échelle.

Lukasiewicz, L. notation, notation préfixée.

M

M out of N, M out of N code, code *m* N dont M.

machine, machine *f*; **accounting m.,** 1. machine comptable; 2. tabulatrice *f*; **adding m.,** machine à additionner; **alphanumeric m.,** machine alphanumérique; **asynchronous m.,** machine asynchrone; **business m.,** machine de gestion; **data processing m.,** machine de traitement de l'information, ordinateur *m*, calculateur *m*; **desk calculating m.,** machine à calculer de bureau; **electrical accounting m. (E.A.M.),** machine comptable électrique; **electronic data processing m.,** calculateur *m* électronique; **numerical m.,** machine numérique; **punched card m. (PCM),** machine à cartes perforées; **punched tape m.,** machine à bande perforée; **synchronous m.,** machine synchrone; **teaching m.**, machine à enseigner; **Turing m.**, simulateur *m* mathématique de calculateur; **m. address,** adresse *f* machine, adresse directe; **m. code,** code *m* machine; **m. cognition,** perception artificielle; **m. cycle,** cycle *m* machine; **m. error,** erreur *f* machine; **m.-independent,** indépendant du type de machine; **m.-independent language,** langage indépendant du (type de) calculateur; **m. instruction,** instruction *f* (en code) machine; **m. instruction code,** code *m* machine; **m. language,** langage *m* machine; **m. language code,** code *m* machine; **m. learning,** apprentissage *m* automatique; **m. operation,** opération *f* machine; **m.-oriented language,** langage orienté vers la machine; **m. pass,** passage *m* (en) machine; **m. processible form,** document *m* exploitable sur machine; **m. readable,** exploitable sur machine; **m.-readable data,** données *f* exploitables sur machine; **m.-readable medium,** support *m* exploitable sur machine; **m. recognizable,** exploitable sur machine; **m. run,** passage *m* (en) machine; **m. script,** information *f* en code machine; **m.-sensible,** exploitable sur machine; **m.-sensible information,** information *f* détectable par (une) machine; **m. spoilt work time,** temps perdu par incidents machine; **m. translation,** traduction *f* automatique; **m. variable,** variable *f* machine; **m. word,** mot *m* machine; **m. word length,** longueur *f* de mot machine.

machinery, computing m., matériel *m* de calcul.

machine tool, machine-outil *f*; **computer-controlled m.t.,** machine-outil commandée par calculateur.

macro, macro; **m. code,** macro-code *m*; **m. coding,** programmation *f* à macro-instructions; **m.-generating program,** macro-générateur *m*; **m.-generator,** macro-générateur *m*; **m.-instruction,** macro-instruction *f*.

macroelement, macroélément *m*.

macrolibrary, bibliothèque *f* de macro-instructions.

macroprogramming, macroprogrammation *f*.

magazine, magasin *m* (d'alimentation); **input m.,** magasin d'alimentation (de cartes); **output m.,** case *f* de réception.

magnet, aimant *m*; **annular m.,** aimant torique; **bar m.,** barreau aimanté, aimant droit; **permanent m.,** aimant permanent.

magnetic, magnétique *adj.*; **m. bubble storage,** mémoire *f* à bulles (*ou* domaines) magnétiques; **m. card,** carte *f* magnétique; **m. card store,** mémoire *f* à cartes (*ou* feuillets) magnétiques; **m. cell,** unité *f* de stockage magnétique; **m. character reader,** lecteur *m* de caractères magnétiques, magnétolecteur *m*; **m. core,** tore *m* magnétique; **m. core storage,** mémoire *f* à tores (magnétiques); **m. delay line,** ligne *f* à retard magnétique; **m. disk,** disque *m* magnétique; **m. disk store (*or* storage),** mémoire *f* à disques magnétiques; **m. drum,** tambour *m* magnétique; **m. drum store (*or* storage),** mémoire *f* à tambour magnétique; **m. film store (*or* storage),** mémoire *f* à film magnétique; **m. head,** tête *f* magnétique; **m. hysteresis,** hystérésis *f* (magnétique); **m. hysteresis loop,** boucle *f* d'hystérésis; **m. induction,** induction *f* magnétique; **m. ink,** encre *f* magnétique; **m. ink character reader,** lecteur *m* de caractères magnétiques; **m. ink character recognition (M.I.C.R.),** reconnaissance *f* de caractères magnétiques codés; **m. intensity,** intensité *f* magnétique; **m. lag,** hystérésis *f*; **m. memory,** mémoire *f* magnétique; **m. memory plate,** matrice *f* de mémoire (à ferrite); **m. printing,** transfert *m* de magnétisation; **m. recorder,** enregistreur *m* magnétique; **m. recording,** enregistrement *m* magnétique; **m. recording medium,** support *m* d'enregistrement magnétique; **m. shift register,** registre *m* (de) décalage magnétique; **m. store (*or* storage),** mémoire *f* magnétique; **m. strip(e) recording,** enregistrement *m* sur piste magnétique; **m. tape,** bande *f* magnétique; **m. tape deck,** unité *f* de bande magnétique, dérouleur *m* de bande magnétique; **m. tape encoder,** enregistreur *m* sur bande magnétique; **m. tape group,** groupe *m* de dérouleurs; **m. tape reader,** lecteur *m* de bande magnétique; **m. tape station,** unité *f* de bande magnétique, dérouleur *m* de bande magnétique; **m. tape store (*or* storage),** mémoire *f* à bande magnétique; **m. tape unit,** unité *f* de bande magnétique, dérouleur *m* de bande magnétique; **m. thin**

film, film *m* mince magnétique; **m. track,** piste *f* magnétique; **m. wire,** fil *m* magnétique; **m. wire store,** mémoire *f* à fil magnétique.

magnetization, magnétisation *f*; **m. curve,** courbe *f* de magnétisation.

magnetized, m. ink character, caractère magnétique codé.

magnetostriction, magnétostriction *f*.

magnetostrictive, magnétostrictif (-ive) *adj.*; **m. delay line,** ligne *f* à retard à magnétostriction; **m. effect,** effet *m* de magnétostriction.

magnitude, 1. grandeur *f*; **2.** valeur absolue.

magtape (*Am.*), bande *f* magnétique.

main, principal *adj.*; **m. distribution frame,** répartiteur *m* d'entrée; **m. file,** fichier principal, fichier *m* maître; **m. frame** (*Am.*), unité centrale de traitement; **m. job,** travail principal; **m. program,** programme principal; **m. routine,** programme principal; **m. sideband,** bande principale; **m. storage,** mémoire principale.

mains, secteur *m*; **m. failure,** panne *f* de secteur; **m. supply,** secteur, alimentation *f* secteur; **m. transformer,** transformateur *m* d'alimentation (secteur).

maintenance, maintenance *f*, entretien *m*; **corrective m.,** entretien correctif, entretien de dépannage, dépannage *m*; **emergency m.,** entretien correctif, entretien de dépannage, dépannage *m*; **file m.,** tenue *f* de fichiers; **preventive m.,** entretien préventif; **program m.,** maintenance de programmes; **remedial m.,** entretien de dépannage; **routine m.,** entretien périodique, entretien courant; **scheduled m.,** entretien périodique; **supplementary m.,** entretien supplémentaire; **m. program,** programme *m* d'aide à l'entretien; **m. routine,** programme *m* d'aide à l'entretien; **m. stand-by time,** temps *m* de garde.

major, m. control change, rupture *f* de contrôle de premier niveau; **m. cycle,** cycle majeur; **m. total,** total *m* de niveau supérieur.

majority, majorité *f*, fonction *f* majoritaire; **m. carrier,** porteur *m* majoritaire; **m. decision element,** circuit *m* de majorité; **m. decision gate,** circuit *m* de majorité; **m. element,** élément *m* de majorité.

make-break, m.-b. operation, opération *f* travail-repos.

makeup, m. time, temps *m* de reprise.

malfunction, mauvais fonctionnement, dérangement *m*; **program-sensitive m.,** mauvais fonctionnement décelable par une séquence particulière de programme; **m. routine,** programme *m* de diagnostic.

management, 1. gestion *f*; **2.** supervision *f*; **automated m.,** gestion automatisée; **automated production m.,** gestion de production automatisée; **computer assisted m.,** gestion automatisée; **data m.,** gestion de(s) données; **job m.,** supervision des travaux; **task m.,** supervision des travaux; **m. information system,** système intégré de gestion.

manipulated, m. variable, variable élaborée.

manipulative, m. indexing, indexation précoordonnée (*Recherche documentaire*).

mantissa, mantisse *f*.

manual, manuel (-elle) *adj.*; **m. control,** contrôle manuel; **m. exchange,** central manuel; **m. input,** introduction manuelle; **m. input unit,** dispositif *m* d'entrée manuelle; **m. operation,** exploitation manuelle; **m. perforator,** perforatrice manuelle; **m.-switch storage,** mémoire *f* à commande manuelle; **m. system,** système manuel; **m. tape relay,** transit manuel par bande perforée; **m. word generator,** dispositif *m* d'entrée manuelle.

manufacturer, original equipment m. (OEM), constructeur *m* de matériel.

map, table *f* d'implantation (en mémoire), topogramme *m*; **Karnaugh m.,** tableau *m* de Karnaugh.

map (to), mettre en correspondance, transformer.

mapping, correspondance *f*, transformation *f*.

margin, marge *f*; **guide m.,** marge de référence (*sur bande perforée*); **receiving m.,** marge de réception; **m. control,** contrôle *m* des marges; **m.-notched card,** carte *f* à encoches marginales; **m.-perforated card,** carte *f* à perforations marginales; **m.-punched card,** carte *f* à perforations marginales.

marginal, m. check, contrôle *m* par marges, test *m* de marges; **m. test(ing),** test *m* de marges, contrôle *m* par marges.

mark, registration m., repère *m* (*OCR*); **m. detection**, lecture *f* de marques (*OCR*); **m. reading**, lecture *f* de marques.

mark(er), marque *f*, drapeau *m*, sentinelle *f*; **beginning of tape m.**, marque de début de bande; **block m.**, marque de bloc; **drum m.**, marque de tambour; **end m.**, marque de fin, marque terminale; **end of disk m.**, marque de fin de disque; **end of file m.**, marque de fin de fichier; **end of tape m.**, marque de fin de bande; **field m.**, marque de zone; **file m.**, marque de fichier; **group m.**, marque de groupe; **record m.**, marque d'enregistrement; **record storage m.**, marque d'enregistrement (en mémoire); **segment m.**, marque de segment; **store m.**, marque de mémoire; **tape m.**, marque de bande; **timing m.**, marque de synchronisation; **word m.**, marque de mot; **m. scanning**, lecture *f* optique de marques; **m. sensing**, lecture *f* de marques.

marker, beginning of information m., marque *f* de début d'information (*sur bande*); **end of data m.**, marque *f* de fin de données.

Markov, M. chain, chaîne *f* de Markov.

mark-sense (to), graphiter.

mask, masque *m*; **holistic m.**, masque holistique; **interrupt m.**, masque d'interruption; **peephole m.**, masque perforé (*OCR*); **program m.**, masque de programme; **weighted area m.**, masque à zones pondérées (*OCR*); **m. matching**, comparaison *f* de masques (*OCR*); **m. register**, registre *m* de masquage.

mask (to), masquer.

masked, m. state, état masqué.

masking, masquage *m*.

mass, masse *f*; **m. memory**, mémoire *f* de très grande capacité, mémoire *f* de masse; **m. storage**, mémoire *f* de masse; **m. storage device**, mémoire *f* de masse.

master, m. card, carte maîtresse; **m. clock**, horloge *f*; **m. control program**, programme principal; **m. data**, données *f* de base; **m. file**, fichier maître, fichier principal; **m. instruction tape (M.I.T.)**, bande *f* d'exploitation; **m. library tape**, bande *f* (de) bibliothèque générale; **m. mode**, mode principal; **m. program**, programme principal; **m. program file**, fichier général des programmes; **m. program tape**, bande *f* d'exploitation; **m. record**, enregistrement principal; **m. routine**, programme *m* superviseur, programme directeur; **m. scheduler**, programmateur principal; **m./slave system**, système *m* à ordinateurs principal et asservi(s); **m. station**, station principale (*ou* maîtresse); **m. tape**, bande maîtresse, bande principale; **m. unit**, unité *f* pilote.

mastergroup, m. link, liaison *f* en groupe tertiaire; **m. section**, section *f* de groupe tertiaire.

match, opération *f* d'équivalence.

match (to), apparier, assortir.

matched, m. filter, filtre *m* de correspondance (*OCR*).

matching, mask m., comparaison *f* de masques (*OCR*); **m. error**, erreur *f* d'adaptation.

materials, matériaux *m*; **ferro-electric m.**, matériaux ferro-électriques; **ferromagnetic m.**, matériaux ferromagnétiques.

mathematical, mathématique *adj.*; **m. check**, contrôle *m* arithmétique; **m. logic**, logique *f* mathématique; **m. model**, modèle *m* mathématique; **m. programming**, programmation *f* mathématique; **m. subroutine**, sous-programme *m* mathématique.

matrix, matrice *f*; adjacency m., matrice d'incidence; **photocell m.**, matrice photoélectrique (*OCR*); **semantic m.**, matrice sémantique; **vertex m.**, matrice associée à un graphe; **m. algebra**, algèbre matricielle; **m. analysis**, analyse matricielle; **m. coefficient**, coefficient matriciel; **m. equation**, équation matricielle; **m. memory**, mémoire matricielle; **m. notation**, notation matricielle; **m. printer**, imprimante *f* à stylets, imprimante à (matrice d')aiguilles, imprimante à mosaïque; **m. store (or storage)**, mémoire (à sélection) matricielle.

maximal, maximal *adj.*

mean, moyen (-enne) *adj.*; **m. repair time**, durée moyenne de réparation; **m. time between failures (m.t.b.f.)**, intervalle moyen entre les pannes, temps moyen de bon fonctionnement; **m. time between overhauls (m.t.b.o.)**, périodicité moyenne des révisions; **m. time to failure (m.t.t.f.)**, temps moyen jusqu'à la panne; **m. time to maintain (m.t.t.m.)**, durée moyenne d'entretien;

m. time to repair (m.t.t.r.), durée moyenne de réparation.

measure, mesure *f*.

measuring, mesure *f*; remote m., télémesure *f*.

mechanical, mécanique *adj*.; m. differential analyser, analyseur différentiel mécanique; m. scanner, analyseur *m* à disque mécanique (*OCR*); m. translation, traduction *f* automatique.

mechanism, mécanisme *m*; access m., mécanisme d'accès; actuating m., dispositif *m* de commande, mécanisme de commande; decision m., organe *m* de décision (*OCR*); integrating m., mécanisme intégrateur; paper advance m., mécanisme d'entraînement de papier; servo m., servomécanisme *m*; tape transport m., (dispositif *m* d')entraînement *m* de bande magnétique; timing m., dispositif *m* de synchronisation.

mechanized, m. data, données *f* exploitables sur machine.

medium, support *m*; automated data m., support exploitable sur machine; blank m., support vierge; data m., support d'information, support de données; empty m., support vierge; input/output m., support d'entrée-sortie; machine-readable m., support exploitable sur machine; magnetic recording m., support d'enregistrement magnétique; storage m., support de mémoire; virgin m., support vierge; m. scale integration (MSI), intégration *f* à moyenne échelle.

meet, ET, conjonction *f*, affirmation *f* connexe, intersection *f* logique; m. operation, opération *f* ET.

megabit, mégabit *m*.

member, print m., porte-caractères *m*.

memorize (to), mémoriser, garder en mémoire.

memory, mémoire *f*; acoustic m., mémoire acoustique; bead m., mémoire à tores de ferrite; circulating m., mémoire cyclique; core m., mémoire à tores (magnétiques); diode-capacity m., mémoire à diodes/condensateurs; drum m., tambour *m* magnétique; dynamic m., mémoire dynamique; external m., mémoire externe; ferrite bead m., mémoire à tores de ferrite; holographic m., mémoire holographique;

internal m., mémoire interne; magnetic m., mémoire magnétique; mass m., mémoire de très grande capacité, mémoire de masse; matrix m., mémoire matricielle; multitape m., mémoire à bandes multiples; non-volatile m., mémoire rémanente, mémoire permanente; optical m., mémoire optique; permanent m., mémoire permanente, mémoire ineffaçable; random access m., mémoire à accès direct, mémoire à accès sélectif; read-only m., mémoire morte, mémoire passive; scratch-pad m., mémoire de travail, mémoire de manœuvre; secondary m., mémoire auxiliaire; serial m., mémoire (en) série; shared m., mémoire en commun, mémoire partagée; static m., mémoire statique; thin film m., mémoire à film mince; virtual m., mémoire virtuelle; volatile m., mémoire non rémanente; working m., mémoire de manœuvre, mémoire de travail; m. address register, registre *m* d'adresse mémoire; m. buffer register, registre-tampon *m* de mémoire; m. capacity, capacité *f* de mémoire; m. cycle, cycle *m* (de) mémoire; m. dump, vidage *m* (de) mémoire; m. exchange, échange *m* (de données) en mémoire; m. guard, protection *f* de mémoire; m. location, position *f* de mémoire; m. print-out, vidage *m* (de) mémoire sur imprimante; m. protect, protection *f* de mémoire; m. protect device, dispositif *m* de protection de mémoire; m. protection, protection *f* de mémoire; m. size, capacité *f* de mémoire.

mercury, mercure *m*; m. delay line, ligne *f* à retard à mercure; m. store (*or* storage), mémoire *f* à mercure; m. tank, réservoir *m* à mercure.

merge, fusion *f*, interclassement *m*.

merge (to), fusionner, interclasser.

merging, sequencing by m., rangement *m* par interclassement; m. sort, tri *m* d'interclassement; tri *m* de fusion.

message, message *m*; book m., message à plusieurs adresses; end of m. (E.O.M.), fin *f* de message; error m., message d'erreur; multiple-address m., message à plusieurs adresses; single-address m., message à adresse unique; start of m., début *m* de message; m. exchange, unité *f* de commutation de messages; m. feedback, renvoi *m* d'information, retour *m* d'information;

m. queuing, gestion *f* de file d'attente de messages; **m. routing**, acheminement *m* de messages; **m. switching**, prise *f* en charge (*ou* commutation *f*) de messages; **m. switching centre**, centre *m* de commutation de messages; **m. switching system**, système *m* de commutation de messages.

messmotor, moteur *m* intégrateur.

meter, compteur *m*, appareil *m* de mesure; **all-purpose m.**, polymètre *m*, appareil de mesure universel; **frequency m.**, fréquencemètre *m*; **modulation factor m.**, modulomètre *m*.

metering, **remote m.**, télémesure *f*.

method, méthode *f*; **access m.**, méthode d'accès; **basic access m.**, méthode d'accès de base; **basic telecommunication access m. (B.T.A.M.)**, méthode d'accès de base en télétraitement; **critical path m. (C.P.M.)**, méthode de chemin critique; **Monte Carlo m.**, méthode de Monte-Carlo; **queued access m.**, méthode d'accès avec file d'attente.

M.I.C.R. (=magnetic ink character recognition), reconnaissance *f* de caractères magnétiques codés.

micro, micro; **m. code**, micro-code *m*; **m. coding**, micro-programmation *f*; **m.-instruction**, micro-instruction *f*.

microcircuit, microcircuit *m*.

microcopier, microcopieuse *f*, duplicateur *m* de microphotographies.

microelectronic, micro-électronique *adj*.

microfiche, microfiche *f*.

microfilm, microfilm *m*; **computer output m.**, microfilm de sortie d'ordinateur, sortie *f* d'ordinateur sur microfilm; **m. printer**, imprimante *f* sur microfilm.

microminiaturization, micro-miniaturisation *f*.

micromodule, micro-élément *m*, micromodule *m*.

microprogram, microprogramme *m*.

microprogramming, microprogrammation *f*.

microsecond, microseconde *f*.

microwave, micro-onde *f*.

middleware, logiciel (*ou* software) adapté à la configuration (*ou* à l'installation).

millimicrosecond, millimicroseconde *f*.

millisecond, milliseconde *f*.

miniaturization, miniaturisation *f*.

mini-computer, mini-ordinateur *m*.

minimal, minimal *adj.*; **m. latency coding**, codage *m* à temps d'accès minimum, programmation *f* à temps d'exécution minimum.

minimum, minimum *m ou adj.*; **m. access code**, code *m* à (temps d')accès minimum; **m. access coding**, codage *m* à accès minimum; **m. access programming**, programmation *f* à temps d'accès minimum; **m. access routine**, programme *m* à temps d'accès minimum; **m. delay coding**, codage *m* à temps d'accès minimum, programmation *f* à temps d'exécution minimum; **m. distance code**, code *m* à distance minimum; **m. interval**, intervalle *m* minimum; **m. latency code**, code *m* à (temps d')accès minimum; **m. latency program**, programme *m* à temps d'accès minimum; **m. latency programming**, programmation *f* à temps d'accès minimum; **m. latency routine**, programme *m* à temps d'accès minimum.

minor, **m. control change**, rupture *f* de contrôle de troisième niveau; **m. cycle**, cycle mineur; **m. failure**, panne mineure; **m. total**, total *m* de niveau inférieur.

minority, minorité *f*, fonction *f* minoritaire; **m. carrier**, porteur *m* minoritaire.

minuend, nombre duquel on soustrait.

minus, **m. zone**, zone *f* «moins».

minute, **lines per m. (LPM)**, lignes *f* par minute.

misfeed, défaut *m* d'alimentation, mauvaise alimentation.

mispocket, erreur *f* de case.

misread, erreur *f* de lecture.

missort, erreur *f* de tri.

mistake, erreur *f*.

M.I.T. (=master instruction tape), bande *f* d'exploitation.

mix, **instruction m.**, sélection représentative d'instructions; **m. gate**, circuit *m* OU.

mixed, **m. base notation**, numération *f* à bases multiples; **m. base numeration**, numération *f* à bases multiples; **m. radix**, à plusieurs bases; **m. radix notation**, numération *f* mixte; **m. radix number**, nombre *m* à base multiple; **m. radix numeration**, numération *f* mixte.

mixer, mélangeur *m*.

mnemonic, mnémonique *adj.*; **m. code**,

code *m* mnémonique; **m. operation code,** code *m* d'opération mnémonique; **m. symbol,** symbole *m* mnémonique.
mnemonics, mnémotechnique *f.*
mod/demod (=**modulator/demodulator**), modulateur-démodulateur *m*, modem *m*.
mode, 1. mode *m*; **2.** état *m*; **access m.,** mode d'accès; **asynchronous m.,** mode asynchrone; **basic control (BC) m.,** mode de base, mode BC, mode 360; **binary m.,** mode binaire; **burst m.,** mode de transfert par paquets, mode continu; **card m.,** mode (d'exploitation) cartes; **compute m.,** état de fonctionnement; **control m.,** mode de contrôle; **conversational m.,** mode conversationnel, mode dialogué; **cycle-stealing m.,** mode d'exploitation en vol de cycles; **echo m.,** mode écho; **emulation m.,** mode d'émulation; **extended control (EC) m.,** mode étendu, mode EC, mode 370; **freeze m., 1.** état d'interruption; **2.** état figé; **hold m.,** état d'interruption; **initial condition m.,** condition initiale; **interactive m.,** mode interactif, mode de dialogue; **interrupt m.,** état d'interruption; **load m.,** mode chargement; **locate m.,** mode localisation; **master m.,** mode principal; **normal m.,** mode normal; **operate m.,** état de fonctionnement; **reset m.,** condition initiale; **simplex m.,** mode (d'exploitation) simplex; **simultaneous m. of working,** mode (d'exploitation) simultané; **slave m.,** mode asservi; **start-stop m.,** mode arythmique; **substitute m.,** mode de substitution; **supervisor m.,** mode (de) superviseur; **synchronous m.,** mode synchrone; **text m.,** mode texte; **transparent m.,** mode transparent; **m. change,** changement *m* de mode.
model, mathematical m., modèle *m* mathématique.
modelling, modélisation *f.*
modem (=**modulator/demodulator**), modulateur-démodulateur *m*, modem *m*.
modification, modification *f*; **address m.,** modification d'adresse; **instruction m.,** modification d'instructions.
modifier, m. register, registre *m* d'index.
modify (to), modifier.
modular, modulaire *adj.*
modularity, modularité *f.*
modulating, m. frequency, fréquence *f* de modulation.
modulation, modulation *f*; **amplitude m. (AM),** modulation d'amplitude; **angle m.,** modulation d'angle; **compound m.,** modulation multiple; **cross m.,** intermodulation *f*, transmodulation *f*; **defective m.,** modulation incorrecte; **differential m.,** modulation différentielle; **double m.,** double modulation; **frequency m. (FM),** modulation de fréquence; **incorrect m.,** modulation incorrecte; **isochronous m.,** modulation isochrone; **low level m.,** modulation à faible puissance; **multiple m.,** modulation multiple; **phase m.,** modulation de phase; **phase-inversion m.,** modulation par inversion de phase; **pulse m.,** modulation par impulsions (*ou* d'impulsions); **pulse-amplitude m. (PAM),** modulation d'impulsions en amplitude; **pulse-code m. (PCM),** modulation par impulsions codées; **pulse-duration m. (PDM),** modulation d'impulsions en durée; **pulse-frequency m.,** modulation d'impulsions en fréquence; **pulse-length m.,** modulation d'impulsions en durée; **pulse-number m.,** modulation d'impulsions en nombre; **pulse-phase m. (PPM),** modulation d'impulsions en phase; **pulse-position m. (PPM),** modulation d'impulsions en position; **pulse-time m.,** modulation d'impulsions dans le temps; **pulse-width m.,** modulation d'impulsions en durée; **significant conditions of a m.,** états significatifs d'une modulation; **start-stop m.,** modulation arythmique; **telegraph m.,** modulation télégraphique; **two-tone m.,** modulation à deux fréquences porteuses; **m. code,** code *m* de modulation; **m. coherence,** cohérence *f* d'une modulation; **m. element,** élément *m* de modulation; **m. factor,** taux *m* de modulation; **m. factor meter,** modulomètre *m*; **m. frequency,** fréquence *f* de modulation; **m. index,** indice *m* de modulation; **m. rate,** rapidité *f* de modulation, vitesse *f* télégraphique; **m. with a fixed reference,** modulation avec référence fixe.
modulator, modulateur *m*; **pulse m.,** modulateur d'impulsions; **telegraph m.,** modulateur télégraphique.
modulator/demodulator, modulateur-démodulateur *m*, modem *m*.
module, élément *m*, module *m*, bloc *m*,

organe *m*, unité *f*; **circuit m.**, élément de circuit; **load m.**, module (de programme) chargeable; **object m.**, module (en langage) objet; **programming m.**, module de programme; **source m.**, module (de programme) source.

modulo N check, contrôle *m* sur reste.

modulo-N residue, reste *m* (d'une division) modulo-N.

modulo 2, m. 2 sum, somme *f* modulo-2.

monadic, m. Boolean operator, opérateur booléen à un seul opérande; **m. operation,** opération *f* à un (seul) opérande.

monitor, 1. (programme *m*) moniteur *m*; **2.** appareil *m* de surveillance (*ou* de contrôle); **m. program,** programme moniteur; **m. routine,** programme moniteur; **m. system,** système *m* d'exploitation; **m. unit,** appareil de surveillance (*ou* de contrôle).

monitor (to), contrôler, surveiller.

monitoring, contrôle *m*, surveillance *f*; **m. key,** clé *f* de surveillance; **m. program,** programme *m* moniteur.

monolithic, monolithique *adj.*; **m. integrated circuit,** circuit intégré monolithique.

monostable, 1. monostable *adj.*; **2.** circuit *m* monostable; **m. circuit,** circuit monostable; **m. multivibrator,** multivibrateur *m* monostable; **m. trigger,** multivibrateur *m* monostable; **m. trigger circuit,** circuit monostable.

Monte Carlo, M. C. method, méthode *f* de Monte-Carlo.

morpheme, morphème *m*.

MOS (=metal oxide semi-conductor) transistor, transistor *m* métal-oxyde-semiconducteur (MOS).

most significant, m.s. character, caractère le plus significatif; **m.s. digit,** chiffre le plus significatif.

motor, moteur *m*; **integrating m.,** moteur intégrateur.

M out of N code, code *m* N dont M.

move (to), 1. transmettre, émettre; **2.** effectuer un transfert (d'information), transférer.

MSI (=medium scale integration), intégration *f* à moyenne échelle.

m.t.b.f. (=mean time between failures), intervalle moyen entre les pannes, temps moyen de bon fonctionnement.

m.t.b.o. (=mean time between overhauls), périodicité moyenne des révisions.

m.t.t.f. (=mean time to failure), temps moyen jusqu'à la panne.

m.t.t.m. (=mean time to maintain), durée moyenne d'entretien.

m.t.t.r. (=mean time to repair), durée moyenne de réparation.

multi-access, à accès *m* multiple.

multi-address, à adresses *f* multiples; **m.-a. instruction,** instruction *f* à adresses multiples.

multichannel, m. link, liaison *f* multivoie; **m. signal,** signal *m* multiplex; **m. system,** système *m* multivoie.

multicircuit, m. carrier telegraphy, télégraphie *f* multivoie par courants porteurs; **m. carrier telephony,** téléphonie *f* multivoie par courants porteurs.

multicomputer, multicalculateur *m*.

multicomputing, m. unit, multicalculateur *m*, multiprocesseur *m*.

multicycle, m. feeding, alimentation *f* (de cartes) à lectures multiples.

multidrop, m. link, liaison *f* multipoints.

multijob, m. operation, traitement *m* multitravaux, exploitation *f* en multiprogrammation.

multilevel, m. address, adresse indirecte; **m. addressing,** adressage indirect.

multiple, multiple *adj.*; **m. access,** accès *m* multiple; **m.-aperture core,** tore *m* à plusieurs trous; **m. arithmetic,** calcul *m* à plusieurs résultats; **m.-aspect indexing,** indexation précoordonnée (*Recherche documentaire*); **m. carrier telephony,** téléphonie *f* multiple à courants porteurs; **m.-channel carrier system,** système *m* multivoie à courants porteurs; **m. connector,** connecteur *m* multiple; **m.-length arithmetic,** fonctionnement *m* en longueur multiple; **m.-length numeral,** nombre *m* en longueur multiple; **m.-length working,** fonctionnement *m* en longueur multiple; **m. modulation,** modulation *f* multiple; **m. precision,** fonctionnement *m* en longueur multiple; **m. programming,** multiprogrammation *f*; **m. punching,** perforation *f* multiple; **m. system,** multicalculateur *m*, multiprocesseur *m*; **m. telephone channel,** voie *f* téléphonique multiple.

multiple-address, m.-a. code, code *m* à

adresses multiples; **m.-a. instruction,** instruction *f* à adresses multiples; **m.-a. message,** message *m* à plusieurs adresses.
multiplex, multiplex *adj*.; **frequency-division m.,** multiplex par partage des fréquences; **time-division m.,** multiplex par partage du temps; **m. channel,** voie *f* multiplex; **m. data terminal,** terminal *m* multiplex (de transmission de données); **m. device,** dispositif *m* multiplex; **m. system,** système *m* multiplex.
multiplex (to), multiplexer.
multiplexed, m. operation, fonctionnement *m* en multiplexage.
multiplexing, multiplexage *m*.
multiplexor, multiplexeur *m*; **m. channel,** canal *m* multiplexeur.
multiplicand, multiplicande *m*.
multiplication, multiplication *f*; **m. time,** durée *f* de multiplication.
multiplier, multiplicateur *m ou adj*.; **analog m.,** multiplicateur analogique; **digital m.,** multiplicateur numérique; **potentiometer m.,** multiplicateur à servomécanisme; **quarter-squares m.,** multiplicateur bicarré; **servo m.,** multiplicateur à servomécanisme; **variable m.,** multiplicateur analogique; **m. factor,** multiplicateur; **m. quotient register,** registre *m* multiplicateur-quotient.
multiply, logical m., ET, conjonction *f*, affirmation *f* connexe, intersection *f* logique; **m. operation,** opération *f* de multiplication.
multiplying, m. punch, calculateur *m* perforateur.
multipoint, m. circuit, circuit *m* multipoint; **m. link,** liaison *f* multipoints.
multi-precision, m.-p. arithmetic, arithmétique *f* à précision multiple.
multiprocessing, multitraitement *m*.
multiprocessor, multicalculateur *m*, multiprocesseur *m*; **m. interleaving,** allocation imbriquée de mémoire (*pour système multiprocesseur*).
multiprogramming, multiprogrammation *f*.
multipurpose, universel (-elle) *adj*., à usages *m* multiples, polyvalent *adj*.
multirange, m. amplifier, amplificateur *m* multigain.
multiread, m. feeding, alimentation *f* (de

cartes) à lectures multiples.
multisequential, m. system, système *m* à multiprogrammation.
multi-spindle, m.-s. disk drive, unité *f* de disques multibroches.
multistation, à stations *f* multiples.
multitape, m. memory, mémoire *f* à bandes multiples.
multitask, m. operation, traitement *m* multi-tâches.
multi-tone, m.-t. circuit, circuit *m* multivoie.
multivibrator, multivibrateur *m*; **astable m.,** multivibrateur astable; **bistable m.,** bascule *f*; **free-running m.,** multivibrateur astable; **monostable m.,** multivibrateur monostable; **one shot m.,** multivibrateur monostable; **single shot m.,** multivibrateur monostable.
Mylar (*Regd. trade mark*), Mylar (*marque déposée*).

N

n, n-address instruction format, format *m* d'instruction à n adresses; **n-ary digit,** chiffre *m* n-aire; **n-core-per-bit store,** mémoire *f* à n tores par bit; **n-level address,** à n niveaux *m* d'adressage; **n-level logic,** logique *f* à n niveaux.
NAK (=negative acknowledge character), (caractère *m*) accusé *m* de réception négatif.
name, 1. nom *m*; 2. identificateur *m*; **condition n.,** nom de condition; **data n.,** nom de données; **file n.,** nom de fichier; **qualified n.,** nom qualifié; **symbolic n.,** nom symbolique.
NAND, NON-ET; **NAND element,** élément *m* NON-ET; **NAND gate,** circuit *m* NON-ET; **NAND operation,** opération *f* NON-ET; **NAND operator,** opérateur *m* NON-ET.
nanosecond, nanoseconde *f*.
napierian, népérien (-enne) *adj*.; **n. base,** base *f* des logarithmes népériens; **n. logarithm,** logarithme népérien.
narrative, commentaire *m*.
natural, naturel (-elle) *adj*.; **n. frequency,** fréquence naturelle; **n. language,** langage

naturel; **n. logarithm,** logarithme naturel.
natural-function, n.-f. generator, générateur *m* de fonctions analytiques.
natural-law, n.-l. function generator, générateur *m* de fonctions analytiques.
naught, zéro.
n-c, n-c contact, contact normalement fermé.
n-core-per-bit, n-c.-p.-b. store (*or* **storage),** mémoire *f* à n tores par bit.
near-end, n.-e. crosstalk, paradiaphonie *f.*
needle, aiguille *f;* **sorting n.,** aiguille de tri.
negate (to), effectuer la fonction NON.
negater, élément *m* NON, inverseur *m.*
negation, 1. négation *f;* **2.** inversion *f,* complémentation *f;* **n. element,** élément *m* d'inversion; **n. gate,** circuit *m* NON.
negative, négatif (-ive) *adj.;* **n. acknowledge character (NAK),** (caractère *m*) accusé *m* de réception négatif; **n. feedback,** contre-réaction *f;* **n. indication,** indication *f* de signe négatif.
negator, élément *m* NON, inverseur *m.*
neper, néper *m.*
nest (to), emboîter.
nesting, 1. inclusion *f;* **2.** emboîtement *m;* **n. loops,** boucles (de programme) emboîtées; **n. store (or storage),** mémoire *f* à liste inversée; **n. subroutines,** sous-programmes emboîtés.
net, n. control station (*Am.*), station *f* de coordination de réseau.
network, 1. réseau *m;* **2.** circuit *m;* **analog n.,** réseau analogique; **balancing n.,** réseau d'équilibrage, équilibreur *m;* **compensating n.,** circuit compensateur; **computer n.,** réseau de calculateurs; **data communications n.,** réseau informatique; **differentiating n.** (*Am.*), montage *m* différentiateur; **equivalent n.,** réseau équivalent; **integrating n.** (*Am.*), montage *m* intégrateur; **leased-line n.,** réseau à lignes privées (*ou* louées); **logic n.,** réseau logique; **private telegraph n.,** réseau télégraphique privé; **private telephone n.,** réseau téléphonique privé; **private wire n.,** réseau à lignes privées (*ou* louées); **public telegraph n.,** réseau télégraphique public; **public telephone n.,** réseau téléphonique public; **ring n.,** réseau en anneau; **star n.,** réseau en étoile; **switched n.,** réseau connecté; **switching n.,** réseau de commutation;

telephone n., réseau téléphonique; **teleprinter n.,** réseau de téléimprimeurs; **telex n.,** réseau télex; **n. analog (device),** réseau d'étude analogique; **n. analyser,** simulateur *m* (d'étude) de réseaux; **n. calculator,** simulateur *m* (d'étude) de réseaux.
neutral, n. zone, zone *f* neutre.
new, n. line character (NL), (caractère *m*) retour *m* à la ligne.
nexus, connexion *f.*
nickel, n. delay line, ligne *f* à retard à nickel.
nine, neuf; **complement on n.,** complément *m* à neuf; **n.-edge leading,** ligne *f* des « 9 » en tête.
nines, casting out n., preuve *f* par neuf; **n. complement,** complément *m* à neuf.
ninety, quatre-vingt-dix; **n. column card,** carte *f* à 90 colonnes.
Nixie, N. tube, tube *m* Nixie.
NL (=**new line character),** (caractère *m*) retour *m* à la ligne.
n-o, n-o contact, contact normalement ouvert.
no address, n. a. instruction, instruction *f* sans adresse.
no-charge, n.-c. machine fault time, temps non imputable dû à une panne machine; **n.-c. nonmachine fault time,** temps non imputable non dû à une panne machine.
node, nœud *m.*
no home, n.h. record, article *m* secondaire, enregistrement indirect.
noise, bruit *m;* **ambient n.,** bruit ambiant; **background n.,** bruit de fond; **impulse n.,** impulsion *f* parasite; **line n.,** bruit de circuit; **random n.,** bruit erratique; **n. factor,** bruit (*Recherche documentaire*); **n. generator,** générateur *m* de bruit; **n. killer,** dispositif *m* antiparasites.
nominal, nominal *adj.;* **n. bandwidth,** largeur *f* de bande nominale; **n. frequency,** fréquence nominale; **n. speed,** vitesse nominale.
non-arithmetic, n.-a. shift, décalage *m* circulaire.
non-conjunction, incompatibilité *f,* opération *f* NON-ET.
non-destructive, n.-d. addition, addition *f* sans effacement; **n.-d. read(ing),** lecture non destructive, lecture sans effacement; **n.-d. readout,** lecture non destructive, lec-

ture sans effacement; **n.-d. storage,** mémoire *f* à lecture non destructive.

non-disjunction, négation *f* connexe, opération *f* NON-OU.

non-dynamic, n.-d. area, zone *f* statique, partie *f* statique.

non-equivalence, non-équivalence *f*; **n.-e. circuit,** circuit *m* de non-équivalence; **n.-e. element,** élément *m* de non-équivalence, élément OU exclusif; **n.-e. gate,** circuit *m* de non-équivalence, circuit OU exclusif; **n.-e. operation,** opération *f* de non-équivalence, exclusion *f* réciproque.

non-equivalent, n.-e.(-to) element, élément *m* de non-équivalence, élément OU exclusif.

non-erasable, n.-e. store (or storage), mémoire *f* fixe, mémoire permanente.

non-existent, n.-e. code, caractère *m* invalide; **n.-e. code check,** contrôle *m* de caractère invalide.

non-linear, n.-l. optimization, programmation *f* non linéaire; **n.-l. programming,** programmation *f* non linéaire.

non-linearity, non-linéarité *f*; **n.-l. distortion,** distorsion *f* de non-linéarité.

non-loaded, n.-l. lines, lignes non chargées.

non-locking, sans maintien *m*; **n.-l. escape,** échappement *m* sans maintien; **n.-l. shift character,** caractère *m* sans maintien (d'un changement de code).

non-oriented, n.-o. graph, graphe non orienté.

non-pageable, non paginable *adj.*

non-polarized, n.-p. return-to-zero recording, enregistrement non polarisé avec retour à zéro.

non-print, n.-p. code, code *m* de non-impression; **n.-p. instruction,** instruction *f* de non-impression.

non-programmed, n.-p. halt, arrêt non programmé.

non-reproducing, n.-r. code, code *m* de non-reproduction.

non-resident, n.-r. routine, programme *m* ne résidant pas en permanence en mémoire.

non-return-to-reference, n.-r.-t.-r. recording, enregistrement *m* non retour à zéro.

non-return-to-zero (N.R.Z.), non retour *m* à zéro; **n.-r.-t.-z. recording,**

enregistrement *m* non retour à zéro.

non-scheduled, n.-s. maintenance time, temps *m* d'entretien non périodique (*ou* non planifié).

non-simultaneous, n.-s. transmission, transmission non simultanée.

non-volatile, n.-v. memory, mémoire rémanente, mémoire permanente; **n.-v. store (or storage),** mémoire rémanente, mémoire permanente.

no-op, n.-o. instruction, instruction *f* factice, instruction de remplissage.

no-operation, n.-o. instruction, instruction *f* factice, instruction de remplissage.

NOR, NON-OU, NI; **NOR circuit,** circuit *m* NON-OU (*ou* NI); **NOR element,** élément *m* NON-OU (*ou* NI), mélangeur-inverseur *m*; **NOR gate,** circuit *m* NON-OU (*ou* NI); **NOR operation,** opération *f* NON-OU (*ou* NI), négation *f* connexe; **NOR operator,** opérateur *m* NON-OU (*ou* NI).

normal, n. binary, binaire pur; **n. direction flow,** sens normal des liaisons (*sur un organigramme*); **n. load,** circuit *m* de charge réel; **n. mode,** mode normal; **n. route,** voie normale; **n. stage punching,** perforation normale.

normalization, pulse n., mise *f* en forme d'impulsions; **signal n.,** mise *f* en forme de signaux.

normalize (to), normaliser.

normalized, n. form, forme normalisée (*en représentation à virgule flottante*).

NOT, NON; **NOT circuit,** circuit *m* NON; **NOT element,** élément *m* NON, inverseur *m*; **NOT gate,** circuit *m* NON; **NOT operation,** opération *f* NON; **NOT operator,** opérateur *m* NON.

NOT-AND, NON-ET; **NOT-AND element,** élément *m* NON-ET, conditionneur-inverseur *m*; **NOT-AND operation,** opération *f* NON-ET.

notation, 1. notation *f*; **2.** numération *f*; **base n.,** numération à base; **binary coded decimal n.,** notation (*ou* numération) décimale (codée en) binaire; **binary coded n.,** représentation codée en binaire; **binary n.,** notation binaire; **biquinary n.,** notation biquinaire; **coded decimal n.,** notation (*ou* numération) décimale codée; **decimal n.,** notation décimale; **fixed-radix n.,** notation (*ou* numération) à base fixe; **hexadecimal n.**, notation hexadécimale; **infix n.**, notation infixée; **Lukasiewicz n.**, notation préfixée; **matrix n.**, notation matricielle; **mixed base n.**, numération à bases multiples; **mixed radix n.**, numération mixte; **octal n.**, notation octale; **parentheses-free n.**, notation préfixée; **Polish n.**, notation préfixée; **polyvalent n.**, notation polyvalente; **positional n.**, numération pondérée, notation pondérée; **prefix n.**, notation préfixée; **radix n.**, numération à base; **sexadecimal n.**, numération sexadécimale; **symbolic n.**, notation symbolique; **ternary n.**, numération ternaire.

NOT-IF-THEN, NOT-IF-THEN operation, exclusion *f*.

nought, zéro; **n. state**, état *m* «zéro».

nought-output, signal *m* de lecture «zéro»; **n. o. signal**, signal *m* de lecture «zéro».

noughts, n. complement, complément *m* à zéro, complément à la base.

n-p, n-p junction, jonction *f* n-p.

n-p-n, n-p-n transistor, transistor *m* n-p-n.

n-p-n-p, n-p-n-p transistor, transistor *m* n-p-n-p.

N.R.Z. (=**non-return-to-zero**), non retour *m* à zéro.

n-type, n-t. semi-conductor, semi-conducteur *m* type n.

nucleus, noyau *m*.

NUL (=**null character**), caractère nul, caractère *m* de remplissage (d'espace *ou* de temps).

null, nul (-lle) *adj.*; **n. character (NUL)**, caractère nul, caractère *m* de remplissage (d'espace *ou* de temps); **n. instruction**, instruction *f* factice, instruction de remplissage; **n. representation**, caractère nul; **n. string**, chaîne *f* vide.

number, 1. nombre *m*; 2. numéro *m*; **binary coded decimal n.**, nombre décimal codé binaire; **binary n.**, nombre binaire; **biquinary coded decimal n.**, nombre décimal codé biquinaire; **biquinary n.**, nombre biquinaire; **call n.**, numéro d'appel; **check n.**, nombre de contrôle; **coded decimal n.**, nombre décimal codé; **decimal n.**, nombre décimal; **dialling n.**, numéro de sélection; **double-length n.**, nombre en longueur double; **double-precision n.**, nom-

bre en double précision; **duodecimal n.**, nombre duodécimal; **floating-point n.**, nombre à virgule flottante; **installation tape n.**, numéro d'identification de bande; **mixed radix n.**, nombre à base multiple; **octal n.**, nombre octal; **operation n.**, numéro d'instruction; **polyvalent n.**, nombre polyvalent; **radix n.**, base *f* (de numération); **random n.**, nombre aléatoire; **reel n.**, numéro d'ordre de bobine; **self-checking n.**, nombre à chiffre-clé de protection; **septenary n.**, nombre septénaire; **sequence n.**, numéro d'ordre; **serial n.**, numéro de série; **slot n.**, numéro de case; **statement n.**, numéro d'instruction; **symbolic n.**, nombre symbolique; **tape serial n.**, numéro de série du fabricant (*de bande*); **uniform random n.**, nombre aléatoire; **n. generator**, générateur *m* de nombres; **n. representation**, numération *f*; **n. (representation) system**, système *m* de numération.

numbering, n. plan (*Am.*), plan *m* de numérotage; **n. scheme**, plan *m* de numérotage.

numeral, nombre *m*, numéral *m*; **binary n.**, nombre binaire; **decimal n.**, nombre décimal; **double-length n.**, nombre en longueur double; **double-precision n.**, nombre en double précision; **multiple-length n.**, nombre en longueur multiple; **octal n.**, nombre octal; **self-checking n.**, nombre à chiffre-clé de protection; **n. system**, système *m* de numération.

numeration, numération *f*; **decimal n.**, numération décimale; **fixed-radix n.**, numération à base fixe; **mixed base n.**, numération à bases multiples; **mixed radix n.**, numération mixte; **pure binary n.**, numération binaire; **radix n.**, numération à base; **n. system**, système *m* de numération.

numeric, numérique *adj.*; **n. character**, caractère *m* numérique, chiffre *m* numérique; **n. character set**, jeu *m* de caractères numériques; **n. character subset**, jeu partiel de caractères numériques; **n. code**, code *m* numérique; **n. coded character set**, jeu *m* de caractères codés numériques; **n. data**, données *f* numériques; **n. representation**, représentation *f* numérique; **n. word**, mot *m* numérique.

numerical, numérique *adj.*; **n. analysis**,

analyse *f* numérique; **n. character,** caractère *m* numérique, chiffre *m* numérique; **n. code,** code *m* numérique; **n. coding,** codage *m* numérique; **n. control,** commande *f* numérique, commande *f* symbolique; **n. data,** données *f* numériques; **n. data code,** code *m* numérique; **n. information,** information *f* numérique; **n. integration,** intégration *f* numérique; **n. machine,** machine *f* numérique; **n. punch,** perforation *f* numérique; **n. representation,** représentation *f* numérique; **n. sorting,** tri *m* numérique; **n. tape,** bande *f* pour la commande numérique de machines-outils; **n. value,** grandeur *f* numérique; **n. word,** mot *m* numérique.

numeric-alphabetic, alphanumérique *adj.*

O

O & M (=**organization and methods**), organisation *f* scientifique du travail (O.S.T.).

object, objet *m*; **o. code,** code *m* objet; **o. computer,** calculateur *m* objet, calculateur d'exécution; **o. configuration,** configuration *f* objet; **o. language,** langage *m* objet, langage généré; **o. module,** module *m* (en langage) objet; **o. program,** programme *m* objet, programme résultant, programme généré; **o. routine,** programme *m* objet, programme résultant, programme généré; **o. tape,** bande *f* programme en langage objet.

O.C.R. (=**optical character recognition**), reconnaissance *f* optique de caractères.

octal, octal *adj.*, de base 8; **binary coded o.,** octal codé binaire; **o. code,** code octal; **o. digit,** chiffre octal; **o. notation,** notation octale; **o. number,** nombre octal; **o. number system,** système *m* de numération octale; **o. numeral,** nombre octal.

octet, octet *m*.

odd, impair *adj.*; **o. parity,** parité impaire; **o. parity check,** contrôle *m* d'imparité (*ou* de parité impaire).

odd-even, o.-e. **check,** contrôle *m* de parité.

OEM (=**original equipment manufacturer**),

constructeur *m* de matériel.

office, calling o., bureau *m* demandeur; **central o.** (*Am.*), centre *m* (*ou* central *m*) téléphonique; **local central o.** (*Am.*), central urbain; **tandem central o.** (*Am.*), central *m* tandem; **telex call o.,** bureau *m* télex; **toll o.** (*Am.*), central interurbain.

offline, autonome *adj.*, non connecté *adj.*, indépendant *adj.*; **o. equipment,** matériel *m* autonome, matériel non connecté, matériel indépendant; **o. operation,** exploitation *f* en (mode) autonome; **o. processing,** traitement *m* (en) différé; **o. storage,** mémoire non connectée; **o. system,** système *m* autonome, système non connecté; **o. working,** fonctionnement *m* (en) autonome.

off-punch, perforation décalée.

offset, décalé *adj.*

offset (*Am.*), maculage *m*; **o. stacker,** case *f* de réception (de cartes) à décalage.

omission, o. **factor,** silence *m* (*Recherche documentaire*).

one, un(e); **binary o.,** «un» binaire; **complement on o.,** complément *m* à un; **o. condition,** état *m* «un».

one-address, à une adresse; **o.-a. code,** instruction *f* à une adresse; **o.-a. instruction,** instruction *f* à une adresse; **o.-a. instruction format,** format *m* d'instruction à une adresse.

one-ahead, o.-a. **addressing,** adressage *m* à progression automatique avancée.

one-core-per-bit, o.-c.-p.-b. **store** (*or* **storage**), mémoire *f* à un tore par bit.

one-digit, o.-d. **adder,** demi-additionneur *m*; **o.-d. subtracter,** demi-soustracteur *m*.

one-for-one, un(e) pour un(e); **o.-f.-o. translator,** traducteur *m* un(e) pour un(e).

one-level, à un niveau; **o.-l. address,** adresse directe, adresse réelle; **o.-l. code,** code réel (*en langage machine*); **o.-l. subroutine,** sous-programme *m* à un niveau.

one-output, signal *m* de lecture «un»; **o.-o. signal,** signal de lecture «un».

one-plus-one, o.-p.-o. **address,** à une adresse d'opérande et une adresse de commande; **o.-p.-o. address instruction format,** format *m* d'instruction à une adresse d'opérande et une adresse de commande.

ones, o. **complement,** complément *m* à un.

one shot, o. s. **multivibrator,** multivibrateur

m monostable; **o. s. operation,** fonctionnement *m* en pas-à-pas.

one state, état *m* «un».

one step, o. s. operation, fonctionnement *m* en pas-à-pas.

one-to-one, o.-t.-o. assembler, assembleur *m* un(e) pour un(e).

one-to-zero, o.-t.-z. ratio, rapport *m* de discrimination (1 à 0).

online, connecté *adj.*; en direct; **o. central file,** fichier central en liaison directe; **o. data reduction,** réduction *f* de données en connecté; **o. equipment,** matériel connecté; **o. operation,** exploitation *f* en (mode) connecté; **o. processing,** traitement *m* en direct, traitement *m* en temps réel; **o. storage,** mémoire connectée; **o. system,** système connecté; **o. typewriter,** machine à écrire connectée; **o. unit,** unité connectée; **o. working,** fonctionnement *m* (en) connecté, fonctionnement en direct.

on-the-fly, o.-t.-f. printer, imprimante *f* à la volée.

open, o.-circuit working, transmission *f* par fermeture de circuit; **o. loop,** circuit ouvert; **o. shop operation,** exploitation *f* en salle ouverte; **o. subroutine,** sous-programme *m* relogeable; **o. wire,** fil (nu) aérien; **o.-wire line,** ligne aérienne.

open-ended, 1. ouvert *adj.*; 2. extensible *adj.*

operand, opérande *m.*

operate, o. mode, état *m* de fonctionnement.

operated, remote o., télécommandé *adj.*

operating, o. area, zone *f* de travail, zone de manœuvre; **o. delays,** retards *m* d'exploitation, retards dus aux opérateurs; **o. limit,** puissance *f* limite admissible; **o. ratio,** taux *m* dzutilisation effective; **o. state,** état *m* de fonctionnement; **o. system,** système *m* d'exploitation.

operation, 1. opération *f*; 2. exploitation *f*; 3. fonctionnement *m*; 4. traitement *m*; **add o.,** opération d'addition; **alternate o.,** exploitation à l'alternat; **AND o.,** opération ET; **arithmetical o.,** opération arithmétique; **asynchronous o.,** fonctionnement asynchrone; **automatic sequential o.,** fonctionnement séquentiel automatique; **auxiliary o.,** opération auxiliaire; **average calculating o.,** opération de calcul moyenne; **biconditional o.,** opération d'équivalence; **binary arithmetical o.,** opération binaire arithmétique; **binary Boolean o.,** opération booléenne diadique; **binary o.,** opération binaire; **book-keeping o.,** opération de service, opération auxiliaire; **Boolean o.,** opération booléenne; **closed shop o.,** exploitation en salle fermée; **collation o.,** opération d'interclassement; **complementary o.,** opération complémentaire; **complete o.,** opération complète; **computer o.,** opération machine; **concurrent o.,** opération simultanée, fonctionnement en parallèle; **conditional implication o.,** 1. inclusion *f*; 2. implication *f*; **control o.,** fonction *f*; **crippled mode o.,** fonctionnement en mode dégradé; **dagger o.,** opération NON-OU (*ou* NI), négation *f* connexe; **decoded o.,** opération décodée; **dial o.,** appel *m* (*ou* sélection *f*) au cadran; **dual o.,** opération inverse (booléenne); **duplex o.,** exploitation en duplex; **dyadic Boolean o.,** opération booléenne diadique; **dyadic o.,** opération binaire à deux opérandes; **either-OR o.,** disjonction *f*; **equivalence o.,** opération d'équivalence; **exclusive-OR o.,** exclusion *f* réciproque, opération de non-équivalence; **fixed-cycle o.,** opération à nombre de cycles fixe; **fixed-point o.,** calcul(s) *m* a virgule fixe; **floating-point o.,** calcul(s) *m* à virgule flottante; **full-duplex o.,** exploitation en duplex; **half-duplex o.,** exploitation (en) semi-duplex; **housekeeping o.,** opération de service, opération auxiliaire; **IF-THEN o.,** implication *f*; **inclusive-OR o.,** disjonction *f*; **independent o.,** opération indépendante; **iterative o.,** opération itérative; **jump o.,** opération de branchement; **logical o.,** opération logique; **machine o.,** opération machine; **make-break o.,** opération travail-repos; **manual o.,** exploitation manuelle; **meet o.,** opération ET; **monadic o.,** opération à un (seul) opérande; **multijob o.,** traitement multi-travaux, exploitation en multiprogrammation; **multiplexed o.,** fonctionnement en multiplexage; **multiply o.,** opération de multiplication; **multitask o.,** traitement multi-tâches; **NAND o.,** opération NON-ET; **non-equivalence o.,** opération de non-équivalence, exclusion *f* réciproque; **NOR**

o., opération NON-OU (*ou* NI), négation *f* connexe; **NOT o.**, opération NON; **NOT-AND o.**, opération NON-ET; **NOT-IF-THEN o.**, exclusion *f*; **offline o.**, exploitation en (mode) autonome; **one shot o.**, fonctionnement en pas-à-pas; **one step o.**, fonctionnement en pas-à-pas; **online o.**, exploitation en (mode) connecté; **open shop o.**, exploitation en salle ouverte; **OR o.**, opération OU; **parallel o.**, exploitation en parallèle; **real-time o.**, fonctionnement en temps réel; **red-tape o.**, opération de service, opération auxiliaire; **repetitive o.**, opération répétitive; **representative calculating o.**, opération de calcul moyenne; **scheduled o.**, exploitation planifiée; **semi-duplex o.**, exploitation (en) semi-duplex; **sequential o.**, exploitation séquentielle; **serial o.**, exploitation en série; **simultaneous o.**, exploitation simultanée; **single shot o.**, fonctionnement en pas-à-pas; **single step o.**, fonctionnement en pas-à-pas; **split-word o.**, opération sur partie de mot; **step-by-step o.**, fonctionnement en pas-à-pas; **synchronous o.**, fonctionnement synchrone; **teleprinter for duplex o.**, téléimprimeur *m* pour service duplex; **transfer o.**, 1. opération de transfert; 2. opération de saut; **transmit o.**, opération de transfert; **true-time o.**, fonctionnement en temps réel; **unary o.**, opération à un (seul) opérande; **o. code**, code *m* d'opération; **o. code field**, zone *f* du code d'opération; **o. control**, (unité *f* de) contrôle *m* des opérations arithmétiques; **o. cycle**, cycle *m* d'exécution (d'une instruction); **o. decoder**, décodeur *m* (du type) d'opération; **o. number**, numéro *m* d'instruction; **o. part**, partie *f* «type d'opération»; **o. register**, registre *m* «type d'opération»; **o. time**, temps *m* d'exploitation, temps opératoire; **o. use time**, temps *m* d'utilisation effective.

operational, o. amplifier, amplificateur *m* calculateur; **o. character**, caractère *m* de commande; **o. research**, recherche opérationnelle; **o. use time**, temps *m* d'utilisation effective.
adj.; **operations, o. analysis**, recherche opérationnelle; **o. research (O.R.)**, recherche opérationnelle.

operator, opérateur *m*; **AND o.**, opérateur ET; **Boolean o.**, opérateur booléen; **com-** plementary o., opérateur complémentaire; **exclusive-OR o.**, opérateur OU exclusif; **inclusive-OR o.**, opérateur OU inclusif; **keypunch o.**, perforatrice *f*, perforeuse *f*; **logical o.**, opérateur logique; **monadic Boolean o.**, opérateur booléen à un seul opérande; **NAND o.**, opérateur NON-ET; **NOR o.**, opérateur NON-OU; **NOT o.**, opérateur NON; **OR o.**, opérateur OU; **relational o.**, opérateur de relation; **telephone o.**, téléphoniste *m ou f*, standardiste *m ou f*; **o. command**, directive *f* (d')opérateur, message *m* (d')opérateur; **o.-connected call**, communication établie par l'opérateur (-trice); **o. part**, partie *f* «type d'opération».

optical, optique *adj.*; **o. bar-code reader**, lecteur *m* optique de marques; **o. character reader**, lecteur *m* optique de caractères; **o. character recognition (O.C.R.)**, reconnaissance *f* optique de caractères; **o. mark reader**, lecteur *m* optique de marques; **o. memory**, mémoire *f* optique; **o. reader**, lecteur *m* optique; **o. scanner**, analyseur *m* optique; **o. scanning**, analyse *f* optique; **o. type font**, ensemble *m* de caractères à lecture optique (*OCR*).

optimalize (to), optimiser.

optimization, linear o., programmation *f* linéaire; **non-linear o.**, programmation *f* non linéaire.

optimize (to), optimiser.

optimum, optimum *m ou adj.*; **o. code**, code *m* optimum; **o. coding**, codage *m* optimum.

optional, facultatif (-ive) *adj.*; en option *f*; **o. device**, dispositif *m* en option, dispositif facultatif; **o. halt instruction**, instruction *f* d'arrêt conditionnel; **o. stop instruction**, instruction *f* d'arrêt conditionnel.

O.R. (=**operations research**), recherche opérationnelle.

OR, réunion *f* logique, mélangeur *m*; **OR circuit**, circuit *m* OU; **OR element**, élément *m* OU, mélangeur; **OR gate**, circuit *m* OU; **OR operation**, opération *f* OU; **OR operator**, opérateur *m* OU.

order, 1. ordre *m*; 2. rangement *m*; **ascending o.**, ordre croissant; **descending o.**, ordre décroissant; **out of o.**, en dérangement *m*, en panne *f*, déréglé *adj.*; **priority o.**, ordre de priorité; **o. code**, code *m* de commande; **o. format**, format *m* d'instruction;

o. structure, format *m* d'instruction; **o. wire,** circuit *m* de service.

order (to), ordonner, mettre en séquence.

ordering, ordonnance *f,* mise *f* en séquence; **o. bias, 1.** écart *m* d'ordre; **2.** séquence préexistante (*dans un tri*).

orders, initial **o.,** ordres initiaux (de programme).

ordinary, o. binary, binaire pur.

organ, arithmetic o., unité *f* arithmétique.

organization, data o., organisation *f* des données.

organization and methods (O & M), organisation *f* scientifique du travail (O.S.T.).

orientation, orientation *f.*

oriented, o. graph, graphe orienté.

origin, origine *f.*

original, o. address, adresse *f* d'origine; **o. document,** document *m* de base; **o. equipment manufacturer (OEM),** constructeur *m* de matériel; **o. language,** langage *m* source.

oscillator, oscillateur *m*; **parametric o.,** oscillateur paramétrique; **phase-locked o.,** oscillateur à blocage de phase.

oscilloscope, oscilloscope *m*; **cathode ray o.,** oscilloscope à rayons cathodiques.

out, o. of contact, hors contact *m*, hors de contact (avec); **o. of line coding,** séquence séparée du programme principal; **o. of order,** en dérangement *m*, en panne *f,* déréglé *adj.*; **o. of service time,** temps *m* de non-disponibilité, temps d'immobilisation.

outer, o. face, côté extérieur (*d'une bande*).

outgoing, o. circuit, circuit *m* de départ.

outline, contour *m*; **character o.,** contour d'un caractère; **o. flowchart,** organigramme *m* sommaire (*ou* général).

out-plant, extérieur *adj.* (*à l'établissement*); **o.-p. system,** système *m* à terminaux extérieurs.

output, de sortie *f,* sortant *adj.*; **o. area,** zone *f* de sortie, zone d'extraction; **o. block,** zone *f* de sortie, zone d'extraction; **o. buffer,** tampon *m* de sortie; **o. channel,** canal *m* de sortie, voie *f* de sortie; **o. circuit,** circuit *m* de sortie; **o. data,** données *f* de sortie; **o. device,** appareil *m* de sortie; **o. equipment,** matériel *m* de sortie, matériel d'extraction; **o. impedance,** impédance *f* de sortie; **o. magazine,** case *f* de réception; **o.**

power, puissance *f* de sortie; **o. process,** sortie *f,* extraction *f*; **o. punch,** perforateur *m* de bande automatique; **o. routine,** programme *m* d'extraction (*ou* de sortie); **o. routine generator,** générateur *m* de programmes de sortie; **o. section,** zone *f* de sortie, zone d'extraction; **o. stacker,** case *f* de réception; **o. state,** état *m* de sortie; **o. storage,** zone *f* de sortie, zone d'extraction; **o. table,** table traçante; **o. unit,** élément *m* de sortie, unité *f* d'extraction; **o. work queue,** file *f* d'attente de sortie des travaux; **o. writer,** programme *m* d'écriture (de fichiers) de sortie.

output, 1. sortie *f,* extraction *f*; **2.** données *f* de sortie; **direct o.,** sortie directe; **indirect o.,** sortie indirecte, sortie différée; **nought-o.,** signal *m* de lecture «zéro»; **one-o.,** signal *m* de lecture «un»; **power o.,** puissance *f* de sortie, puissance débitée; **pulse power o.,** puissance *f* de sortie des impulsions; **read o.,** signal *m* de (sortie) lecture; **real-time o.,** sortie en temps réel; **zero o.,** signal *m* de lecture «zéro».

output (to), extraire, sortir.

overflow, 1. débordement *m*; **2.** dépassement *m* de capacité; **characteristic o.,** dépassement de capacité de la caractéristique; **o. bucket,** emplacement *m* de débordement (en mémoire); **o. (check) indicator,** indicateur *m* de dépassement de capacité; **o. position,** position *f* de dépassement de capacité; **o. record,** enregistrement *m* en débordement; **o. route,** voie *f* de débordement; **o. stacking,** réception *f* en case alternée.

overhauls, mean time between o., périodicité moyenne des révisions.

overhead, o. bit, bit *m* supplémentaire.

overlap, 1. simultanéité *f*; **2.** chevauchement *m*.

overlay, 1. recouvrement *m*; **2.** segment *m* de recouvrement; **primary o.,** segment de recouvrement principal; **subordinate o.,** segment de recouvrement secondaire; **o. supervisor,** superviseur *m* de segments de recouvrement.

overload, surcharge *adj.*; **o. level** (*Am.*), puissance *f* limite admissible.

over-modulation, surmodulation *f.*

overpunch(ing), 1. perforation *f* hors texte; **2.** double perforation *f.*

overrun, engorgement *m*.
overwrite (to), écrire par remplacement.
own, o. coding, séquence *f* (complémentaire) d'utilisateur.

P

P.A.B.X. (=private automatic branch exchange), installation privée automatique.
pack, 1. tassement *m*; **2.** paquet *m* (de cartes); **disk p.**, chargeur *m* de disques amovible; **test p.**, jeu *m* d'essai (*sur cartes*).
pack (to), 1. condenser; **2.** grouper.
package, 1. produit-programme *m*; **2.** bloc *m* logique, boîtier *m*.
packed, p. decimal, décimal condensé.
packet, p. switching, commutation *f* de paquets.
packing, p. density, densité *f* d'enregistrement.
pad, attenuation p., atténuateur *m* fixe; **p. character**, caractère *m* de remplissage (de temps).
pad (to), garnir, remplir.
padding, garnissage *m*, remplissage *m*.
page, page *f*; **active p.**, page active; **fixed p.**, page sédentaire, page fixée; **p.-at-a-time printer**, imprimante *f* page par page; **p. data set**, ensemble de données constitué de pages; **p. entry**, renvoi *m* d'organigramme en entrée; **p. exit**, renvoi *m* d'organigramme en sortie; **p. fixing**, fixation *f* de page; **p. frame**, cadre *m* de page; **p. frame table**, table *f* des cadres de page; **p. printer**, imprimante *f* page par page; **p. reader**, lecteur *m* de pages; **p. table (PGT)**, table *f* des pages; **p. turning**, transfert *m* de page; **p. wait condition**, attente *f* de page.
page (to), paginer.
pageable, paginable *adj*.
paged, p. file, fichier organisé (*ou* subdivisé) en pages.
page-in, chargement *m* de page.
page-out, renvoi *m* de page.
paging, pagination *f*; **demand p.**, pagination sur demande; **p. supervisor**, superviseur *m* de pagination.
pair, binary p., bascule *f*; **pulse p.**, paire *f* d'impulsions; **trigger p.**, bascule *f*.
paired, p. cable, câble *m* à paires.

PAM (=pulse-amplitude modulation), modulation *f* d'impulsions en amplitude.
panel, 1. panneau *m* (de commande); **2.** tableau *m* de connexions; **control p.**, tableau de commande; **graphic p.**, panneau d'affichage graphique; **jack p., 1.** tableau de connexions; **2.** tableau de jacks; **patch p.**, panneau de raccordement.
panic, p. button, interrupteur *m* de secours.
paper, papier *m*; **carbon p.**, papier-carbone *m*; **co-ordinate p.**, papier quadrillé; **fan-folded p.**, papier (en continu) à pliage paravent; **teletype p.**, bande *f* de téléimprimeur; **p. advance mechanism**, mécanisme *m* d'entraînement de papier; **p. drive**, entraînement *m* de papier; **p. low condition**, indication *f* de fin de papier; **p. slew**, saut *m* de papier; **p. tape**, bande perforée; **p. tape code**, code *m* de bande perforée; **p. tape loop**, bande *f* pilote; **p. tape punch**, perforateur *m* de bande; **p. tape punching**, perforation *f* de bande; **p. tape reader**, lecteur *m* de bande perforée; **p. tape reproducer**, reproductrice *f* de bande perforée; **p. tape unit**, unité *f* de bande perforée; **p. tape verifier**, vérificatrice *f* de bande perforée; **p. throw**, saut *m* de papier; **p. throw character**, caractère *m* de saut de papier.
parallel, parallèle *adj*.; en parallèle; **p. access**, accès *m* parallèle; **p. arithmetic**, arithmétique *f* (en) parallèle; **p. computer**, calculateur simultané; **p. feed**, alimentation *f* ligne par ligne; **p. flow**, déroulement *m* des travaux en parallèle; **p. full adder**, additionneur *m* parallèle; **p. full subtracter**, soustracteur *m* parallèle; **p. half adder**, demi-additionneur *m* parallèle; **p. half subtracter**, demi-soustracteur *m* parallèle; **p. operation**, exploitation *f* en parallèle; **p. printer**, imprimante *f* parallèle; **p. processing**, traitement *m* en parallèle, traitement *m* en simultanéité; **p. programming**, programmation *f* (en) parallèle; **p. running**, exploitation *f* en parallèle; **p. search storage**, mémoire *f* associative; **p. storage**, mémoire *f* (en) parallèle; **p. series converter**, convertisseur *m* parallèle-série; **p. transfer**, transfert *m* parallèle; **p. transmission**, transmission *f* parallèle; **p. work-flow**, déroulement *m* des travaux en parallèle.

parameter, paramètre *m*; **preset p.**, paramètre prédéterminé, paramètre prédéfini; **program p.**, paramètre de programme; **p. card**, carte *f* paramètre; **p. word**, mot *m* paramètre.

parametric, **p. oscillator**, oscillateur *m* paramétrique.

parasitic, parasite *adj.*; **p. current**, courant *m* parasite; **p. effect**, effet *m* parasite; **p. frequency**, fréquence *f* parasite; **p. signal**, signal *m* parasite; **p. suppressor**, éliminateur *m* de parasites, dispositif *m* antiparasites.

parentheses-free, **p.-f. notation**, notation préfixée.

parity, parité *f*; **even p.**, parité paire; **odd p.**, parité impaire; **p. bit**, bit *m* de parité; **p. check**, contrôle *m* de parité; **p. error**, erreur *f* de parité.

part, partie *f*; **address p.**, partie adresse (d'une instruction); **fixed-point p.**, mantisse *f*; **fractional p.**, mantisse *f* (*en représentation à virgule flottante*); **function p.**, partie «type d'opération»; **operation p.**, partie «type d'opération»; **operator p.**, partie «type d'opération».

partial, partiel (-elle) *adj.*; **p. arithmetic**, calcul *m* à un seul résultat; **p. carry**, report partiel; **p. disturbed one-output signal**, signal *m* de sortie «un» en sélection partielle avec perturbation; **p. disturbed response signal**, signal *m* de sortie en sélection partielle avec perturbation; **p. disturbed response voltage**, signal *m* de sortie en sélection partielle avec perturbation; **p. disturbed zero-output signal**, signal *m* de sortie «zéro» en sélection partielle avec perturbation; **p. drive pulse**, impulsion *f* de commande (d'intensité) partielle; **p. product**, produit partiel, produit *m* intermédiaire; **p. read pulse**, impulsion (de commande) partielle de lecture; **p.-select input pulse**, impulsion (de commande) partielle d'écriture; **p.-select output pulse**, impulsion (de commande) partielle de lecture; **p. sum**, somme partielle; **p. undisturbed one-output signal**, signal *m* de sortie «un» en sélection partielle sans perturbation; **p. undisturbed response signal**, signal *m* de sortie en sélection partielle sans perturbation; **p. undisturbed response voltage**, signal *m* de sortie en sélection partielle sans

perturbation; **p. undisturbed zero-output signal**, signal *m* de sortie «zéro» en sélection partielle sans perturbation; **p. write pulse**, impulsion (de commande) partielle d'écriture.

partially, **p. switched cell**, élément perturbé.

partition, partition *f*; **virtual storage p.**, partition de mémoire virtuelle.

partition (to), segmenter.

partitioned, **p. data set**, ensemble *m* de données compartimenté.

partitioning, segmentation *f*, fractionnement *m*, compartimentage *m*.

parts, **p. list**, nomenclature *f* (de pièces).

party, **called p.**, demandé *m*; **calling p.**, demandeur *m*; **p. line**, ligne partagée.

pass, passe *f*, passage *m*; **machine p.**, passage (en) machine.

pass-band, bande passante.

passive, passif (-ive) *adj.*; **p. circuit**, circuit passif; **p. element**, élément passif.

patch, 1. raccordement *m*; 2. correction *f* provisoire (de programme); **p. panel**, panneau *m* de raccordement; **p.-program plugboard**, tableau *m* de connexions auxiliaire.

patch (to), 1. raccorder; 2. corriger (un programme).

patchboard, tableau *m* de connexions.

patchcord, connecteur *m*, fiche *f* de connexion.

patchplug, connecteur *m*, fiche *f* de connexion.

path, chemin *m*, voie *f*.

pattern, 1. modèle *m*; 2. profil *m*; 3. configuration *f*; 4. dessin *m*; **bit p.**, profil binaire; **land p.**, modèle de circuit, dessin du dépôt conducteur; **p. recognition**, reconnaissance *f* de formes (*OCR*); **p. sensitive fault**, incident *m* décelable par une disposition particulière des données.

P.A.X. (=**private automatic exchange**), bureau privé automatique.

P.B.X. (=**private branch exchange**), installation *f* d'abonné avec postes supplémentaires.

P C M (=**pulse-code modulation**), modulation *f* par impulsions codées.

P C M (=**punched card machine**), machine *f* à cartes perforées.

P D M (=**pulse-duration modulation**),

modulation f d'impulsions en durée.

peak, p. current, courant m de crête, courant m de pointe.

pecker, palpeur m.

peek-a-boo, p.-a-b. check, contrôle visuel.

peephole, p. mask, masque perforé (*OCR*).

pen, light p., crayon lumineux, marqueur lumineux, stylet lumineux, luminostyle m.

pence, p. conversion equipment, dispositif m de conversion de pence.

pencil, crayon m; **conductive p.,** crayon à mine conductrice.

pentode, pentode f.

percentage, p. occupied time, coefficient m d'occupation (*d'un faisceau de circuits*).

perception, artificial p., perception artificielle.

perforated, perforé *adj.*; **p. tape,** bande perforée; **p.-tape retransmitter,** retransmetteur m à bande perforée, reperforateur-transmetteur m; **p.-tape teletypewriter,** téléimprimeur m à bande perforée.

perforation, perforation f; **chadless p.,** perforation partielle; **chad type p.,** perforation complète; **p. rate,** vitesse f de perforation (de bande).

perforator, perforateur m, perforatrice f; **key p.,** perforatrice à clavier; **keyboard p.,** perforateur à clavier, clavier perforateur; **manual p.,** perforatrice manuelle; **printer p.** (*Am.*), récepteur perforateur imprimeur, reperforateur imprimeur; **printing keyboard p.,** perforateur imprimeur à clavier, clavier perforateur avec impression; **receiving p.,** récepteur perforateur, reperforateur m; **tape p.,** perforateur de bande.

performance, transmission p., qualité f de transmission; **p. evaluation,** évaluation f de(s) performance(s); **p. period,** durée f de fonctionnement.

period, période f; **charging p.,** période de taxation; **digit p.,** durée f d'impulsion; **performance p.,** durée f de fonctionnement; **regeneration p.,** période de régénération; **retention p.,** période de rétention; **scan p.,** période de balayage (*ou* d'analyse); **word p.,** période de mot.

peripheral, périphérique m *ou adj.*; **buffered p.,** périphérique à mémoire-tampon; **p. buffer,** tampon m de périphérique; **p. control unit,** unité f de commande de périphériques; **p. equipment,** unité f périphérique; **p. interface channel,** canal m d'interface avec périphériques; **p.-limited,** limité par le (*ou* subordonné au) débit des périphériques; **p. processor,** processeur m auxiliaire; **p. store,** mémoire f périphérique; **p. transfer,** transfert m périphérique (*ou* entre périphériques); **p. unit,** unité f périphérique.

permanent, permanent *adj.*; **p. connection,** connexion permanente; **p. fault,** panne permanente; **p. magnet,** aimant permanent; **p. memory,** mémoire permanente, mémoire f ineffaçable; **p. store (or storage),** mémoire permanente, mémoire f fixe.

permutation, permutation f; **p. index,** index m de permutation, index permuté (*Recherche documentaire*).

permuted, p.-title index, index m de permutation, index permuté (*Recherche documentaire*).

P.E.R.T. (=**Program Evaluation and Review Technique**), P.E.R.T.

pertinency, p. factor, pertinence f (*Recherche documentaire*).

PGT (=**page table**), table f des pages.

phantom, p. circuit, circuit m fantôme.

phase, phase f; **compiling p.,** phase de compilation; **execute p.,** phase d'exécution; **run p.,** phase d'exécution; **p. distortion,** distorsion f de phase; **p. equalizer,** compensateur m de phase; **p.-inversion modulation,** modulation f par inversion de phase; **p.-locked oscillator,** oscillateur m à blocage de phase; **p. modulation,** modulation f de phase; **p. shift,** déphasage m.

phoneme, phonème m.

photocell, cellule f photo-électrique; **p. matrix,** matrice f photo-électrique (*OCR*).

photoelectric, p. reader, lecteur m photo-électrique.

photogravure, photogravure f.

phototypesetting, photocomposition f.

photovoltaic, p. cell, cellule f photovoltaïque.

physical, physique *adj.*; **p. record,** enregistrement m physique.

pick (to), choisir, sélectionner.

picker, p. arm, bras m d'alimentation; **p. belt,** courroie f d'alimentation.

picosecond, picoseconde f.

picture, 1. image *f*; **2.** modèle *m*.

piezoelectric, piézoélectrique *adj.*; **p. effect,** effet *m* piézoélectrique.

pilot, group (reference) p., onde *f* pilote de groupe primaire; **reference p.,** onde *f* pilote; **regulating p.,** onde *f* pilote de régulation; **supergroup reference p.,** onde *f* pilote de groupe secondaire; **switching (control) p.,** onde *f* pilote de commutation; **synchronizing p.,** onde *f* pilote de synchronisation; **p. card,** carte-pilote *f*; **p. channel,** voie *f* d'onde (porteuse) pilote; **p. system,** système *m* pilote; **p.-wire regulator,** régulateur *m* à fil pilote.

pin, p. contact, contact *m* à broche; **p. feed,** entraînement *m* par picots, entraînement *m* par ergots.

pinboard, tableau *m* à aiguilles.

pinch, p. lever, levier *m* pinceur; **p. roller,** rouleau *m* pinceur.

pinfeed, p. platen, dispositif *m* d'entraînement par ergots.

ping-pong, travail *m* en bascule (sur deux dérouleurs).

pitch, array p., pas longitudinal, interligne *m*; **character p.,** entraxe *m* de caractères; **feed p.,** pas *m* d'entraînement; **row p.,** pas longitudinal, interligne *m*; **track p.,** entraxe *m* de pistes.

place, emplacement *m*, position *f*; **digit p.,** emplacement de chiffre, rang *m* (d'un chiffre).

plan, numbering p. (*Am.*), plan *m* de numérotage.

planar, p. graph, graphe *m* planaire.

plane, digit p., plan *m* de mémoire.

planning, 1. planning *m*; **2.** planification *f*; **product p.,** planning de production.

plant (to), implanter.

plate, aperture p., plaque *f* à trous; **magnetic memory p.,** matrice *f* de mémoire (à ferrite).

plated, p. circuit, circuit imprimé; **p. wire store,** mémoire *f* à fils plaqués, mémoire *f* à couche mince sur fil.

platen, cylindre *m* (d'impression); **pinfeed p.,** dispositif *m* d'entraînement par ergots.

playback, p. head, tête *f* de lecture.

PL/1, PL/1.

plot (to), tracer.

plotter, traceur *m* (de courbes), table traçante; **data p.,** traceur de courbes;

digital incremental p., traceur de courbes incrémental; **incremental p.,** traceur incrémental; **X-Y p.,** traceur de courbes.

plotting, p. board, table traçante, table de report; **p. table,** table traçante.

plug, fiche *f* (de connexion); **banana p.,** fiche banane; **cordless p.,** cavalier *m*.

plugboard, tableau *m* de connexions; **detachable p.,** tableau de connexions amovible; **patch-program p.,** tableau de connexions auxiliaire; **removable p.,** tableau de connexions amovible; **p. chart,** schéma *m* de connexions, relevé *m* de connexions.

plugging, p. chart, schéma *m* de connexions, relevé *m* de connexions.

plug-in, p.-i. unit, plaquette *f* embrochable (*ou* interchangeable).

plug-to-plug, p.-t.-p. compatible, à connexion *f* compatible, directement connectable.

plus, p. zone, zone *f* «plus».

p-n, p-n junction, jonction *f* p-n; **p-n junction transistor,** transistor *m* à jonction p-n.

pneumatic, p. computer, ordinateur *m* à fluides.

p-n-p, p-n-p transistor, transistor *m* p-n-p.

p-n-p-n, p-n-p-n transistor, transistor *m* p-n-p-n.

pocket, case *f*; **reject p.,** case (de) rebut; **sorter p.,** case de tri, case de réception de trieuse; **p. gate,** clapet *m* (de case).

pocketing, réception *f* en case.

point, 1. virgule *f*; **2.** point *m*; **3.** emplacement *m*; **adjustable p.,** virgule réglable; **arithmetic p.,** virgule; **assumed decimal p.,** virgule implicite; **binary p.,** virgule (en) binaire; **decimal p.,** virgule décimale, signe décimal; **dump p.,** point de contrôle, point de reprise; **entry p.,** point d'entrée; **index p.,** point machine; **load p.,** point de départ de lecture *ou* d'écriture (*d'une bande*); **radix p.,** séparation *f* fractionnaire, emplacement de la virgule; **re-entry p.,** point de retour; **rerun p.,** point de reprise; **restart p.,** point de reprise; **set p.,** point de réglage; **p. mode display,** affichage *m* par points; **p.-to-p. link,** liaison *f* point à point; **p.-to-p. transmission,** transmission (directe) entre deux points.

pointer, pointeur *m*.

polar, p. direct-current system (*Am.*),

transmission f par double courant.
polarity, polarité f.
polarized, polarisé *adj.*; **p. return-to-zero recording**, enregistrement polarisé avec retour à zéro.
Polish, P. notation, notation préfixée.
poll (to), appeler.
polling, appel sélectif *(de terminaux)*; **p. list**, liste f d'appel (sélectif).
polymorphic, p. system, système m polymorphe.
polyphase, polyphasé *adj.*
polyvalence, polyvalence f.
polyvalent, polyvalent *adj.*; **p. notation**, notation polyvalente; **p. number**, nombre polyvalent.
position, position f, emplacement m; **bit p.**, position binaire; **code p.**, emplacement de perforation *(bande)*; **controlling p.**, position directrice; **digit p.**, emplacement de chiffre, rang m (d'un chiffre); **highest significant p.**, position la plus significative; **high order p.**, position la plus significative; **low order p.**, position la moins significative; **overflow p.**, position de dépassement de capacité; **print p.**, position d'impression; **punch(ing) p.**, emplacement de perforation *(carte)*; **sign p.**, position du signe; **p. pulse**, impulsion f de contrôle.
positional, p. notation, numération pondérée, notation pondérée; **p. representation**, représentation pondérée.
positioning, p. arm, bras m de positionnement.
positive, p. feedback, réaction f.
post, p. printer, postmarqueuse f.
post (to), annoter, signaler, enregistrer, inscrire.
post-edit (to), mettre en forme des résultats (de calcul).
posting, facsimile p., report m.
post-installation, p.-i. review, revue f après installation.
post-mortem, p.-m. dump, vidage m post-mortem; **p.-m. program**, programme m post-mortem, programme m d'autopsie; **p.-m. routine**, programme m post-mortem, programme m d'autopsie.
post-slew *(Am.)*, saut m après impression.
post-write, p.-w. disturb pulse, impulsion f de perturbation après écriture.
potentiometer, potentiomètre m; **induc-**

tive **p.**, potentiomètre bobiné; **resolving p.**, potentiomètre à variation sinusoïdale; **sine-cosine p.**, potentiomètre à variation sinusoïdale; **p. multiplier**, multiplicateur m à servomécanisme.
powder, antisetoff p., poudre f antimaculage *(OCR)*.
powdered, p. iron core, noyau m à poudre de fer.
power, 1. puissance f; **2.** exposant m; **apparent p.**, puissance apparente; **available p.**, puissance (maximum) disponible; **output p.**, puissance de sortie; **p. dump**, coupure f d'alimentation électrique; **p.-off indicator**, indicateur m de débranchement; **p.-on indicator**, indicateur m de branchement; **p. output**, puissance f de sortie, puissance débitée; **p. supply**, alimentation f, source f d'énergie.
PPM (=pulse-phase modulation), modulation f d'impulsions en phase.
PPM (=pulse-position modulation), modulation f d'impulsions en position.
P-pulse, impulsion f de contrôle.
pragmatics, pragmatisme m.
preamplifier, préamplificateur m; **differential p.**, préamplificateur différentiel.
preanalysis, analyse f préparatoire.
precision, précision f; **double p.**, double précision; **multiple p.**, fonctionnement m en longueur multiple; **single p.**, simple précision; **triple p.**, triple précision.
predefined, p. process, processus prédéfini.
predicate, prédicat m.
pre-edit (to), pré-éditer.
prefix, p. notation, notation préfixée.
preliminary, p. review, revue f préliminaire.
preparation, data p., saisie f de données.
preprinted, préimprimé *adj.*
preprocessor, programme m de prétraitement, pré-processeur m.
prepunched, préperforé *adj.*
pre-read, p.-r. disturb pulse, impulsion f de perturbation avant lecture; **p.-r. head**, tête f de prélecture.
preselect (to), présélectionner.
preselection, présélection f.
presence, p. bit, bit m indicateur de présence.
preserve (to), conserver, mettre en réserve.

preset, p. parameter, paramètre prédéterminé, paramètre prédéfini.
preset (to), 1. prérégler; **2.** mettre à la valeur initiale, initialiser.
pre-slew (*Am.*), saut *m* avant impression.
presort, tri *m* préalable.
press-button, bouton-poussoir *m*.
pre-store (to), pré-enregistrer.
presumptive, p. address, adresse *f* de base, adresse origine; **p. instruction,** instruction *f* sous forme initiale.
preventive, p. maintenance, entretien préventif; **p. maintenance time,** temps *m* d'entretien préventif.
prewired, précâblé *adj.*; **p. circuit,** circuit précâblé.
p.r.f. (=**pulse repetition** (*or* **recurrence**) **frequency**), fréquence *f* de répétition des impulsions.
primary, p. failure, défaillance *f* primaire; **p. instruction,** instruction *f* élémentaire; **p. overlay,** segment *m* de recouvrement principal; **p. route,** voie *f* primaire; **p. storage,** mémoire principale.
principal, p. test section, section principale d'essais.
print, impression *f*; **p. bar,** barre *f* d'impression; **p. barrel,** cylindre *m* d'impression; **p. chain,** chaîne *f* d'impression; **p. contrast ratio,** taux *m* de contraste d'impression; **p. control character,** caractère *m* de contrôle d'impression; **p. format,** format *m* d'impression; **p. hammer,** marteau *m* d'impression; **p. line,** ligne *f* d'impression; **p. member,** porte-caractères *m*; **p. position,** position *f* d'impression; **p. roll,** rouleau *m* d'impression, cylindre *m* d'impression; **p. wheel,** roue *f* d'impression.
print (to), imprimer.
printed, p. circuit, circuit imprimé; **p. circuit board,** (plaque(tte) *f* à) circuit imprimé; **p. circuit card,** (plaque(tte) *f* à) circuit imprimé; **p. form,** imprimé *m*.
printer, imprimante *f*; **bar p.,** imprimante à barres; **barrel p.,** imprimante à la volée; **chain p.,** imprimante à chaîne; **character-at-a-time p.,** imprimante caractère par caractère; **character p.,** imprimante caractère par caractère; **dot p.,** imprimante par points; **electrostatic p.,** imprimante électrostatique; **high-speed p.,** imprimante rapide; **hit-on-the-fly p.,** imprimante à la volée; **line-at-a-time p.,** imprimante (ligne) par ligne; **line p.,** imprimante (ligne) par ligne; **matrix p.,** imprimante à stylets, imprimante à (matrice d')aiguilles, imprimante à mosaïque; **microfilm p.,** imprimante sur microfilm; **on-the-fly p.,** imprimante à la volée; **page-at-a-time p.,** imprimante page par page; **page p.,** imprimante page par page; **parallel p.,** imprimante parallèle; **post p.,** postmarqueuse *f*; **serial p.,** imprimante série; **stylus p.,** imprimante à stylets, imprimante à (matrice d')aiguilles; **wheel p.,** imprimante à roues; **wire p.,** imprimante à stylets, imprimante à (matrice d')aiguilles; **xerographic p.,** imprimante xérographique; **p. perforator** (*Am.*), récepteur *m* perforateur imprimeur, reperforateur *m* imprimeur; **p. ribbon,** ruban *m* d'imprimante.
printing, background p., impression *f* du fond (*OCR*); **end p.,** impression *f* en bout de carte; **line p.,** impression *f* (ligne) par ligne; **magnetic p.,** transfert *m* de magnétisation; **p. equipment,** matériel *m* d'impression; **p. keyboard perforator,** perforateur *m* imprimeur à clavier, clavier *m* perforateur avec impression; **p. reperforator,** récepteur *m* perforateur imprimeur, reperforateur *m* imprimeur.
print-out, sortie *f* d'imprimante, état imprimé; **dynamic p.-o.,** impression *f* dynamique; **memory p.-o.,** vidage *m* (de) mémoire sur imprimante; **static p.-o.,** impression différée.
print restore, p. r. code, code *m* de reprise d'impression.
priority, priorité *f*; **dispatching p.,** priorité de prise en charge; **limit p.,** priorité limite; **program p.,** priorité de programme; **p. indicator,** indicatif *m* de priorité; **p. order,** ordre *m* de priorité; **p. processing,** traitement *m* par priorités.
private, privé *adj.*; **p. automatic branch exchange (P.A.B.X.),** installation privée automatique; **p. automatic exchange (P.A.X.),** bureau privé automatique; **p. branch exchange (P.B.X.),** installation *f* d'abonné avec postes supplémentaires; **p. exchange (P.X.),** central privé; **p. (leased) line,** ligne privée; **p. line service,** service *m* à ligne privée; **p. telegraph network,** réseau télégraphique privé; **p. telephone network,**

réseau téléphonique privé; **p. wire network,** réseau *m* à lignes privées (*ou* louées); **p. wire service,** service *m* à ligne privée.

probability, probabilité *f*; **p. theory,** théorie *f* des probabilités.

probe, sense p., crayon *m* émetteur.

problem, problème *m*; **benchmark p.,** problème de référence, problème d'évaluation comparative; **check p.,** problème de contrôle, problème-test *m*; **queuing p.,** problème de file d'attente; **test p.,** problème de contrôle, problème-test *m*; **trouble location p.,** problème de localisation de panne; **p. board,** tableau *m* de connexions; **p. definition,** définition *f* de problème; **p. description,** dossier *m* d'application; **p. file,** dossier *m* d'exploitation; **p. folder,** dossier *m* d'exploitation; **p.-oriented language,** langage orienté vers le problème; **p. program,** programme *m* de production.

procedure, procédure *f*; **aborting p.,** procédure d'abandon; **catalogued p.,** procédure cataloguée; **p. division,** division *f* «traitement» (*COBOL*); **p.-oriented language,** langage orienté vers le traitement.

proceed, p.-to-select signal, signal *m* d'invitation à numéroter; **p.-to-send signal,** signal *m* d'invitation à transmettre; **p.-to-transmit signal,** signal *m* d'invitation à transmettre.

process, 1. processus *m*; **2.** procédé *m*; **3.** traitement *m*; **input p.,** entrée *f*, introduction *f*; **input/output p.,** transfert radial, opération *f* d'entrée-sortie; **irreversible p.,** processus irréversible; **irreversible magnetic p.,** transformation *f* magnétique irréversible; **iterative p.,** processus itératif; **output p.,** sortie *f*, extraction *f*; **predefined p.,** processus prédéfini; **recursive p.,** processus récurrent; **reversible p.,** processus réversible; **reversible magnetic p.,** transformation *f* magnétique réversible; **transput p.,** transfert radial, opération *f* d'entrée-sortie; **p. chart,** organigramme *m* (de traitement de l'information), ordinogramme *m*; **p. control,** contrôle *m* de processus industriels; **p. control computer,** calculateur *m* de contrôle de processus industriels; **p.-limited,** limité par la vitesse de traitement.

processing, traitement *m*; **administrative**

data p., informatique *f* de gestion, traitement de l'information en gestion; **automatic data p.,** traitement automatique de l'information, traitement automatique des données; **background p.,** traitement non prioritaire; **batch p., 1.** traitement par lots, traitement différé; **2.** traitement en série; **business data p.,** informatique *f* de gestion, traitement de l'information en gestion; **centralized data p.,** traitement centralisé de l'information; **commercial data p.,** informatique *f* de gestion; **conversational data p.,** traitement de l'information (en mode) conversationnel; **data p.,** informatique *f*, traitement de l'information, traitement des données; **demand p.,** traitement immédiat, traitement à la demande; **electronic data p. (E.D.P.),** traitement électronique de l'information (*ou* des données); **foreground p.,** traitement prioritaire; **immediate p.,** traitement immédiat, traitement à la demande; **industrial data p.,** informatique industrielle; **information p.,** informatique *f*, traitement de l'information; **inline p.,** traitement immédiat; **integrated data p. (I.D.P.),** traitement intégré des données, traitement unifié des données; **list p.,** traitement de liste; **offline p.,** traitement (en) différé; **online p.,** traitement en direct, traitement en temps réel; **parallel p.,** traitement en parallèle, traitement en simultanéité; **priority p.,** traitement par priorités; **query p.,** traitement d'interrogations; **random p.,** traitement non ordonné; **real-time p.,** traitement en temps réel; **remote batch p.,** traitement groupé à distance; **remote data p.,** téléinformatique *f*; **remote p.,** télétraitement *m*, traitement à distance; **scientific data p.,** informatique *f* scientifique; **sequential p.,** traitement séquentiel; **serial p.,** traitement en série; **stacked job p.,** traitement par programmes groupés; **word p.,** traitement de texte; **p. program,** programme *m* d'exploitation.

processor, machine *f* de traitement de l'information, unité *f* de traitement de l'information, processeur *m*; **central p.,** unité centrale de traitement; **data p.,** machine de traitement de l'information, ordinateur *m*, calculateur *m*; **front-end p.,** processeur frontal, ordinateur frontal; **peripheral p.,**

processeur auxiliaire; **remote p.,** téléprocesseur *m*; **satellite p.,** processeur satellite; **p. error interrupt,** interruption *f* sur erreur de parité; **p.-limited,** limité par la vitesse de traitement.

product, produit *m*; **arithmetic p.,** produit arithmétique; **intermediate p.,** produit partiel, produit intermédiaire; **logical p.,** ET, conjonction *f*, affirmation *f* connexe, intersection *f* logique; **partial p.,** produit partiel, produit intermédiaire; **p. planning,** planning *m* de production.

production, production *f*; **p. control,** contrôle *m* de production; **p. routine,** programme *m* de production, passage *m* de production; **p. time,** temps *m* d'exploitation réelle.

productive, p. time, temps *m* d'exploitation réelle.

professional, computer p., informaticien (-enne).

program, programme *m*; **assembly p.,** assembleur *m*, programme d'assemblage; **background p.,** programme non prioritaire; **bootstrap input p.,** programme d'amorçage; **checking p.,** programme de contrôle; **coded p.,** programme codé, programme enregistré; **compiling p.,** compilateur *m*, programme de compilation; **computer p.,** programme de calculateur; **control p.,** programme de contrôle, programme de commande; **conversion p.,** programme de conversion; **diagnostic p.,** programme de diagnostic; **executive p.,** programme superviseur, programme directeur; **externally stored p.,** programme sur support externe; **general p.,** programme général; **generating p.,** programme générateur; **heuristic p.,** programme heuristique; **housekeeping p.,** programme de service, programme auxiliaire; **incomplete p.,** programme paramétrable; **input p.,** (sous-)programme d'introduction; **internally stored p.,** programme enregistré; **interpretive p.,** programme interprétatif; **library p.,** programme de bibliothèque; **load p.,** programme de chargement; **macro-generating p.,** macro-générateur *m*; **main p.,** programme principal; **maintenance p.,** programme d'aide à l'entretien; **master (control) p.,** programme principal; **minimum latency p.,** programme

à temps d'accès minimum; **monitor p.,** programme moniteur; **monitoring p.,** programme moniteur; **object p.,** programme objet, programme résultant, programme généré; **post-mortem p.,** programme post-mortem, programme d'autopsie; **problem p.,** programme de production; **processing p.,** programme d'exploitation; **re-enterable p.,** programme rentrant, programme invariant; **re-entrant p.,** programme rentrant, programme invariant; **relocatable p.,** programme translatable, programme relogeable; **report p.,** programme d'édition; **segmented p.,** programme segmenté; **self-triggered p.,** programme à lancement automatique; **service p.,** programme de service; **simulator p.,** programme de simulation; **snapshot p.,** programme d'analyse sélective; **sorting p.,** programme de tri; **source p.,** programme source *m*; **specific p.,** programme particulier; **stalled p.,** programme figé (*ou* bloqué); **standard p.,** programme standard; **stored p.,** programme enregistré; **subject p.,** programme source; **supervisory p.,** programme superviseur; **target p.,** programme objet, programme résultant, programme généré; **test p.,** programme d'essai, programme de test; **trace p.,** programme d'analyse, programme de dépistage; **translating p.,** programme traducteur; **utility p.,** programme de service; **p. address counter,** registre *m* (d'adresse) d'instruction; **p. board,** tableau *m* de connexions; **p. bug,** erreur *f* dans un programme; **p. card,** carte *f* (de) programme; **p. checkout,** mise *f* au point de programme; **p. compatibility,** compatibilité *f* des programmes; **p. compiler,** compilateur *m*, programme de compilation; **p. control,** commande *f* par calculateur; **p.-controlled sequential computer,** ordinateur *m* à séquence contrôlée par programme; **p. controller,** contrôleur *m* d'exécution de programme; **p. control unit,** contrôleur *m* d'exécution de programme; **p. counter,** registre *m* (d'adresse) d'instruction; **p. design,** analyse *f* organique; **p. development time,** durée *f* de mise au point de programmes; **p. documentation,** dossier *m* de programmation; **p. drum,** tambour *m* (de) programme; **p. error,** erreur *f* de programme; **p. file,** fichier *m* de programmes; **p. generator,** générateur *m* de programmes; **p. indicator code,** code *m* d'identification de programme; **p. library,** bibliothèque *f* de programmes; **p. maintenance,** maintenance *f* de programmes; **p. mask,** masque *m* de programme; **p. parameter,** paramètre *m* de programme; **p. priority,** priorité *f* de programme; **p. register,** registre *m* de programme; **p.-sensitive error,** erreur due au programme; **p.-sensitive fault,** incident *m* décelable par une séquence particulière de programme; **p.-sensitive malfunction,** mauvais fonctionnement décelable par une séquence particulière de programme; **p. specification,** spécification *f* du programme; **p. status word,** mot *m* d'état de programme; **p. step,** pas *m* de programme; **p. storage,** mémoire *f* (à) programme; **p. tape,** bande *f* programme; **p. test,** essai *m* de programme; **p. testing,** essai *m* de programme; **p. testing time,** durée *f* d'essai de programmes.

program (to), programmer, rédiger un programme.

programmed, p. check, contrôle *m* par programme, contrôle programmé; **p. dump,** vidage programmé; **p. halt,** arrêt programmé; **p. logic,** logique programmée; **p. marginal check,** contrôle *m* par marges programmé; **p. stop,** arrêt programmé; **p. switch,** renvoi *m* multiple.

programmer, programmeur *m*.

programming, programmation *f*; **automatic p.,** programmation automatique; **dynamic p.,** programmation dynamique; **heuristic p.,** programmation heuristique; **interpretive p.,** programmation en pseudo-instructions; **linear p. (LP),** programmation linéaire; **mathematical p.,** programmation mathématique; **minimum access p.,** programmation à temps d'accès minimum; **minimum latency p.,** programmation à temps d'accès minimum; **multiple p.,** multiprogrammation *f*; **non-linear p.,** programmation non linéaire; **parallel p.,** programmation (en) parallèle; **random access p.,** programmation à accès sélectif; **sequential p.,** programmation séquentielle; **serial p.,** programmation (en) série; **structured p.,** programmation structurée; **sym-** **bolic p.,** programmation (en langage) symbolique; **p. aids,** aides *f* à la programmation; **p. flowchart,** organigramme *m* de programmation; **p. flow diagram,** organigramme *m* de programmation; **p. language,** langage *m* de programmation; **p. module,** module *m* de programme; **p. system,** système *m* de programmation.

progress, p. report, rapport *m* d'avancement (des travaux).

proof, p. total, total *m* de contrôle.

propagated, p. error, erreur répercutée.

property, p. detector, système *m* de reconnaissance (*OCR*); **p. sort,** tri *m* par caractéristiques.

proportional, proportionnel (-elle) *adj.*; **p. control,** commande proportionnelle.

protect, memory p., protection *f* de mémoire.

protected, p. location, emplacement protégé.

protection, protection *f*; **file p.,** protection de fichiers; **memory p.,** protection de mémoire; **storage p.,** protection de mémoire; **p. character,** caractère *m* de substitution; **p. key,** indicatif *m* de protection.

proving, p. time, temps *m* d'essai.

pseudo, p.-code, pseudo-code *m*; **p.-instruction,** pseudo-instruction *f*.

pseudo-random, p.-r. number sequence, séquence *f* de nombres pseudo-aléatoires.

p-type, p-t. semi-conductor, semi-conducteur *m* type p.

public, p. telegraph network, réseau télégraphique public; **p. telephone network,** réseau téléphonique public.

puller, crystal p., four *m* d'étirage de cristaux.

pulling, crystal p., tirage *m* d'un monocristal.

pulse, impulsion *f*; **clock p.,** impulsion de synchronisation, impulsion d'horloge; **commutator p.,** impulsion de contrôle; **dial p.,** impulsion de cadran; **drive p.,** impulsion de commande; **emitter p.,** impulsion de distributeur; **enable p.,** impulsion complémentaire (de validation); **full drive p.,** impulsion de commande (d'intensité) intégrale; **full read p.,** impulsion (de commande) de lecture; **full write p.,** impulsion (de commande) d'écriture; **gating p.,** impulsion sélectrice, impulsion de déclenchement;

half p., impulsion de demi-intensité; **inhibit p.**, impulsion de blocage, impulsion d'inhibition; **partial drive p.**, impulsion de commande (d'intensité) partielle; **partial read p.**, impulsion (de commande) partielle de lecture; **partial-select input p.**, impulsion (de commande) partielle d'écriture; **partial-select output p.**, impulsion (de commande) partielle de lecture; **partial write p.**, impulsion (de commande) partielle d'écriture; **position p.**, impulsion de contrôle; **post-write disturb p.**, impulsion de perturbation après écriture; **P-p.**, impulsion de contrôle; **pre-read disturb p.**, impulsion de perturbation avant lecture; **read(ing) p.**, impulsion (de commande) de lecture; **read-out p.**, impulsion (de commande) de lecture; **reset p.**, impulsion de rétablissement; **set p.**, impulsion d'excitation; **sprocket p.**, impulsion de synchronisation; **synchronizing p.**, impulsion de synchronisation; **timing p.**, impulsion de synchronisation; **write (or writing) p.**, impulsion (de commande) d'écriture, impulsion d'enregistrement; **p. amplifier**, amplificateur *m* d'impulsions; **p. amplitude**, amplitude *f* d'impulsion; **p.-amplitude modulation (PAM)**, modulation *f* d'impulsions en amplitude; **p. circuit**, circuit *m* d'impulsions; **p.-code modulation (PCM)**, modulation *f* par impulsions codées; **p. coder**, générateur *m* d'impulsions codées; **p. counter**, compteur *m* d'impulsions; **p. decay time**, durée *f* d'extinction de l'impulsion; **p. duration**, durée *f* d'impulsion; **p.-duration modulation (PDM)**, modulation *f* d'impulsions en durée; **p. frequency**, fréquence *f* d'impulsion; **p.-frequency modulation**, modulation *f* d'impulsions en fréquence; **p. generator**, générateur *m* d'impulsions; **p. group**, train *m* d'impulsions; **p. integrator**, intégrateur *m* d'impulsions; **p. length**, durée *f* d'impulsion; **p.-length modulation**, modulation *f* d'impulsions en durée; **p. metering system**, système *m* de comptage par impulsions; **p. modulated transmission**, émission modulée par impulsions; **p. modulated wave**, onde modulée par impulsions; **p. modulation**, modulation *f* par impulsions (*ou* d'impulsions); **p. modulator**, modulateur *m* d'impulsions; **p. normalization**, mise *f* en forme d'impulsions; **p.-number modula-**

tion, modulation *f* d'impulsions en nombre; **p. pair**, paire *f* d'impulsions; **p.-phase modulation (PPM)**, modulation *f* d'impulsions en phase; **p.-position modulation (PPM)**, modulation *f* d'impulsions en position; **p. power output**, puissance *f* de sortie des impulsions; **p. regeneration**, mise *f* en forme d'impulsions; **p. regenerator**, régénérateur *m* d'impulsions; **p. repeater**, répéteur *m* d'impulsions; **p. repetition (or recurrence) frequency (p.r.f.)**, fréquence *f* de répétition des impulsions; **p. repetition (or recurrence) rate**, taux *m* de répétition des impulsions; **p. reshaping**, remise *f* en forme d'impulsions; **p. rise time**, durée *f* d'établissement de l'impulsion; **p. selection circuit**, circuit *m* de sélection à impulsions; **p. shape**, forme *f* des impulsions; **p. shaping**, mise *f* en forme d'impulsions; **p. signal**, impulsion; **p. spacing**, espacement *m* des impulsions; **p. spectrum**, spectre *m* d'impulsions; **p. standardization**, mise *f* en forme d'impulsions; **p. string**, train *m* d'impulsions; **p. test**, méthode *f* d'essai par impulsions; **p.-time modulation**, modulation *f* d'impulsions dans le temps; **p. train**, train *m* d'impulsions; **p.-train generator**, générateur *m* de trains d'impulsions; **p. transformer**, transformateur *m* d'impulsions; **p. transmission system**, système *m* de transmission par émission d'impulsions; **p. transmitter**, émetteur *m* d'impulsions; **p. triple**, groupe *m* de trois impulsions; **p. width**, durée *f* d'impulsion; **p.-width modulation**, modulation *f* d'impulsions en durée.

pulsing, key p. (*Am.*), envoi *m* de signaux au clavier; **p. signal**, signal *m* de numérotation.

punch, 1. perforation *f*; **2.** perforateur *m*, perforatrice *f*; **automatic p.**, perforateur automatique; **automatic feed p.**, perforateur à alimentation automatique (de cartes); **automatic tape p.**, perforateur de bande automatique; **calculating p.**, calculateur *m* perforateur; **card p.**, perforateur de cartes; **card reader p.**, lecteur-perforateur *m* de cartes; **double p.**, double perforation; **duplicating card p.**, perforateur duplicateur de cartes; **electronic calculating p.**, calculateur *m* perforateur électronique; **eleven p.**, perforation «onze»; **gang p.,** reproduction f de constantes (*depuis une carte sur les suivantes*); **hand(-feed) p.,** perforatrice à alimentation manuelle; **keyboard p.,** perforatrice à clavier; **multiplying p.,** calculateur m perforateur; **numerical p.,** perforation numérique; **output p.,** perforateur de bande automatique; **paper tape p.,** perforateur de bande; **reproducing p.,** reproductrice f; **spot p.,** perforatrice à perforation unique; **summary p.,** perforateur récapitulateur, poinçonneuse récapitulatrice; **tape p.,** perforateur de bande; **twelve p.,** perforation «douze»; **X p.,** perforation «X», perforation «11»; **Y p.,** perforation «Y», perforation «12»; **zone p.,** perforation hors-texte; **p. card,** carte perforée; **p. die,** matrice f de perforation; **p. knife,** poinçon m; **p. position,** emplacement m de perforation (*carte*); **p. tape code,** code m de bande perforée.

punch (to), perforer.

punched, perforé *adj.*; **p. card,** carte perforée; **p. card machine (PCM),** machine f à cartes perforées; **p. tape,** bande perforée; **p. tape code,** code m de bande perforée; **p. tape machine,** machine f à bande perforée.

punching, perforation f; **accumulated total p.,** total m de contrôle perforé; **card p.,** perforation de cartes; **control p.,** perforation de contrôle; **designation p.,** perforation de contrôle; **double p.,** double perforation; **function p.,** perforation de contrôle; **interstage p.,** perforation intercalée; **multiple p.,** perforation multiple; **normal stage p.,** perforation normale; **paper tape p.,** perforation de bande; **p. position,** emplacement m de perforation (*carte*); **p. rate,** vitesse f de perforation; **p. station,** poste m de perforation; **p. track,** piste f de perforation.

pure, p. binary numeration, numération f binaire.

purge, p. date, date f de péremption.

purification, data p., validation f des données.

push-button, bouton-poussoir m; **p.-b. switching,** commutation f par bouton(s)-poussoir(s).

push down, p. d. dialling, appel m par boutons-poussoirs; **p. d. list,** liste refoulée, liste inversée; **p. d. stack,** pile refoulée; **p. d.**

store (*or* **storage),** mémoire f à liste inversée.

push-pull, p.-p. amplifier, amplificateur m push-pull, amplificateur symétrique; **p.-p. circuit,** montage m symétrique, montage push-pull.

push up, p. u. list, liste directe; **p. u. storage,** mémoire f à liste directe.

P.X. (=**private exchange),** central privé.

Q

quad, quarte f.

quadded, q. cable, câble m à quartes.

quad-pair, q.-p. cable, câble m à paires câblées en étoile.

quadruplex, q. system, système m quadruplex.

qualified, q. name, nom qualifié.

qualifier, qualificateur m.

quality, q. index, indice m de qualité.

quantification, quantification f.

quantity, quantité f; **double-precision q.,** quantité en double précision; **scalar q.,** grandeur f scalaire; **vector q.,** grandeur vectorielle.

quantization, quantification f; **q. distortion,** distorsion f de quantification.

quantize (to), quantifier.

quantizer, quantificateur m.

quantum, quantum m.

quarter-squares, q.-s. multiplier, multiplicateur bicarré.

quartet, quartet m.

quartz, q. delay line, ligne f à retard à quartz.

quasi, q.-instruction, pseudo-instruction f.

query, q. processing, traitement m d'interrogations.

question, question f; **encoded q.,** question codée.

queue, file f d'attente; **input work q.,** file d'attente d'entrée des travaux; **output work q.,** file d'attente de sortie des travaux; **task q.,** file d'attente des travaux (*ou* des tâches); **q. control block,** zone f de contrôle de file d'attente.

queued, q. access, accès m par file d'attente; **q. access method,** méthode f d'accès avec file d'attente.

queuing, message q., gestion f de file d'attente de messages; **q. problem,** problème m de file d'attente.
quibinary, q. code, code m quibinaire.
quick, q. access store (or storage), mémoire f à accès rapide.
quinary, biquinaire *adj.*
quintet, quintet m.
quotient, quotient m.

R

rack, bâti m, châssis m.
radial, r. transfer, transfert radial, opération f d'entrée-sortie.
radio, r. communication, radiocommunication f; **r. frequency (RF),** haute fréquence; **r. link,** liaison hertzienne.
radix, base f (de numération); **floating-point r.,** base (de numération) à virgule flottante, base de séparation flottante; **mixed r.,** à plusieurs bases; **r. complement,** complément m à la base, complément m à zéro; **r.-minus-one complement,** complément m à la base moins un, complément restreint; **r. notation,** numération f à base; **r. number,** base (de numération); **r. numeration,** numération f à base; **r. point,** séparation f fractionnaire, emplacement m de la virgule; **r. scale,** numération f à base.
random, r. access, accès m aléatoire, accès sélectif; **r. access device,** appareil m à accès direct, appareil m à accès sélectif; **r. access memory,** mémoire f à accès direct, mémoire f à accès sélectif; **r. access programming,** programmation f à accès sélectif; **r. access store (or storage),** mémoire f à accès direct, mémoire f à accès sélectif; **r. failure,** défaillance f aléatoire; **r. noise,** bruit m erratique; **r. number,** nombre m aléatoire; **r. number generator,** générateur m de nombres aléatoires; **r. number sequence,** séquence f de nombres aléatoires; **r. processing,** traitement non ordonné.
random-walk, cheminement m aléatoire.
range, balanced error r., plage f d'erreurs à valeur moyenne nulle; **dynamic r.,** portée f dynamique; **error r.,** plage f d'erreurs.
rank, niveau m.

rank (to), ranger.
rapid, r. access storage, mémoire f à accès rapide.
rate, taux m; **average data-transfer r.,** vitesse effective de transfert de données, débit effectif; **average transmission r.,** vitesse effective de transfert de données, débit effectif; **bit r.,** débit m binaire, vitesse f de transmission de bits; **bit error r.,** taux d'erreurs sur les bits; **block error r.,** taux d'erreurs sur les blocs; **character error r.,** taux d'erreurs sur les caractères; **clock r.,** fréquence f d'horloge, fréquence de base; **data signalling r.,** vitesse f de transmission de données; **data transfer r.,** taux de transfert de données; **effective data-transfer r.,** vitesse effective de transfert de données, débit effectif; **effective transmission r.,** vitesse effective de transfert de données, débit effectif; **element error r.,** taux d'erreurs sur les éléments; **error r.,** taux d'erreurs; **instantaneous data-transfer r.,** vitesse instantanée de transfert de données, débit instantané; **instantaneous transmission r.,** vitesse instantanée de transfert de données, débit instantané; **modulation r.,** rapidité f de modulation, vitesse f télégraphique; **perforation r.,** vitesse f de perforation (de bande); **pulse repetition (or recurrence) r.,** taux de répétition des impulsions; **punching r.,** vitesse f de perforation; **reading r.,** vitesse f de lecture; **residual error r.,** taux d'erreurs résiduelles; **sampling r.,** taux d'échantillonnage; **scanning r.,** taux d'analyse; **signalling r.,** vitesse f de transmission de signaux; **telephone r.,** tarif m téléphonique; **telex r.,** tarif m télex; **transfer r.,** débit m, vitesse f de transmission; **undetected error r.,** taux d'erreurs résiduelles.
rated, r. speed, vitesse nominale.
rates, call r., tarification f des communications.
ratio, rapport m, taux m; **activity r.,** taux d'activité; **availability r.,** taux de disponibilité; **break-make r.,** rapport d'impulsions; **carrier-to-noise r.,** écart m entre porteuse et bruit; **deviation r.,** rapport de déviation; **error r.,** taux d'erreurs; **file activity r.,** taux d'activité d'un fichier; **one-to-zero r.,** rapport de discrimination (1 à 0); **operating r.,** taux d'utilisation effective;

print contrast r., taux de contraste d'impression; **recall r.,** taux de succès (*Recherche documentaire*); **relevance r.,** pertinence *f* (*Recherche documentaire*); **residual error r.,** taux d'erreurs résiduelles; **selection r.,** rapport de sélection; **serviceability r.,** taux de service; **signal-to-noise r.,** rapport signal/bruit; **squareness r.,** taux de rectangularité; **utilization r.,** taux d'utilisation.

raw, r. data, données brutes (*ou* non traitées).

R C T L (=resistor-capacitor-transistor logic), logique *f* à résistances, condensateurs et transistors.

read, lecture *f*; **destructive r.,** lecture destructive, lecture avec effacement; **non-destructive r.,** lecture non destructive, lecture sans effacement; **scatter r.,** lecture avec éclatement; **r. alert,** incident *m* de lecture; **r. error,** erreur *f* de lecture; **r. half-pulse,** impulsion *f* de demi-intensité de lecture; **r. head,** tête *f* de lecture; **r. output (signal),** signal *m* de (sortie) lecture; **r, pulse,** impulsion *f* (de commande) de lecture; **r. punch unit,** lecteur-perforateur *m*; **r. screen,** fenêtre *f* de lecture; **r. time,** temps *m* d'accès; **r. while writing,** lecture et écriture simultanées; **r. wire,** fil *m* de lecture.

read (to), lire.

readable, machine r., exploitable sur machine.

read-back, r.-b. check, contrôle *m* par écho.

reader, lecteur *m*; **badge r.,** lecteur de jetons, lecteur de «badges»; **card r.,** lecteur de cartes; **character r.,** lecteur de caractères; **continuous stationery r.,** lecteur de documents en continu (*OCR*); **film r.,** lecteur de film; **high-speed r.,** lecteur rapide; **magnetic character r.,** lecteur de caractères magnétiques, magnétolecteur *m*; **magnetic ink character r.,** lecteur de caractères magnétiques; **magnetic tape r.,** lecteur de bande magnétique; **optical bar-code r.,** lecteur optique de marques; **optical character r.,** lecteur optique de caractères; **optical mark r.,** lecteur optique de marques; **optical r.,** lecteur optique; **page r.,** lecteur de pages; **paper tape r.,** lecteur de bande perforée; **photoelectric r.,** lecteur photo-électrique; **tally r.,** lecteur de bandes imprimées (*de caisses enregistreuses, etc.*); **tape r.,** lecteur de bande perforée.

reader-punch, card r.-p., lecteur-perforateur *m* de cartes.

read-in (to), introduire en mémoire, enregistrer.

reading, lecture *f*; **demand r.,** lecture à la demande; **destructive r.,** lecture destructive, lecture avec effacement; **double-pulse r.,** lecture par double impulsion; **mark r.,** lecture de marques; **non-destructive r.,** lecture non destructive, lecture sans effacement; **regenerative r.,** lecture avec ré-enregistrement; **reverse r.,** lecture arrière; **r. head,** tête *f* de lecture; **r. pulse,** impulsion *f* (de commande) de lecture; **r. rate,** vitesse *f* de lecture; **r. speed,** vitesse *f* de lecture; **r. station,** poste *m* de lecture; **r. track,** piste *f* de lecture.

read-only, r.-o. memory, mémoire morte, mémoire passive; **r.-o. store (*or* storage),** mémoire morte, mémoire passive.

read-out, destructive r.-o., lecture destructive, lecture avec effacement; **non-destructive r.-o.,** lecture non destructive, lecture sans effacement; **r.-o. pulse,** impulsion *f* (de commande) de lecture.

read-out (to), extraire de la mémoire, sortir.

read/write, r./w. check, contrôle *m* de lecture/écriture; **r./w. check indicator,** indicateur *m* de contrôle de lecture/écriture; **r./w. head,** tête *f* de lecture/écriture.

ready, r. condition, état *m* de disponibilité.

real, r. storage, mémoire réelle; **r. storage page table (RSPT),** table *f* des pages réelles, table *f* RSPT.

real-time, (en) temps réel; **r.-t. clock,** horloge *f* à signaux horaires; **r.-t. control,** commande *f* en temps réel; **r.-t. input,** introduction *f* en temps réel, entrée *f* en temps réel; **r.-t. input/output,** entrée-sortie *f* en temps réel; **r.-t. operation,** fonctionnement *m* en temps réel; **r.-t. output,** sortie *f* en temps réel; **r.-t. processing,** traitement *m* en temps réel; **r.-t. simulation,** simulation *f* en temps réel; **r.-t. system,** système *m* en temps réel; **r.-t. working,** fonctionnement *m* en temps réel.

rearrange (to), réordonner.

recall, r. factor, taux *m* de succès (*Recherche documentaire*); **r. ratio,** taux *m* de succès (*Recherche documentaire*).

receiver, 1. récepteur *m*; **2.** case *f* de réception de cartes; **data r.**, récepteur de données; **facsimile r.**, récepteur de facsimilé; **telemetering r.**, récepteur de télémesure; **telephone r.**, récepteur téléphonique; **r. response time**, temps *m* de réponse (d'un récepteur).

receiving, r. margin, marge *f* de réception; **r. perforator**, récepteur *m* perforateur, reperforateur *m*.

receiving-end, r.-e. crossfire, courant perturbateur côté réception.

reception, diversity r., réception *f* en diversité; **space diversity r.**, réception *f* par diversité dans l'espace.

recognition, reconnaissance *f*; **character r.**, reconnaissance de caractères; **magnetic ink character r. (M.I.C.R.)**, reconnaissance de caractères magnétiques codés; **optical character r. (O.C.R.)**, reconnaissance optique de caractères; **pattern r.**, reconnaissance de formes (*OCR*).

recognizable, machine r., exploitable sur machine.

record, 1. enregistrement *m*; **2.** article *m*; **3.** rubrique *f*; **4.** fiche *f*; **5.** relevé *m*; **addition r.**, enregistrement supplémentaire; **amendment r.**, enregistrement (de) mouvement, enregistrement (de) détail; **chained r.**, enregistrement chaîné; **change r.**, enregistrement (de) mouvement, enregistrement (de) détail; **control r.**, enregistrement de gestion, ordre *m* de gestion; **data r.**, enregistrement (de données); **deletion r.**, enregistrement d'annulation; **duplicate r.**, enregistrement en double, enregistrement redondant; **duplicated r.**, enregistrement dupliqué; **fixed-length r.**, enregistrement en longueur fixe; **header r.**, enregistrement en-tête; **home r.**, article primaire, enregistrement direct; **leader r.**, enregistrement en-tête; **logical r.**, article logique; **master r.**, enregistrement principal; **no home r.**, article secondaire, enregistrement indirect; **overflow r.**, enregistrement en débordement; **physical r.**, enregistrement physique; **reference r.**, liste *f* de référence; **spanned r.**, enregistrement morcelé; **trailer r.**, enregistrement complémentaire, article secondaire; **transaction r.**, enregistrement (de) mouvement, enregistrement (de)

détail; **variable-length r.**, enregistrement en longueur variable; **r. blocking**, groupage *m* d'enregistrements; **r. circuit**, ligne *f* d'annotrice; **r. count**, nombre *m* d'enregistrements; **r. format**, disposition *f* d'enregistrement, modèle *m* d'enregistrement; **r. gap**, espace *m* entre enregistrements; **r. head**, tête *f* d'enregistrement; **r. layout**, dessin *m* d'enregistrement, disposition *f* d'enregistrement; **r. length**, longueur *f* d'enregistrement; **r. mark**, marque *f* d'enregistrement; **r. separator**, séparateur *m* d'enregistrements; **r. separator character**, caractère *m* de séparation d'enregistrements; **r. storage mark**, marque *f* d'enregistrement (en mémoire).

record (to), 1. enregistrer; **2.** relever.

recorder, enregistreur *m*; **data r.**, enregistreur de données; **electromechanical r.**, enregistreur électromecanique; **film r.**, enregistreur sur film; **magnetic r.**, enregistreur magnétique.

recording, enregistrement *m*; **double pulse r.**, enregistrement par double impulsion; **electron beam r. (EBR)**, enregistrement électronique sur microfilm; **group coded r. (GCR)**, enregistrement par groupes de caractères; **magnetic r.**, enregistrement magnétique; **magnetic strip(e) r.**, enregistrement sur piste magnétique; **non-polarized return-to-zero r.**, enregistrement non polarisé avec retour à zéro; **non-return to reference r.**, enregistrement non retour à zéro; **non-return-to-zero r.**, enregistrement non retour à zéro; **polarized return-to-zero r.**, enregistrement polarisé avec retour à zéro; **return-to-bias r.**, enregistrement avec retour à l'état prédéterminé; **return-to-reference r.**, enregistrement avec retour à zéro; **source r.**, enregistrement source; **r. density**, densité *f* d'enregistrement; **r. head**, tête *f* d'enregistrement; **r. trunk** (*Am.*), ligne *f* d'annotatrice.

records, grouped r., articles groupés; **grouping of r.**, groupement *m* d'articles.

rectangular, rectangulaire *adj.*; **r. integration**, intégration *f* rectangulaire.

rectifier, (tube *m*) redresseur *m* ou *adj.*

recursion, récurrence *f*.

recursive, récurrent *adj.*; **r. function**, fonction récurrente; **r. process,** processus récurrent.

red-tape, r.-t. operation, opération *f* de service, opération auxiliaire.

reduction, réduction *f*; **data r.,** réduction de données; **online data r.,** réduction de données en connecté.

redundancy, redondance *f*; **r. check,** contrôle *m* par redondance.

redundant, redondant *adj.*; superflu *adj.*; **r. character,** caractère *m* de complément, caractère *m* de garnissage; **r. check,** contrôle *m* par redondance; **r. code,** code redondant.

reel, bobine *f*; **end of r.,** fin *f* de bobine; **feed r.,** bobine d'alimentation, bobine émettrice; **file r.,** bobine émettrice, bobine dérouleuse; **take-up r.,** bobine réceptrice, bobine enrouleuse; **r. number,** numéro *m* d'ordre de bobine.

re-enterable, rentrant *adj.*; **r. program,** programme rentrant, programme invariant.

re-entrant, r. program, programme rentrant, programme invariant.

re-entry, r. point, point *m* de retour.

reference, référence *f*; **external r.,** référence symbolique externe; **modulation with a fixed r.,** modulation *f* avec référence fixe; **r. address,** adresse *f* de base, adresse origine; **r. axis,** axe *m* de référence; **r. edge,** bord *m* de référence; **r. field,** champ *m* (magnétique) de référence; **r. level,** niveau *m* de référence; **r. listing,** liste *f* de référence; **r. pilot,** onde *f* pilote; **r. record,** liste *f* de référence; **r. supply,** alimentation *f* de référence; **r. time,** moment *m* de référence.

reflectance, réflectance *f* (*OCR*); **background r.,** réflectance de fond (*OCR*); **ink r.,** réflectance de l'encre (*OCR*).

reflected, r. binary code, code binaire réfléchi.

reflection, réflexion *f*; **r. coefficient,** coefficient *m* de réflexion.

reflective, réfléchissant *adj.*; **r. spot,** spot réfléchissant.

regenerate (to), régénérer.

regeneration, régénération *f*, restauration *f*; **pulse r.,** mise *f* en forme d'impulsion; **signal r.,** mise *f* en forme de signaux; **r. period,** période *f* de régénération.

regenerative, r. feedback, réaction *f*; **r. reading,** lecture *f* avec ré-enregistrement; **r. store (*or* storage),** mémoire *f* à régénération; **r. track,** piste *f* à régénération.

regenerator, régénérateur *m*; **pulse r.,** régénérateur d'impulsions.

region, région *f*; **virtual storage r.,** région de mémoire virtuelle.

regional, r. centre, centre régional.

register, registre *m*; **accumulator r.,** registre d'accumulateur; **address r.,** registre d'adresse; **arithmetic r.,** registre arithmétique; **B r.,** registre d'index; **base r.,** registre de base; **carry r.,** registre de report; **check r.,** registre de contrôle, registre de vérification; **circulating r.,** registre de décalage cyclique; **console display r.,** registre d'unité de visualisation; **control r.,** registre (d'adresse) d'instruction; **current instruction r.,** registre d'instruction en cours; **delay line r.,** registre à ligne à retard; **exchange r.,** registre de mémoire; **flip-flop r.,** registre à bascules; **index r.,** registre d'index; **input/output r.,** registre d'entrée-sortie; **input r.,** registre d'entrée; **instruction address r.,** registre de contrôle de séquence; **instruction r.,** registre d'instruction; **magnetic shift r.,** registre (de) décalage magnétique; **mask r.,** registre de masquage; **memory address r.,** registre d'adresse mémoire; **memory buffer r.,** registre-tampon *m* de mémoire; **modifier r.,** registre d'index; **multiplier quotient r.,** registre multiplicateur-quotient; **operation r.,** registre «type d'opération»; **program r.,** registre de programme; **return code r.,** registre de code de retour; **sequence control r.,** registre de contrôle de séquence; **sequence r.,** registre de contrôle de séquence; **shift(ing) r.,** registre (de) décalage; **standby r.,** registre de réserve; **storage r.,** registre de mémoire; **r. capacity,** capacité *f* de registre; **r. designator,** indicateur *m* de registre; **r. length,** longueur *f* de registre.

registration, repérage *m*; **r. mark,** repère *m* (*OCR*).

regrouping, regroupement *m*; **r. converter,** convertisseur *m* de regroupement.

regular, r. binary, binaire pur.

regulating, r. pilot, onde *f* pilote de

régulation.

regulation, régulation *f*; **voltage r.,** régulation de tension.

regulator, régulateur *m*; **pilot-wire r.,** régulateur à fil pilote.

reject, r. pocket, case *f* (de) rebut.

reject (to), rejeter, éliminer.

rejection, opération *f* NON-OU (*ou* NI), négation *f* connexe; **r. gate,** circuit *m* NON-OU (*ou* NI).

relational, r. operator, opérateur *m* de relation.

relationship, control r., interdépendance *f*.

relative, relatif (-ive) *adj.*; **r. address,** adresse relative; **r. addressing,** adressage relatif; **r. code,** code relatif; **r. coding,** codage relatif; **r. error,** erreur relative; **r. level,** niveau relatif de puissance.

relay, relais *m*; **automatic tape r.,** retransmission *f* automatique par bande perforée; **call(ing) r.,** relais d'appel; **cut-off r.,** relais de coupure; **electronic r.,** relais électronique; **line r.,** relais de ligne; **manual tape r.,** transit manuel par bande perforée; **supervisory r.,** relais de supervision; **switching r.,** relais de commutation; **tape r.,** transit *m* par bande perforée; **telegraph r.,** relais télégraphique; **telephone r.,** relais téléphonique; **thermionic r.,** relais thermionique; **time r.,** relais temporisé; **torn tape r.** (*Am.*), transit manuel par bande perforée; **r. amplifier,** amplificateur-relais *m*; **r. automatic system,** système *m* automatique tout à relais; **r. calculator,** calculateur *m* à relais; **r. centre,** centre-relais *m*.

release, r. guard signal, signal *m* de libération de garde.

release (to), libérer, relâcher.

relevance, r. ratio, pertinence *f* (*Recherche documentaire*).

reliability, fiabilité *f*; **data r.,** fiabilité des données; **system r.,** fiabilité du système.

relocatable, relogeable *adj.*, translatable *adj.*; **r. address,** adresse *f* relogeable, adresse translatable; **r. program,** programme *m* translatable, programme relogeable; **r. routine,** programme *m* translatable, programme relogeable.

relocate (to), reloger, translater.

relocation, réallocation *f*; **dynamic memory r.,** réallocation dynamique de mémoire; **r. dictionary,** liste *f* des adresses relogeables (*ou* translatables).

remainder, reste *m*.

remedial, r. maintenance, entretien *m* de dépannage.

remote, r. access, accès *m* à distance; **r. batch entry,** soumission *f* de travaux à distance par lots; **r. batch processing,** traitement groupé à distance; **r. calculator,** calculateur *m* de télégestion, calculateur *m* à distance; **r. computing system,** système *m* de télétraitement; **r. console,** console *f* de télétraitement; **r. control,** commande *f* à distance, télécommande *f*; **r. control equipment,** matériel commandé à distance, matériel télécommandé; **r.-controlled station,** station télécommandée, station télérégulée; **r. control signal,** signal *m* de télécommande; **r. data processing,** téléinformatique *f*; **r. data station,** station *f* à distance; **r. data terminal,** terminal *m* à distance; **r. debugging,** mise *f* au point à distance; **r. entry services (RES),** soumission *f* de travaux à distance; **r. inquiry,** interrogation *f* à distance; **r. job entry (RJE),** soumission *f* de travaux à distance; **r. measuring,** télémesure *f*; **r. metering,** télémesure *f*; **r. operated,** télécommandé; **r. processing,** télétraitement *m*, traitement *m* à distance; **r. processor,** téléprocesseur *m*; **r. station,** station *f* à distance; **r. testing,** essais *m* à distance.

removable, r. plugboard, tableau *m* de connexions amovible.

reorder (to), réordonner.

repair, réparation *f*, remise *f* en état; **mean time to r. (m.t.t.r.),** durée moyenne de réparation; **r. delay time,** temps *m* d'attente de réparation; **r. time,** temps *m* de réparation.

repeater, répéteur *m*; **line r.,** répéteur de ligne; **pulse r.,** répéteur d'impulsions; **telephone r.,** répéteur téléphonique; **r. station,** station *f* de répéteurs.

repeating, r. coil, translateur *m*.

reperforator, récepteur *m* perforateur, reperforateur *m*; **printing r.,** récepteur perforateur imprimeur, reperforateur imprimeur; **r. switching,** commutation *f* avec retransmission par bande perforée.

repertoire (*or* **repertory**), répertoire *m*; **character r.,** répertoire de caractères; **instruction r.,** répertoire d'instructions.

repetition, répétition *f*; **automatic r.,** répétition automatique; **r. instruction,** in truction *f* de répétition.

repetitive, répétitif (-ive) *adj.*; **r. addressing,** adressage *m* à progression automatique; **r. operation,** opération répétitive.

report, 1. rapport *m*; **2.** état *m*; **error r.,** liste *f* d'erreurs; **progress r.,** rapport d'avancement (des travaux); **r. generation,** génération *f* (de programmes) d'édition; **r. program,** programme *m* d'édition; **r. program generator,** générateur *m* (de programmes) d'édition.

reporting, production *f* (*ou* impression *f*) d'états.

representation, représentation *f*; **analog r.,** représentation analogique; **binary coded decimal r.,** numération décimale (codée en) binaire, représentation (en) décimal codé binaire; **binary incremental r.,** représentation par accroissements binaires; **binary r.,** représentation binaire; **coded r.,** combinaison *f* de code, élément *m* de code; **data r.,** représentation de données; **decimal r.,** représentation décimale; **deleted r.,** oblitération *f*; **digital r.,** représentation numérique (*ou* numérale); **discrete r.,** représentation discrète; **excess-fifty r.,** représentation majorée de cinquante; **fixed-point r.,** représentation à virgule fixe, numération *f* à séparation fixe; **floating-point r.,** représentation à virgule flottante, numération *f* à virgule flottante; **incremental r.,** représentation par accroissements; **null r.,** caractère nul; **number r.,** numération *f*; **numeric(al) r.,** représentation numérique; **positional r.,** représentation pondérée; **ternary incremental r.,** représentation par accroissements à valeur ternaire; **variable-point r.,** représentation à virgule variable, numération *f* à séparation variable.

representative, r. calculating operation, opération *f* de calcul moyenne.

reproduce (to), reproduire.

reproducer, 1. reproductrice *f*; **2.** duplicatrice *f*; **card r.,** reproductrice de cartes; **paper tape r.,** reproductrice de bande perforée; **tape r.,** reproducteur *m* de bande.

reproducing, r. punch, reproductrice *f*.

reproduction, r. code, code *m* de reproduction.

reprographics, reprographie *f*.

request, r. repeat system, système détecteur d'erreurs avec demande de répétition.

rerun, r. point, point *m* de reprise; **r. routine,** programme *m* de reprise.

rerun (to), repasser, effectuer un nouveau passage.

RES (=remote entry services), soumission *f* de travaux à distance (RES).

rescue, r. dump, vidage *m* de sauvegarde.

research, recherche *f*; **operational r.,** recherche opérationnelle; **operations r. (O.R.),** recherche opérationnelle.

reservation, réservation *f*.

reserve, r. circuit, circuit *m* de secours.

reserve (to), réserver.

reserved, réservé *adj.*; **r. area,** zone réservée; **r. word,** mot réservé.

reset, remise *f* à l'état initial, réinitialisation *f*, rétablissement *m*; **automatic r.,** rétablissement automatique; **cycle r.,** réinitialisation du compteur de cycles; **r. cycle,** cycle *m* de remise à l'état initial (*ou* antérieur); **r. mode,** condition initiale; **r. pulse,** impulsion *f* de rétablissement.

reset (to), remettre à l'état initial, réinitialiser, rétablir, restaurer.

reshaping, pulse r., remise *f* en forme d'impulsions; **signal r.,** remise *f* en forme de signaux.

resident, core memory r., résidant en mémoire; **r. routine,** programme *m* résidant en mémoire.

residual, r. error, erreur résiduelle; **r. error rate,** taux *m* d'erreurs résiduelles; **r. error ratio,** taux *m* d'erreurs résiduelles.

residue, modulo-n r., reste *m* (*d'une division*) modulo-n; **r. check,** contrôle *m* sur reste.

resistance, résistance *f*; **colour-bleeding r.,** résistance au déteintage; **smudge r.,** résistance au maculage; **wear r.,** résistance à l'usure; **r.-coupled amplifier,** amplificateur *m* à couplage par résistance.

resistor, résistance *f*; **r.-capacitor-transistor logic (RCTL),** logique *f* à résistances, condensateurs et transistors; **r.-transistor logic (RTL),** logique *f* à résistances et transistors.

resolution, résolution *f*; **logical r.** résolution d'opérations logiques; **r. error,** erreur *f* de résolution.

resolving, r. potentiometer, potentiomètre *m* à variation sinusoïdale.

response, réponse *f*; **frequency r.,** réponse de (*ou* en) fréquence; **spectral r.,** réponse spectrale; **r. duration,** temps *m* de réponse; **r. time,** temps *m* de réponse.

restart, r. point, point *m* de reprise.

restart (to), repartir, reprendre.

restitution, restitution *f*; **isochronous r.,** restitution isochrone; **significant conditions of a r.,** états significatifs d'une restitution.

restore (to), restaurer, remettre à l'état initial.

restorer, direct current r., régénérateur *m* de composante continue.

result, résultat *m*; **intermediate r.,** résultat intermédiaire.

retention, rétention *f*; **r. period,** période *f* de rétention.

retransmitter, retransmetteur *m*; **perforated-tape r.,** retransmetteur à bande perforée, reperforateur-transmetteur *m*.

retrieval, récupération *f*; **data r.,** recherche *f* de données; **document r.,** recherche *f* documentaire; **false r.,** bruit *m* (*Recherche documentaire*); **information r.,** recherche *f* de l'information, recherche documentaire.

retrieve (to), retrouver, récupérer.

retrofit (to), mettre à niveau.

return, carriage r., retour *m* de chariot; **r. address,** adresse *f* de retour; **r. code,** code *m* de retour (sur programme); **r. code register,** registre *m* de code de retour; **r. instruction,** instruction *f* de retour, instruction *f* de raccordement (*vers le programme principal*); **r.-to-bias recording,** enregistrement *m* avec retour à l'état prédéterminé; **r.-to-reference recording,** enregistrement *m* avec retour à zéro; **r.-to-zero (R.Z.),** retour *m* à zéro.

reusable, réutilisable *adj*.

reverse, r. direction flow, sens *m* inverse des liaisons (*sur un organigramme*); **r. reading,** lecture *f* arrière.

reverser, sign r., inverseur *m* de signe.

reversible, r. counter, compteur *m* réversible, compteur-décompteur *m*; **r. magnetic process,** transformation *f* magnétique réversible; **r. process,** processus *m* réversible.

review, revue *f*, révision *f*; **post-installation r.,** revue après installation; **preliminary r.,** revue préliminaire.

revolution, tour *m*, rotation *f*.

revolver, r. track, piste *f* à régénération.

rewind, rebobinage *m*; **high-speed r.,** rebobinage rapide.

rewind (to), rebobiner, réenrouler.

rewrite (to), réenregistrer, récrire.

R F (=radio frequency), haute fréquence.

ribbon, ruban *m*; **carbon r.,** ruban-carbone *m*; **ink r.,** ruban encreur; **printer r.,** ruban d'imprimante.

right, r. justified, 1. justifié à droite; 2. cadré à droite; **r. shift,** décalage *m* à droite.

right-justify (to), 1. justifier à droite; 2. cadrer à droite.

ring, anneau *m*; **file guard r.,** anneau d'interdiction d'écriture; **file protection r.,** anneau de protection d'écriture; **write inhibit r.,** anneau d'interdiction d'écriture; **write (permit) r.,** anneau d'autorisation d'écriture; **r. network,** réseau *m* en anneau; **r. shift,** décalage *m* circulaire.

ringing, selective r., appel sélectif; **r. key,** clé *f* d'appel.

ripple-through, r.-t. carry, report *m* rapide.

rise, r. time, temps *m* de montée.

RJE (=remote job entry), soumission *f* de travaux à distance.

r.m.s. (=root-mean-square), efficace *adj*.

rod, ferrite r., bâtonnet *m* de ferrite.

role, r. indicator, indicateur *m* de rôle (*Recherche documentaire*).

roll, rouleau *m*; **print r.,** rouleau d'impression, cylindre *m* d'impression.

rollback, r. routine, programme *m* de reprise.

rollback (to), repasser, effectuer un nouveau passage.

roller, rouleau *m*; **pinch r.,** rouleau pinceur.

roll in (to), rappeler en mémoire centrale.

roll out (to), transférer en mémoire auxiliaire.

room, switch r., salle *f* de commutation.

root, r. segment, segment principal.

root mean square (r.m.s.), efficace *adj*.; **r.m.s. current,** intensité *f* efficace; **r.m.s. value,** valeur *f* efficace; **r.m.s. voltage,** tension *f* efficace.

rotary, r. dial, cadran rotatif; **r. switch,** commutateur rotatif.

rotate, permutation f circulaire.

round, r. brackets, parenthèses f.

round (to), arrondir.

rounding, r. error, erreur f d'arrondi.

round-off, arrondi m; **r.-o. error,** erreur f d'arrondi.

round off (to), arrondir.

route, voie f; **auxiliary r.,** voie auxiliaire; **direct r.,** voie directe; **emergency r.,** voie de secours; **normal r.,** voie normale; **overflow r.,** voie de débordement; **primary r.,** voie primaire; **secondary r.,** voie secondaire.

routine, 1. programme m; 2. routine f; **algorithmic r.,** programme algorithmique; **assembly r.,** assembleur m, programme d'assemblage; **automatic r.,** programme automatique; **auxiliary r.,** programme auxiliaire; **checking r.,** programme de contrôle; **checkout r.,** programme de mise au point; **closed r.,** programme fermé, programme en boucle; **compiling r.,** compilateur m, programme de compilation; **complete r.,** programme figé; **condensing r.,** programme de condensation (des programmes); **control r.,** programme superviseur, programme directeur; **conversion r.,** programme de conversion; **debugging aid r.,** programme d'aide à la mise au point; **diagnostic r.,** programme de diagnostic; **edit r.,** (programme) éditeur m; **end of file r.,** programme de traitement de fin de fichier; **end of run r.,** programme de fin d'exécution; **end of tape r.,** programme de traitement de fin de bande; **error r.,** programme de traitement en cas d'erreur; **error-correcting r.,** programme de correction d'erreurs; **error-correction r.,** programme de correction d'erreurs; **error-detection r.,** programme de détection d'erreurs; **executive r.,** programme superviseur, programme directeur; **fixed r.,** programme fixe; **floating-point r.,** programme à virgule flottante; **general r.,** programme général; **generalized r.,** programme polyvalent; **generating r.,** programme générateur; **heuristic r.,** programme heuristique; **housekeeping r.,** programme de service, programme auxiliaire; **incomplete r.,** programme paramétrable; **input r.,** programme d'introduction (*ou* d'entrée); **interpreter r.,** programme interprétatif; **interpretive r.,** programme interprétatif; **interrupt r.,** programme de traitement des interruptions; **iterative r.,** programme itératif; **library r.,** programme de bibliothèque; **loading r.,** (programme) chargeur m, programme de chargement; **main r.,** programme principal; **maintenance r.,** programme d'aide à l'entretien; **malfunction r.,** programme de diagnostic; **master r.,** programme superviseur, programme directeur; **minimum access r.,** programme à temps d'accès minimum; **minimum latency r.,** programme à temps d'accès minimum; **monitor r.,** programme moniteur; **non-resident r.,** programme ne résidant pas en permanence en mémoire; **object r.,** programme objet, programme résultant, programme généré; **output r.,** programme d'extraction (*ou* de sortie); **post-mortem r.,** programme post-mortem, programme d'autopsie; **production r.,** programme de production; **relocatable r.,** programme translatable, programme relogeable; **rerun r.,** programme de reprise; **resident r.,** programme résidant en mémoire; **rollback r.,** programme de reprise; **selective tracing r.,** programme d'analyse sélective, programme de dépistage sélectif; **sequence checking r.,** programme de contrôle de séquence; **service r.,** programme de service; **simulator r.,** programme de simulation; **source r.,** programme source; **specific r.,** programme particulier; **stored r.,** programme enregistré; **supervisory r.,** programme superviseur; **target r.,** programme objet, programme résultant, programme généré; **test r.,** programme d'essai, programme de test; **trace r.,** programme d'analyse, programme de dépistage; **tracing r.,** programme d'analyse, programme de dépistage; **translating r.,** programme traducteur; **utility r.,** programme de service; **working r.,** programme de production; **r. check,** contrôle m par programme, contrôle programmé; **r. library,** bibliothèque f de programmes; **r. maintenance,** entretien m périodique, entretien courant; **r. maintenance time,** temps m d'entretien périodique (*ou* courant); **r.**

test, essai *m* périodique, essai courant.

routing, acheminement *m*; **alternate r.,** voie *f* de déroutement, déviation *f*; **message r.,** acheminement de messages; **r. channel,** voie *f* d'acheminement; **r. code,** indicatif *m*; **r. indicator,** indicatif *m* d'acheminement; **r. time,** durée *f* d'acheminement.

row, rangée *f*, ligne *f*; **card r.,** ligne (*sur une carte*); **check r.,** rangée de contrôle; **r. binary,** binaire par rangée; **r. binary card,** carte *f* binaire par rangée; **r. pitch,** pas *m* longitudinal, interligne *m*.

RSPT (=**real storage page table**), table *f* des pages réelles, table *f* RSPT.

RTL (=**resistor-transistor logic**), logique *f* à résistances et transistors.

rub-out, r.-o. character, caractère *m* d'oblitération.

run, computer r., passage *m* (en) ordinateur, passage *m* (en) machine; **end of r.,** fin *f* d'exécution; **machine r.,** passage *m* (en) machine; **production r.,** passage *m* de production; **test r.,** passage *m* d'essai; **r. book,** dossier *m* d'exploitation; **r. chart,** organigramme *m* d'exploitation; **r. diagram,** organigramme *m* d'exploitation; **r. duration,** durée *f* d'exécution (*d'un passage en machine*); **r. phase,** phase *f* d'exécution; **r. time,** durée *f* d'exploitation.

running, dry r., contrôle *m* de programmation sur papier; **parallel r.,** exploitation *f* en parallèle; **r. accumulator,** accumulateur circulant; **r. state,** état *m* de marche, état opérationnel.

R.Z. (=**return-to-zero**), retour *m* à zéro.

S

sample (to), échantillonner.

sampling, échantillonnage *m*; **s. rate,** taux *m* d'échantillonnage.

sapphire, silicon on s. (SOS), silicium *m* sur saphir.

satellite, s. processor, processeur *m* satellite.

saturating, s. field, champ *m* (magnétique) de saturation; **s. integrator,** intégrateur *m* par accroissements.

saturation, saturation *f*.

sawtooth, s. wave, oscillation *f* en dents de scie.

scalar, s. quantity, grandeur *f* scalaire.

scale, binary s., notation *f* binaire; **radix s.,** numération *f* à base; **two s.,** notation *f* binaire; **s. coefficient,** échelle *f*, facteur *m* de multiplication (*ou* de division); **s. factor,** échelle *f*, facteur *m* de multiplication (*ou* de division); **s. of two,** notation *f* binaire.

scaling, s. factor, échelle *f*, facteur *m* de multiplication (*ou* de division).

scan, s. period, période *f* de balayage (*ou* d'analyse).

scan (to), explorer, balayer.

scanner, analyseur *m*, explorateur *m*; **bar-code s.,** analyseur de code à bâtonnets; **flying spot s.,** analyseur à spot mobile; **mechanical s.,** analyseur à disque mécanique (*OCR*); **optical s.,** analyseur optique; **TV camera s.,** analyseur à caméra de télévision (*OCR*); **visual s.,** analyseur optique.

scanning, balayage *m*, analyse *f*; **mark s.,** lecture *f* optique de marques; **optical s.,** analyse optique; **s. rate,** taux *m* d'analyse.

scatter, s. loading, chargement éclaté; **s. read,** lecture *f* avec éclatement.

scatter (to), ventiler, dégrouper.

scatter/gather, ventilation *f*/regroupement *m*.

scheduled, s. maintenance, entretien *m* périodique; **s. maintenance time,** temps *m* d'entretien périodique (*ou* planifié); **s. operation,** exploitation planifiée.

scheduler, programmateur *m*; **job s.,** programmateur de travaux; **master s.,** programmateur principal.

scheduling, ordonnancement *m*, planification *f*.

scheme, coding s., codification *f*, code *m*; **numbering s.,** plan *m* de numérotage.

scientific, s. computer, ordinateur *m* scientifique; **s. data processing,** informatique *f* scientifique; **s. language,** langage *m* scientifique.

scratch, s. tape, bande *f* de manœuvre.

scratch-pad, s.-p. memory, mémoire *f* de travail, mémoire de manœuvre; **s.-p. storage,** mémoire *f* de travail, mémoire de manœuvre.

screen, écran *m*; **cathode s.,** écran cathodique; **read s.,** fenêtre *f* de lecture.

screen (to), faire un tri préalable.

script, machine s., information *f* en code machine.

search, recherche *f*, compulsation *f*; **area s.,** recherche de zone; **binary s.,** recherche binaire, recherche dichotomique; **chain(ing) s.,** recherche en chaine; **conjunctive s.,** recherche par groupe de mots-clés (*Recherche documentaire*); **dichotomizing s.,** recherche dichotomique; **disjunctive s.,** recherche par mot-clé unique (*Recherche documentaire*); **Fibonacci s.,** recherche (dichotomique) de Fibonacci; **literature s.,** recherche documentaire; **s. card,** carte chercheuse; **s. cycle,** cycle *m* de recherche; **s. key,** clé *f* (*ou* indicatif *m*) de recherche; **s. time,** temps *m* de recherche.

search (to), rechercher.

searching, s. storage, mémoire associative.

second, s.-generation computer, calculateur *m* de deuxième génération; **s.-level address,** adresse indirecte à deux niveaux; **s.-level addressing,** adressage indirect à deux niveaux; **s.-order subroutine,** sous-programme *m* de second niveau; **s. remove subroutine,** sous-programme *m* de second niveau.

secondary, s. failure, défaillance *f* secondaire; **s. memory,** mémoire *f* auxiliaire; **s. route,** voie *f* secondaire; **s. store (*or* storage),** mémoire *f* secondaire.

section, section *f*; **arithmetic s.,** unité *f* arithmétique; **control s.,** section de contrôle; **group s.,** section de groupe primaire; **input s.,** zone *f* d'entrée, zone d'introduction; **mastergroup s.,** section de groupe tertiaire; **output s.,** zone *f* de sortie, zone d'extraction; **principal test s.,** section principale d'essais; **supergroup s.,** section de groupe secondaire; **test s.,** section d'essais.

section (to), segmenter.

sector, secteur *m*.

seek, recherche *f*; **s. address,** adresse *f* de recherche; **s. area,** zone *f* de recherche (accélérée).

seek (to), rechercher, chercher.

see-saw, s.-s. circuit, inverseur *m* de polarité.

segment, segment *m*; **root s.,** segment principal; **s. mark,** marque *f* de segment; **s. table (SGT),** table *f* des segments.

segment (to), segmenter.

segmented, s. program, programme segmenté.

segments, segments *m*; **exclusive s.,** segments (secondaires) à implantation exclusive; **inclusive s.,** segments (secondaires) à implantation simultanée.

seizing, s. signal, signal *m* de prise.

select (to), sélectionner, choisir.

selected, s. cell, élément sélectionné.

selecting, sélection *f*.

selection, sélection *f*; **address s.,** sélection d'adresse; **coincident-current s.,** sélection par courants simultanés; **keyboard s.,** numérotation *f* au clavier, sélection au clavier; **s. check,** contrôle *m* de sélection; **s. control,** (unité *f* de) contrôle *m* de sélection (d'instructions); **s. ratio,** rapport *m* de sélection.

selective, s. calling, appel sélectif; **s. digit emitter,** émetteur *m* de signaux, distributeur *m*; **s. dump,** vidage sélectif; **s. fading,** fading sélectif, évanouissement sélectif; **s. ringing,** appel sélectif; **s. trace,** programme *m* d'analyse sélective; **s. tracing routine,** programme *m* d'analyse sélective, programme *m* de dépistage sélectif.

selectivity, sélectivité *f*; **adjacent channel s.,** sélectivité adjacente.

selector, sélecteur *m*; **digit s.,** sélecteur de perforation; **s. channel,** canal *m* de sélection.

self, s.-adapting, auto-adaptateur (-trice) *adj.*, (auto-)adaptatif (-ive) *adj.*; **s.-checking code,** code détecteur d'erreurs; **s.-checking number,** nombre *m* à chiffre-clé de protection; **s.-checking numeral,** nombre *m* à chiffre-clé de protection; **s.-demarcating code,** code auto-délimité; **s.-organizing,** auto-organisateur (-trice) *adj.*; **s.-resetting loop,** boucle *f* à auto-rétablissement; **s.-triggered program,** programme *m* à lancement automatique.

semanteme, sémantème *m*.

semantic, sémantique *adj.*; **s. error,** erreur *f* sémantique; **s. matrix,** matrice *f* sémantique.

semantics, sémantique *f*.

semi-automatic, s.-a. message switching centre, centre *m* semi-automatique de commutation de messages; **s.-a. system,** système *m* semi-automatique.

semi-conductor, semi-conducteur *m ou adj.*; **intrinsic s.-c.,** semi-conducteur intrinsèque; **n-type s.-c.,** semi-conducteur type n; **p.-type s.-c.,** semi-conducteur type p.

semi-duplex, s.-d. operation, exploitation *f* (en) semi-duplex.

sending, key s., envoi *m* de signaux au clavier.

send/receive, automatic s./r., téléimprimeur *m* automatique d'émission-réception.

sense, s. probe, crayon émetteur; **s. signal,** signal *m* de (sortie) lecture; **s. switch,** inverseur *m*; **s. winding,** fil *m* de lecture; **s. wire,** fil *m* de lecture.

sense (to), détecter, lire.

sensible, machine-s., exploitable sur machine.

sensing, mark s., lecture *f* de marques; **s. device,** 1. dispositif *m* de lecture; 2. détecteur *m*, capteur *m*, palpeur *m*; **s. station,** poste *m* de lecture.

sensitivity, sensibilité *f*; **deflection s.,** sensibilité de déviation.

sensor, 1. dispositif *m* de lecture; 2. détecteur *m*, capteur *m*, palpeur *m*.

sentinel, drapeau *m*, marque *f*, sentinelle *f*.

separating, s. character, caractère séparateur (d'informations).

separator, séparateur *m*; **information s. (IS),** caractère séparateur (d'informations); **record s.,** séparateur d'enregistrements; **unit s.,** séparateur d'unités; **word s.,** séparateur de mots.

septenary, s. number, nombre *m* septénaire.

septet, septet *m*.

sequence, séquence *f*; **calling s.,** séquence d'appel; **collation (or collating) s.,** séquence (*ou* ordre *m*) d'interclassement; **control s.,** séquence (d'exécution) des instructions; **pseudo-random number s.,** séquence de nombres pseudo-aléatoires; **random number s.,** séquence de nombres aléatoires; **s. access,** accès séquentiel; **s. check,** contrôle *m* de séquence; **s. checking routine,** programme *m* de contrôle de séquence; **s. control register,** registre *m* de contrôle de séquence; **s.-controlled calculator,** calculateur *m* automatique à séquence contrôlée; **s. counter,** registre *m* (d'adresse)

d'instruction; **s. error,** erreur *f* de séquence; **s. number,** numéro *m* d'ordre; **s. register,** registre *m* de contrôle de séquence.

sequence (to), ordonner, mettre en séquence.

sequencing, mise *f* en séquence; **s. by merging,** rangement *m* par interclassement.

sequential, séquentiel (-elle) *adj.*; **s. access,** accès séquentiel; **s. access storage,** mémoire *f* à accès séquentiel; **s. computer,** calculateur séquentiel, calculateur *m* (en) série; **s. control,** mode séquentiel; **s. (logic) element,** élément logique séquentiel; **s. operation,** exploitation séquentielle; **s. processing,** traitement séquentiel; **s. programming,** programmation séquentielle; **s. scheduling system,** système séquentiel de prise en charge de travaux; **s.-stacked job control,** contrôle *m* de séquence des travaux.

serial, en série *f*; **s. access,** accès *m* en série; **s. arithmetic,** arithmétique *f* (en) série; **s. computer,** calculateur séquentiel, calculateur *m* (en) série; **s. feed,** alimentation *f* colonne par colonne; **s. flow,** déroulement *m* des travaux en série; **s. full adder,** additionneur *m* série; **s. full subtracter,** soustracteur *m* série; **s. half adder,** demi-additionneur *m* série; **s. half subtracter,** demi-soustracteur *m* série; **s. memory,** mémoire *f* (en) série; **s. number,** numéro *m* de série; **s. operation,** exploitation *f* en série; **s.-parallel,** série-parallèle *adj.*; **s. printer,** imprimante *f* série; **s. processing,** traitement *m* en série; **s. programming,** programmation *f* (en) série; **s. storage,** mémoire *f* (en) série; **s. transfer,** transfert *m* en série; **s. transmission,** transmission *f* série; **s. work-flow,** déroulement *m* des travaux en série.

serialize (to), convertir de parallèle à série.

series, série *f*; **time s.,** série dans le temps.

service, service *m*; **automatic teleprinter s.,** liaison *f* automatique par téléimprimeur; **field s.,** service d'entretien en clientèle; **full-duplex s.,** service duplex; **half-duplex s.,** service semi-duplex; **private line (or wire) s.,** service à ligne privée; **telegraph s.,** service télégraphique; **telephone s.,** service téléphonique; **teleprinter s.,** service de téléimprimeurs; **telex s.,** service télex; **s. bit,**

bit *m* de service; **s. bureau,** service de travaux à façon, façonnier *m*; **s. program,** programme *m* de service; **s. routine,** programme *m* de service.
service (to), entretenir.
serviceability, s. ratio, taux *m* de service.
serviceable, s. time, temps *m* disponible.
services, remote entry s. (RES), soumission *f* de travaux à distance.
servicing, s. time, temps *m* de maintenance.
servo, servomécanisme *m*; **s. mechanism,** servomécanisme; **s. multiplier,** multiplicateur *m* à servomécanisme.
set, ensemble *m*, jeu *m*; **alphabetic(al) character s.,** jeu de caractères alphabétiques; **alphabetic(al) coded character s.,** jeu de caractères codés alphabétiques; **alphanumeric character s.,** jeu de caractères alphanumériques; **alphanumeric coded character s.,** jeu de caractères codés alphanumériques; **calling s.,** poste appelant; **catalogued data s.,** ensemble de(s) données cataloguées; **character s.,** jeu de caractères, répertoire *m* de caractères; **coded character s.,** jeu de caractères codés; **code s.,** jeu de représentations, jeu d'éléments de code; **computer instruction s.,** répertoire *m* d'instructions de calculateur; **concatenated data s.,** ensemble de données enchaînées; **data s., 1.** ensemble de données; **2.** unité *f* de transmission; **four-wire terminating s.,** termineur *m*; **indexed sequential data s.,** ensemble de données (organisé) en séquentiel indexé; **instruction s.,** répertoire *m* d'instructions; **interleaved carbon s.,** liasse carbonée; **level measuring s.,** décibelmètre *m*; **numeric character s.,** jeu de caractères numériques; **numeric coded character s.,** jeu de caractères codés numériques; **page data s.,** ensemble de données constitué de pages; **partitioned data s.,** ensemble de données compartimenté; **telephone data s.,** unité *f* de transmission téléphonique; **user's s.,** poste *m* (d')utilisateur; **s. point,** point *m* de réglage; **s. pulse,** impulsion *f* d'excitation; **s. theory,** théorie *f* des ensembles.
set (to), 1. placer; **2.** régler.
setting, trap s., déclenchement *m* d'un déroutement.
set-up, montage *m*; **s.-u. diagram,** schéma

m d'implantation, schéma d'installation, schéma de montage; **s.-u. time,** temps *m* de préparation.
seven-bit, s.-b. byte, septet *m*.
sexadecimal, s. notation, numération sexadécimale.
sextet, sextet *m*.
SGT (=segment table), table *f* des segments.
shaft, s. position encoder, codeur *m* de position angulaire.
shape, forme *f*; **pulse s.,** forme des impulsions.
shaping, pulse s., mise *f* en forme d'impulsions; **signal s.,** mise *f* en forme de signaux; **s. circuit,** circuit *m* de mise en forme.
shared, partagé *adj.*, en commun; **s. file,** fichier partagé, fichier *m* en commun; **s. files system,** système *m* à fichiers communs; **s. line,** ligne partagée; **s. memory,** mémoire *f* en commun, mémoire partagée.
sharing, time s., partage *m* de temps.
sheet, coding s., feuille *f* de programmation.
Sheffer, S. stroke, NON-ET; **S. stroke gate,** circuit *m* NON-ET.
shift, 1. décalage *m*; **2.** glissement *m*; **arithmetic(al) s.,** décalage arithmétique; **carrier s.,** déplacement *m* de la porteuse; **case s.,** inversion *f*; **circular s.,** décalage circulaire; **cyclic s.,** décalage circulaire; **end-around s.,** décalage circulaire; **figures s.,** inversion *f* «chiffres»; **frequency s.,** déplacement *m* de fréquence; **left s.,** décalage à gauche; **letters s.,** inversion *f* «lettres»; **logic(al) s.,** décalage logique; **non-arithmetic s.,** décalage circulaire; **phase s.,** déphasage *m*; **right s.,** décalage à droite; **ring s.,** décalage circulaire; **s.-lock keyboard,** clavier *m* avec garde d'inversion; **s. register,** registre *m* (de) décalage.
shift (to), décaler.
shift-in, s.-i. character (SI), caractère *m* en code, caractère de commande de code normal.
shifting, s. register, registre *m* (de) décalage.
shift-out, s.-o. character (so), caractère *m* hors code, caractère de commande de code spécial.
short, s. word, mot incomplet.
short-circuit, court-circuit *m*.
SI (=shift-in character), caractère *m* en code,

caractère de commande de code normal.

side, côté *m*, face *f* (*d'un disque*); **line s.**, côté ligne; **local s.**, côté matériel; **s. circuit**, circuit combinant; **s. circuit loading coil**, bobine *f* de charge de circuit combinant.

sideband, bande latérale; **main s.**, bande principale; **transmitted s.** (*Am.*), bande principale; **vestigial s.**, bande résiduelle.

sideways, **s. feed(ing)**, alimentation *f* ligne par ligne.

sight, **s. check**, contrôle visuel.

sight-check (to), mirer (des cartes).

sign, signe *m*; **call s.**, indicatif *m* d'appel; **special s.**, caractère spécial; **s. bit**, bit *m* de signe; **s. changer**, inverseur *m* de signe; **s.-changing amplifier**, amplificateur inverseur (*ou* changeur) de signe; **s. character**, caractère *m* de signe; **s. check indicator**, indicateur *m* de contrôle de signe; **s. digit**, chiffre *m* de signe; **s. field**, zone *f* de signe; **s. position**, position *f* du signe; **s. reverser**, inverseur *m* de signe; **s. reversing amplifier**, amplificateur inverseur (*ou* changeur) de signe.

signal, signal *m*; **acknowledgement s.**, signal (d')accusé de réception; **alphabetic(al) s.**, signal alphabétique; **answer s.**, signal de réponse; **basic s.**, signal de base; **call-confirmation s.**, signal de confirmation d'appel; **call connected s.**, signal de connexion; **calling s.**, signal d'appel; **carriage return s.**, signal de retour du chariot; **carry-complete s.**, signal de fin de report; **character s.**, signal de caractère; **clear-back s.**, signal de raccrochage; **clear-forward s.**, signal de fin (de communication); **clearing s.**, signal de libération; **clock s.**, signal d'horloge; **command s.**, signal de commande; **control s.**, signal de commande; **correcting s.**, signal de correction; **data s.**, signal de données; **dialling s.**, signal de sélection; **disconnect s.** (*Am.*), signal de fin (de communication); **disturbed one-output s.**, signal de sortie «un» avec perturbation; **disturbed response s.**, signal de sortie avec perturbation; **disturbed zero-output s.**, signal de sortie «zéro» avec perturbation; **enabling s.**, signal de validation; **end-of-block s.**, signal de fin de bloc; **end-of-call s.**, signal de fin de conversation; **end-of-message s.**, signal de fin de message; **engaged s.**, signal

d'occupation; **error s.**, signal d'erreur; **faulty s.**, signal erroné; **feedback control s.**, signal de régulation par réaction; **guard s.**, signal de garde; **impulsing s.**, signal d'appel par impulsions; **inhibiting s.**, signal d'interdiction; **interfering s.**, signal parasite, signal perturbateur; **interrupt s.**, signal d'interruption; **multichannel s.**, signal multiplex; **nought-output s.**, signal de lecture «zéro»; **one-output s.**, signal de lecture «un»; **parasitic s.**, signal parasite; **partial disturbed one-output s.**, signal de sortie «un» en sélection partielle avec perturbation; **partial disturbed response s.**, signal de sortie en sélection partielle avec perturbation; **partial disturbed zero-output s.**, signal de sortie «zéro» en sélection partielle avec perturbation; **partial undisturbed one-output s.**, signal de sortie «un» en sélection partielle sans perturbation; **partial undisturbed response s.**, signal de sortie en sélection partielle sans perturbation; **partial undisturbed zero-output s.**, signal de sortie «zéro» en sélection partielle sans perturbation; **proceed-to-select s.**, signal d'invitation à numéroter; **proceed-to-send s.**, signal d'invitation à transmettre; **proceed-to-transmit s.**, signal d'invitation à transmettre; **pulse s.**, impulsion *f*; **pulsing s.**, signal de numérotation; **read output s.**, signal de (sortie) lecture; **release guard s.**, signal de libération de garde; **remote control s.**, signal de télécommande; **seizing s.**, signal de prise; **sense s.**, signal de (sortie) lecture; **start s.**, signal de mise en marche; **start dialling s.** (*Am.*), signal d'invitation à transmettre; **start-of-block s.**, signal de début de bloc; **stop s.**, signal d'arrêt; **supervisory s.**, signal de supervision; **switching s.**, signal de commutation; **telegraph s.**, signal télégraphique; **teleprinter s.**, signal de téléimprimeur; **undisturbed one-output s.**, signal de sortie «un» sans perturbation; **undisturbed output s.**, signal de sortie sans perturbation; **undisturbed response s.**, signal de sortie sans perturbation; **undisturbed zero-output s.**, signal de sortie «zéro» sans perturbation; **zero-output s.**, signal de lecture «zéro»; **s. attenuation**, atténuation *f* de signaux; **s. conditioning**, conditionnement *m* de signaux; **s.-conversion equipment**, équipement *m* de conversion de signaux; **s. distance,** distance *f* inter-signaux; **s. element, 1.** élément *m* de signal; **2.** (*Am.*) intervalle *m* unitaire; **s. level,** niveau *m* de signal de contraste (*OCR*); **s. normalization,** mise *f* en forme de signaux; **s. regeneration,** mise *f* en forme de signaux; **s. reshaping,** mise *f* en forme de signaux; **s. shaping,** mise *f* en forme de signaux; **s. standardization,** mise *f* en forme de signaux; **s.-to-noise ratio,** rapport *m* signal/bruit; **s. transformation,** transformation *f* de signaux.

signalling, amplitude-change s., (formation *f* des signaux par) modulation *f* d'amplitude; **automatic s., 1.** signalisation *f* automatique; **2.** transmission *f* automatique des signaux; **frequency-change s.,** (formation *f* des signaux par) modulation *f* de fréquence; **frequency-exchange s.,** modulation *f* par mutation des fréquences; **frequency-shift s.,** modulation *f* par déplacement de fréquence; **s. rate,** vitesse *f* de transmission de signaux.

signals, correction from s., correction *f* sans courants spéciaux.

sign-changing, s.-c. amplifier, amplificateur inverseur (*ou* changeur) de signe.

signed, s. field, zone *f* algébrique.

significance, 1. signification *f*; **2.** poids *m*.

significant, significatif (-ive) *adj.*; **s. conditions of a modulation,** états significatifs d'une modulation; **s. conditions of a restitution,** états significatifs d'une restitution; **s. digit,** chiffre significatif; **s. digits, 1.** chiffres significatifs; **2.** mantisse *f* (*en représentations à virgule flottante*); **s. figures,** chiffres significatifs; **s. instants,** instants significatifs; **s. interval,** intervalle significatif.

sign-reversing, s.-r. amplifier, amplificateur inverseur (*ou* changeur) de signe.

silicon, s. on sapphire (SOS), silicium *m* sur saphir.

simple, s. buffering, utilisation *f* de tampon unique.

simplex, simplex *adj.*, unidirectionnel (-elle) *adj.*; **s. channel,** voie *f* simplex; **s. circuit,** communication *f* simplex; **s. line,** ligne *f* simplex; **s. mode,** mode *m* (d'exploitation) simplex.

simulate (to), simuler.

simulation, simulation *f*; **real-time s.,** simulation en temps réel.

simulator, simulateur *m*; **s. program,** programme *m* de simulation; **s. routine,** programme *m* de simulation.

simultaneity, simultanéité *f*.

simultaneous, simultané *adj.*; **s. access,** accès simultané; **s. carry,** report simultané; **s. computer,** calculateur simultané; **s. input/output,** entrée-sortie simultanées; **s. mode of working,** mode *m* (d'exploitation) simultané; **s. operation,** exploitation simultanée; **s. transmission,** transmission simultanée.

sine, s. wave, onde sinusoïdale.

sine-cosine, s.-c. potentiometer, potentiomètre *m* à variation sinusoïdale.

single, s.-address, à une adresse; **s.-address code,** code *m* à une adresse; **s.-address instruction,** instruction *f* à une adresse; **s.-address message,** message *m* à adresse unique; **s. column duodecimal coding,** codage duodécimal sur une colonne; **s. crystal,** monocristal *m*; **s.-current transmission,** transmission *f* par simple courant; **s.-ended amplifier,** amplificateur *m* à une sortie (*ou* à sortie simple); **s. error,** erreur *f* simple; **s.-level address,** adresse directe, adresse réelle; **s. precision,** simple précision *f*; **s.-sheet feeding,** alimentation *f* de feuilles individuelles; **s. shot multivibrator,** multivibrateur *m* monostable; **s. shot operation,** fonctionnement *m* en pas-à-pas; **s. sideband transmission,** émission *f* sur bande latérale unique; **s. step operation,** fonctionnement *m* en pas-à-pas.

sink, data s., collecteur *m* de données.

site, hole s., emplacement *m* de perforation.

six, s.-bit byte, sextet *m*.

size, grandeur *f*, capacité *f*; **item s.,** grandeur d'article; **memory s.,** capacité de mémoire.

skeletal, s. code, code *m* paramétrable; **s. coding,** codage *m* à instruction paramétrable.

skew, 1. désalignement *m*; **2.** inclinaison *f*.

skip, saut *m*; **tape s.,** saut de bande; **s. code,** code *m* de saut (de papier); **s. instruction,** instruction *f* de saut, instruction de branchement.

skip (to), sauter.

slave, s. **application**, application *f* en mode asservi; s. **computer**, ordinateur asservi, ordinateur *m* satellite; s. **mode**, mode asservi; s. **station**, station asservie; s. **system**, système asservi.

slew, saut *m*; **paper s.**, saut de papier; **post-s.** (*Am.*), saut après impression; **pre-s.** (*Am.*), saut avant impression; s. **character**, caractère *m* de saut.

slot, case *f*; s. **group**, groupe *m* de cases; s. **number**, numéro *m* de case.

slow, s. **storage**, mémoire lente.

S.L.T. (=**solid logic technology**), technologie *f* des circuits logiques transistorisés et/ou miniaturisés.

smooth (to), 1. lisser; 2. filtrer.

smudge, ink s., bavochure *f* (*OCR*); s. **resistance**, résistance *f* au maculage.

smudging, maculage *m*.

snapshot, s. **dump**, vidage dynamique sélectif; s. **program**, programme *m* d'analyse sélective.

so (=**shift-out character**), caractère *m* hors code, caractère *m* de commande de code spécial.

socket, 1. plot *m*; 2. douille *f*.

software, logiciel *m*, (ensemble *m* de) programmes *m* (nécessaires à l'exploitation d'un système informatique), «software».

SOH (=**start of heading character**), caractère *m* debut d'en-tête.

solid, s. **logic technology (S.L.T.)**, technologie *f* des circuits logiques transistorisés et/ou miniaturisés.

solid-state, s.-s. **component**, composant transistorisé, composant *m* à semi-conducteur(s); s.-s. **computer**, calculateur transistorisé; s.-s. **device**, dispositif *m* à semi-conducteurs, dispositif transistorisé.

solution, graphic s., solution *f* graphique.

solver, **structural engineering system s.** **(STRESS)**, langage *m* mathématique pour le calcul de la résistance des matériaux.

son, s. **tape**, bande *f* de troisième génération.

sonic, s. **delay line**, ligne *f* à retard acoustique.

sort, tri *m*; **backward s.**, tri décroissant; **block s.**, tri par sous-groupes (d'indicatif); **digital s.**, tri numérique; **forward s.**, tri croissant; **four-tape s.**, tri à quatre dérouleurs; **merging s.**, tri d'interclassement, tri de fusion; **property s.**, tri par caractéristiques; **tape s.**, tri sur bande magnétique; s. **generator**, générateur *m* de programmes de tri; s. **key**, clé *f* (*ou* indicatif *m*) de tri.

sort (to), trier.

sorter, trieuse *f*; **document s.**, trieuse de documents; s. **pocket**, case *f* de tri, case *f* de réception de trieuse.

sorter-reader, trieuse-lectrice *f*.

sorting, tri *m*; **alphanumeric s.**, tri alphanumérique; **numerical s.**, tri numérique; s. **needle**, aiguille *f* de tri; s. **program**, programme *m* de tri; s. **routine generator**, générateur *m* de programmes de tri.

SOS (=**silicon on sapphire**), silicium *m* sur saphir.

source, source *f*; **data s.**, source de données; s. **code**, code *m* source; s. **data**, données *f* de base; s. **data automation**, automatisation *f* des données de base; s. **deck**, paquet *m* de cartes en langage source; s. **document**, document *m* de base; s. **language**, langage *m* source; s. **library**, bibliothèque *f* de programmes source; s. **module**, module *m* (de programme) source; s. **program**, programme *m* source; s. **program library**, bibliothèque *f* de programmes source; s. **recording**, enregistrement *m* source; s. **routine**, programme *m* source.

SP (=**space character**), caractère *m* espace.

space, espace *m*; **interblock s.**, espace interblocs; **interword s.**, espace entre mots; **line s.**, interligne *m*, espacement vertical; **switching s.**, espace de commutation; **word s.**, espace occupé par un mot; **working s.**, mémoire *f* de travail, mémoire de manœuvre; s. **character (SP)**, caractère *m* espace; s. **code**, code *m* (de commande) d'espace; s. **diversity**, diversité *f* dans l'espace; s. **diversity reception**, réception *f* par diversité dans l'espace; s. **suppression**, suppression *f* d'espaces.

spacing, pulse s., espacement *m* des impulsions.

span, plage *f*.

spanned, s. **record**, enregistrement morcelé.

special, spécial *adj.*; s. **character**, caractère spécial; s. **device**, dispositif spécial; s. **feature**, dispositif spécial; s. **purpose computer**, calculateur spécialisé; s. **sign**, caractère spécial; **s. symbol,** caractère spécial.

specific, s. address, adresse absolue, adresse réelle; **s. addressing,** adressage absolu, adressage réel; **s. code,** code réel (*en langage machine*); **s. coding,** codage absolu; **s. program,** programme particulier; **s. routine,** programme particulier.

specification, program s., spécification *f* du programme.

spectral, s. response, réponse spectrale.

spectrum, pulse s., spectre *m* d'impulsions.

speed, vitesse *f*; **effective s.,** vitesse effective; **effective transmission s.,** vitesse effective de transmission; **full s.,** vitesse maximale; **line s.,** vitesse de ligne; **nominal s.,** vitesse nominale; **rated s.,** vitesse nominale; **reading s.,** vitesse de lecture; **telegraph s.,** vitesse télégraphique; **transmission s.,** vitesse de transmission; **traverse s.,** vitesse de défilement (*d'une bande*).

splicer, colleuse *f* de bande.

split, column s., séparation *f* de colonne; **s. catalog(ue),** catalogue éclaté; **s.-word operation,** opération *f* sur partie de mot.

split (to), séparer, subdiviser, fractionner.

spool, bobine *f* (vide); **blank s.,** bobine (*de bande perforée*) sans enregistrement; **take-off s.,** bobine émettrice, bobine dérouleuse; **take-up s.,** bobine réceptrice, bobine enrouleuse; **virgin s.,** bobine (*de bande perforée*) vierge.

spooler, enrouleur *m*, bobineuse *f*.

sporadic, s. fault, panne intermittente.

spot, spot *m*; **flying s.,** spot mobile; **reflective s.,** spot réfléchissant; **s. punch,** perforatrice *f* à perforation unique.

sprocket, s. hole, perforation *f* d'entraînement; **s. pulse,** impulsion *f* de synchronisation.

square, s. brackets, crochets *m*.

square-law, s.-l. detection, détection *f* parabolique.

squareness, s. ratio, taux *m* de rectangularité.

squeezeout, ink s., écrasage *m*.

stack, pile *f*; **core s.,** bloc *m* de mémoire; **head s.,** groupe *m* de têtes de lecture/écriture; **push down s.,** pile refoulée; **storage s.,** 1. bloc *m* de mémoire; 2. pile de données (*en mémoire*).

stacked, s. job processing, traitement *m* par

programmes groupés.

stacker, case *f* de réception; **card s.,** case de réception de cartes; **input s.,** magasin *m* d'alimentation (de cartes); **offset s.,** case de réception (de cartes) à décalage; **output s.,** case de réception.

stacking, overflow s., réception *f* en case alternée.

stalled, s. program, programme figé (*ou* bloqué).

standard, standard *m ou adj.,* norme *f*; **s. form,** forme normalisée (*en représentations à virgule flottante*); **s. interface,** interface *m* standard; **s. program,** programme *m* standard; **s. subroutine,** sous-programme *m* standard.

standardization, pulse s., mise *f* en forme d'impulsions; **signal s.,** mise *f* en forme de signaux.

standardize (to), normaliser, standardiser.

standby, de secours, en réserve; **s. application,** application *f* avec système(s) auxiliaire(s) (*ou* de secours); **s. block,** bloc *m* de réserve, bloc de secours; **s. equipment,** matériel *m* de secours, matériel en réserve; **s. register,** registre *m* de réserve.

standby-on-nines, s.-o.-n. carry, report bloqué sur neuf.

star, s. network, réseau *m* en étoile.

start, s. button, interrupteur *m* de mise en route; **s. dialling signal**(*A m.*), signal *m* d'invitation à transmettre; **s. element,** élément *m* de départ; **s. key,** interrupteur *m* de mise en route; **s.-of-block signal,** signal *m* de début de bloc; **s. of heading character (SOH),** caractère *m* début d'en-tête; **s. of message,** début *m* de message; **s. of text,** début *m* de texte; **s. of text character (STX),** caractère *m* début de texte; **s. signal,** signal *m* de mise en marche; **s. time,** temps *m* d'accélération.

starting up, mise *f* en route, démarrage *m*, amorçage *m*.

start-stop, s.-s. apparatus, appareil *m* arythmique; **s.-s. code,** code *m* arythmique; **s.-s. mode,** mode *m* arythmique; **s.-s. modulation,** modulation *f* arythmique; **s.-s. system,** système *m* arythmique; **s.-s. transmission,** transmission *f* arythmique.

state, 1. état *m*; 2. condition *f*; **dormant s.,**

état d'inactivité; **input s.**, état d'entrée; **masked s.**, état masqué; **nought s.**, état «zéro»; **one s.**, état «un»; **operating s.**, état de fonctionnement; **output s.**, état de sortie; **running s.**, état de marche, état opérationnel; **stopped s.**, état d'arrêt; **supervisory s.**, état superviseur; **zero s.**, état «zéro».

statement, 1. instruction *f* (*en langage source*); 2. état *m*; **conditional s.**, instruction conditionnelle; **declarative s.**, instruction de déclaration (*en COBOL*); **execute s.**, instruction d'exécution; **job control s.**, ordre *m* de contrôle des travaux; **job s.**, ordre *m* de début des travaux; **s. number**, numéro *m* d'instruction.

static, statique *adj.*; **s. check**, contrôle *m* statique; **s. dump**, vidage *m* (de) mémoire à l'arrêt; **s. error**, erreur *f* statique; **s. magnetic cell**, unité *f* de stockage magnétique; **s. memory**, mémoire *f* statique; **s. print-out**, impression différée; **s. store** (*or* **storage**), mémoire *f* statique, stockage permanent; **s. subroutine**, sous-programme *m* non paramétrable; **s. test**, contrôle *m* statique.

staticize (to), 1. convertir de série à parallèle; 2. prendre en charge (une instruction de programme).

staticizer, convertisseur *m* série-parallèle.

station, 1. station *f*; 2. poste *m*; **accepting s.**, station de réception; **attended s.**, station surveillée; **auxiliary s.**, 1. station auxiliaire; 2. station téléalimentée; **brush s.**, poste de lecture (par balais); **called s.**, station appelée; **calling s.**, station appelante; **control s.**, station de commande; **encoding s.**, poste d'encodage; **inquiry s.**, poste d'interrogation, poste de consultation; **input s.**, poste de saisie de données; **magnetic tape s.**, unité *f* de bande magnétique, dérouleur *m* de bande magnétique; **master s.**, station principale (*ou* maîtresse); **net control s.** (*Am.*), station de coordination de réseau; **punching s.**, poste de perforation; **reading s.**, poste de lecture; **remote-controlled s.**, station télécommandée, station télérégulée; **remote (data) s.**, station à distance; **repeater s.**, station de répéteurs; **sensing s.**, poste de lecture; **slave s.**, station asservie; **tape s.**, unité *f* de bande magnétique, dérouleur *m* de bande

magnétique; **telephone s.**, poste téléphonique; **telex s.**, poste télex; **tributary s.**, station tributaire; **s. battery**, alimentation *f* (en électricité) d'une station.

stationery, **continuous s.**, papier *m* en continu.

step, 1. instruction *f*; 2. étape *f*; **job s.**, étape de travail; **program s.**, pas *m* de programme; **s. change**, variation *f* discrète; **s. counter**, compteur *m* des phases d'une opération.

step (to), faire progresser.

step-by-step, **s.-b.-s. operation**, fonctionnement *m* en pas-à-pas; **s.-b.-s. switch**, commutateur *m* pas-à-pas; **s.-b.-s. system**, système *m* pas-à-pas.

stepped, **s. addressing**, adressage *m* à progression automatique avancée; **s. start-stop system**, système arythmique cadencé.

sticker, marque réfléchissante (*de bande magnétique*).

stochastic, stochastique *adj.*

stop, arrêt *m*; **automatic s.**, arrêt automatique; **coded s.**, arrêt codé, arrêt programmé; **conditional s.**, arrêt conditionnel; **dynamic s.**, arrêt sur boucle (*de programme*); **form s.**, arrêt (de) fin de papier; **hoot s.**, arrêt avec signal sonore; **loop s.**, arrêt sur boucle; **programmed s.**, arrêt programmé; **s. bit**, élément *m* d'arrêt; **s. code**, code *m* d'arrêt; **s. element**, élément *m* d'arrêt; **s. instruction**, instruction *f* d'arrêt; **s. signal**, signal *m* d'arrêt; **s. time**, temps *m* de décélération.

stop (to), arrêter.

stopped, **s. state**, état *m* d'arrêt.

storage, 1. mémoire *f*; 2. stockage *m*, mémorisation *f*; **acoustic s.**, mémoire acoustique; **associative s.**, mémoire associative; **auxiliary s.**, mémoire auxiliaire; **backing s.**, mémoire auxiliaire; **buffer s.**, mémoire tampon; **capacitor s.**, mémoire à condensateurs; **cathode ray s.**, mémoire à tube cathodique; **changeable s.**, mémoire interchangeable; **circulating s.**, mémoire circulante, mémoire cyclique; **condenser s.**, mémoire à condensateurs; **constant s.**, zone *f* de constantes; **content-addressed s.**, mémoire associative; **core s.**, mémoire à tores (magnétiques); **cryogenic s.**, mémoire cryogénique; **cyclic s.**, mémoire circulante, mémoire cyclique;

data s., stockage de données; **dedicated s.**, mémoire réservée; **delay line s.**, mémoire à ligne à retard; **destructive s.**, mémoire à lecture destructive; **direct access s.**, mémoire à accès direct, mémoire à accès sélectif; **disk s.**, mémoire à disques; **drum s.**, mémoire à tambour magnétique; **dynamic s.**, mémoire cyclique, mémoire dynamique; **electrostatic s.**, mémoire électrostatique; **erasable s.**, mémoire effaçable; **external page s.**, mémoire auxiliaire de pages; **external s.**, mémoire externe; **fast access s.**, mémoire à accès rapide; **fast s.**, mémoire rapide; **fixed s.**, mémoire fixe, mémoire permanente; **flip-flop s.**, mémoire à bascules; **high-speed s.**, mémoire à accès rapide; **immediate access s.**, mémoire à accès immédiat; **input s.**, zone f d'entrée, zone d'introduction; **input/output s.**, zone f d'entrée-sortie; **instantaneous s.**, mémoire à accès immédiat; **instruction s.**, zone f (de stockage) d'instruction(s), zone de programme; **intermediate s.**, mémoire de manœuvre; **internal s.**, mémoire interne; **low-speed s.**, mémoire lente; **magnetic bubble s.**, mémoire à bulles (*ou* domaines) magnétiques; **magnetic core s.**, mémoire à tores (magnétiques); **magnetic disk s.**, mémoire à disques magnétiques; **magnetic drum s.**, mémoire à tambour magnétique; **magnetic film s.**, mémoire à film magnétique; **magnetic s.**, mémoire magnétique; **magnetic tape s.**, mémoire à bande magnétique; **main s.**, mémoire principale; **manual-switch s.**, mémoire à commande manuelle; **mass s.**, mémoire de masse; **matrix s.**, mémoire (à sélection) matricielle; **mercury s.**, mémoire à mercure; **n-core-per-bit s.**, mémoire à n tores par bit; **nesting s.**, mémoire à liste inversée; **non-destructive s.**, mémoire à lecture non destructive; **non-erasable s.**, mémoire fixe, mémoire permanente; **non-volatile s.**, mémoire rémanente, mémoire permanente; **offline s.**, mémoire non connectée; **one-core-per-bit s.**, mémoire à un tore par bit; **online s.**, mémoire connectée; **output s.**, zone f de sortie, zone d'extraction; **parallel s.**, mémoire (en) parallèle; **parallel search s.**, mémoire associative; **permanent s.**, mémoire fixe, mémoire permanente; **primary s.**, mémoire principale; **program**

s., mémoire (à) programme; **push down s.**, mémoire à liste inversée; **push up s.**, mémoire à liste directe; **quick access s.**, mémoire à accès rapide; **random access s.**, mémoire à accès direct, mémoire à accès sélectif; **rapid access s.**, mémoire à accès rapide; **read-only s.**, mémoire morte, mémoire passive; **real s.**, mémoire réelle; **regenerative s.**, mémoire à régénération; **scratch-pad s.**, mémoire de travail, mémoire de manœuvre; **searching s.**, mémoire associative; **secondary s.**, mémoire auxiliaire; **sequential access s.**, mémoire à accès séquentiel; **serial s.**, mémoire (en) série; **slow s.**, mémoire lente; **static s.**, mémoire statique, stockage permanent; **switch s.**, mémoire à commande manuelle; **temporary s.**, mémoire de travail, mémoire de manœuvre; **virtual equals real (V=R) s.**, mémoire virtuelle=réelle (*ou* V=R); **virtual s.**, mémoire virtuelle; **volatile s.**, mémoire non rémanente; **working s.**, mémoire de travail, mémoire de manœuvre; **s. allocation**, allocation f de mémoire; **s. area**, zone f de mémoire, zone de stockage; **s. block**, zone f de mémoire; **s. buffer**, mémoire tampon; **s. capacity**, 1. capacité f de stockage; 2. capacité f de mémoire; **s. cell**, élément m de mémoire; **s. core**, tore m; **s. device**, dispositif m de mémorisation, mémoire; **s. exchange**, échange m (de données) en mémoire; **s. fill**, garnissage m de mémoire; **s. key**, indicatif m de protection (de mémoire); **s. keyboard**, clavier m à transfert; **s. medium**, support m de mémoire; **s. protection**, protection f de mémoire; **s. register**, registre m de mémoire; **s. stack**, 1. bloc m de mémoire; 2. pile f de données (*en mémoire*); **s. tube**, tube-mémoire m.

store, mémoire f; **acoustic s.**, mémoire acoustique; **active s.**, mémoire active; **addressable s.**, mémoire adressable; **associative s.**, mémoire associative; **automatic s.**, mémoire interne; **auxiliary s.**, mémoire auxiliaire; **backing s.**, mémoire auxiliaire; **beam s.**, mémoire à faisceau(x); **B s.**, registre m d'index; **buffer s.**, mémoire tampon; **capacitor s.**, mémoire à condensateurs; **cathode ray tube s.**, mémoire à tube cathodique; **circulating s.**, mémoire circulante, mémoire cyclique; **computer s.,** mémoire interne; **content-addressed s.,** mémoire associative; **co-ordinate s.,** mémoire (à sélection) matricielle; **core s.,** mémoire à tores (magnétiques); **cryogenic s.,** mémoire cryogénique; **cyclic s.,** mémoire circulante, mémoire cyclique; **data carrier s.,** mémoire à support amovible; **delay line s.,** mémoire à ligne à retard; **direct access s.,** mémoire à accès direct, mémoire à accès sélectif; **electrostatic s.,** mémoire électrostatique; **erasable s.,** mémoire effaçable; **exchangeable disk s.,** mémoire à disques amovibles; **external s.,** mémoire externe; **fast access s.,** mémoire à accès rapide; **fast s.,** mémoire rapide; **file s.,** mémoire (à) fichier; **fixed s.,** mémoire fixe, mémoire permanente; **immediate access s.,** mémoire à accès immédiat; **inherent s.,** mémoire interne; **interchangeable disk s.,** mémoire à disques amovibles; **internal s.,** mémoire interne; **magnetic card s.,** mémoire à cartes (ou feuillets) magnétiques; **magnetic disk s.,** mémoire à disques magnétiques; **magnetic drum s.,** mémoire à tambour magnétique; **magnetic film s.,** mémoire à film magnétique; **magnetic s.,** mémoire magnétique; **magnetic tape s.,** mémoire à bande magnétique; **magnetic wire s.,** mémoire à fil magnétique; **matrix s.,** mémoire (à sélection) matricielle; **mercury s.,** mémoire à mercure; **n-core-per-bit s.,** mémoire à n tores par bit; **nesting s.,** mémoire à liste inversée; **non-erasable s.,** mémoire fixe, mémoire permanente; **non-volatile s.,** mémoire rémanente, mémoire permanente; **one-core-per-bit s.,** mémoire à un tore par bit; **peripheral s.,** mémoire périphérique; **permanent s.,** mémoire fixe, mémoire permanente; **plated wire s.,** mémoire à fils plaqués, mémoire à couche mince sur fil; **push down s.,** mémoire à liste inversée; **quick access s.,** mémoire à accès rapide; **random access s.,** mémoire à accès direct, mémoire à accès sélectif; **read-only s.,** mémoire morte, mémoire passive; **regenerative s.,** mémoire à régénération; **secondary s.,** mémoire auxiliaire; **static s.,** mémoire statique; **thin film s.,** mémoire à film mince; **two-core-per-bit s.,** mémoire à deux tores par bit; **uniformly accessible s.,** mémoire à accès direct, mémoire à accès sélectif; **volatile s.,** mémoire rémanente; **word organized s.,** mémoire organisée en mots; **working s.,** mémoire de travail, mémoire de manœuvre; **writable s.,** mémoire active; **s. allocation,** allocation f de mémoire; **s. capacity,** capacité f de mémoire; **s. cycle,** cycle m (de) mémoire; **s. dump,** vidage m (de) mémoire; **s. mark,** marque f de mémoire.

store (to), ranger en mémoire, mémoriser, stocker.

store and forward, prise f en charge (ou commutation f) de messages.

stored, s. program, programme enregistré; **s. program computer,** calculateur m à programme enregistré; **s. routine,** programme enregistré.

straight, s. binary, binaire pur; **s.-line coding,** codage m en succession.

stream, bit s., signal m binaire; **input job s.,** flot m des travaux en entrée; **s.-oriented transmission,** transmission f en continu (*PL/1*).

STRESS (=structural engineering system solver), langage m mathématique pour le calcul de la résistance des matériaux.

string, 1. chaîne f; **2.** monotonic f; **alphabetic(al) s.,** chaîne (de caractères) alphabétique(s); **binary element s.,** chaîne d'éléments binaires; **bit s.,** chaîne de chiffres binaires; **character s.,** chaîne de caractères; **null s.,** chaîne vide; **pulse s.,** train m d'impulsions; **symbol s.,** chaîne de symboles; **unit s.,** chaîne unitaire; **s. break,** rupture f de monotonie; **s. length,** longueur f de monotonie.

strip, connecting s., barrette f.

strobe (to), échantillonner.

stroke, segment m; **character s.,** segment de caractère; **Sheffer s.,** NON-ET; **s. analysis,** analyse f par traits élémentaires (ou segments) (*OCR*); **s. centreline,** ligne médiane d'un segment; **s. edge,** bord m de segment; **s. width,** largeur f de segment.

structural, s. engineering system solver (STRESS), langage m mathématique pour le calcul de la résistance des matériaux.

structure, list s., structure f de liste; **order s.,** format m d'instruction.

structured, s. programming, programmation structurée.

stub, s. card, carte *f* à volet.
study, étude *f*; **application s.,** étude d'application; **feasibility s.,** étude de praticabilité (*ou* préalable); **time s.,** étude des temps.
stunt, s. box, coffret *m* de commande.
STX (=**start of text character**), caractère *m* début de texte.
style, type s., style *m* du caractère.
stylus, s. input device, crayon lumineux, marqueur lumineux, stylet lumineux, luminostyle *m*; **s. printer,** imprimante *f* à stylets, imprimante à (matrice d')aiguilles.
SUB (=**substitute character**), caractère *m* substitut.
sub-assembly, sous-ensemble *m*.
sub-band, sous-bande *f*.
sub-carrier, intermediate s.-c., sous-porteuse *f* intermédiaire.
sub-centre, sous-centre *m*.
subject, s. program, programme *m* source.
subminiature, subminiature *adj*.
subordinate, s. overlay, segment *m* de recouvrement secondaire.
subprogram, sous-programme *m*.
subroutine, sous-programme *m*; **closed s.,** sous-programme fermé; **dating s.,** sous-programme dateur; **direct insert s.,** sous-programme relogeable; **division s.,** sous-programme de division; **dynamic s.,** sous-programme paramétrable; **editing s.,** sous-programme éditeur; **first-order s.,** sous-programme de premier niveau; **first remove s.,** sous-programme de premier niveau; **inline s.,** sous-programme relogeable; **library s.,** sous-programme de bibliothèque; **linked s.,** sous-programme fermé; **mathematical s.,** sous-programme mathématique; **one-level s.,** sous-programme à un niveau; **open s.,** sous-programme relogeable; **second-order s.,** sous-programme de second niveau; **second remove s.,** sous-programme de second niveau; **standard s.,** sous-programme standard; **static s.,** sous-programme non paramétrable; **two-level s.,** sous-programme à deux niveaux; **s. call,** appel *m* d'un sous-programme; **s. library,** bibliothèque *f* de sous-programmes.
subroutines, nesting s., sous-programmes emboîtés.
subscriber, abonné *m*; **calling s.,** abonné demandeur; **telephone s.,** abonné au téléphone; **telex s.,** abonné au (service) télex; **s. line,** ligne *f* d'abonné; **s.'s loop,** ligne *f* d'abonné.
subscript, indice inférieur.
subscripting, indiçage *m*.
subsequence, s. counter, compteur *m* auxiliaire.
subset, 1. sous-ensemble *m*; **2.** modem *m*; **alphabetic(al) character s.,** jeu partiel de caractères alphabétiques; **alphanumeric character s.,** jeu partiel de caractères alphanumériques; **character s.,** jeu partiel de caractères, sous-ensemble de caractères; **digital s., 1.** ensemble *m* de données; **2.** unité *f* de transmission; **numeric character s.,** jeu partiel de caractères numériques.
substitute, s. character (SUB), caractère *m* substitut; **s. mode,** mode *m* de substitution.
substitution, substitution *f*; **address s.,** substitution d'adresses.
substrate, substrat *m*.
subsystem, sous-système *m*; **job entry s. (JES),** sous-système de soumission des travaux.
subtracter, soustracteur *m*; **adder-s.,** additionneur/soustracteur *m*; **digital s.,** soustracteur numérique; **full s.,** soustracteur complet; **half s.,** demi-soustracteur *m*; **one-digit s.,** demi-soustracteur *m*; **parallel full s.,** soustracteur parallèle; **parallel half s.,** demi-soustracteur *m* parallèle; **serial full s.,** soustracteur série; **serial half s.,** demi-soustracteur *m* série; **three-input s.,** soustracteur à trois entrées; **two-input s.,** soustracteur à deux entrées.
subtraction, soustraction *f*.
subtrahend, diminuteur *m*, quantité *f* à soustraire.
suffix, indice inférieur.
sum, somme *f*; **arithmetic s.,** somme arithmétique; **check s.,** total *m* de contrôle; **logical s.,** disjonction *f*, réunion *f*, opération *f* OU; **modulo 2 s.,** somme modulo-2; **partial s.,** somme partielle; **s. check,** contrôle *m* par totalisation (*ou* addition); **s. check digit,** chiffre *m* de contrôle de totalisation.
summary, 1. résumé *m*; **2.** récapitulatif (-ive) *adj*.; **s. card,** carte récapitulative; **s. punch,** perforateur récapitulateur,

poinçonneuse récapitulatrice.
summation, s. check, contrôle *m* par totalisation (*ou* addition).
summer, additionneur *m* analogique.
summing, s. amplifier, amplificateur *m* de sommation; **s. integrator,** intégrateur additionneur.
superconductivity, supraconductivité *f*, supraconductibilité *f*.
superconductor, supraconducteur *m ou adj*.
supergroup, groupe *m* secondaire; **s. allocation,** répartition *f* des groupes secondaires; **s. link,** liaison *f* en groupe secondaire; **s. reference pilot,** onde *f* pilote de groupe secondaire; **s. section,** section *f* de groupe secondaire.
superposed, s. circuit, circuit superposé.
superscript, indice supérieur.
supervision, surveillance *f*, supervision *f*.
supervisor, (programme *m*) superviseur *m ou adj*.; **overlay s.,** superviseur de segments de recouvrement; **paging s.,** superviseur de pagination; **s. lock,** verrouillage *m* du superviseur; **s. mode,** mode *m* (de) superviseur.
supervisory, s. channel, voie *f* de surveillance, voie *f* de supervision; **s. control,** commande *f* de surveillance; **s. instruction,** instruction *f* de contrôle d'exécution; **s. program,** programme *m* superviseur; **s. relay,** relais *m* de supervision; **s. routine,** programme *m* superviseur; **s. signal,** signal *m* de supervision; **s. state,** état *m* superviseur.
supplementary, supplémentaire *adj*.; **s. maintenance,** entretien *m* supplémentaire; **s. maintenance time,** temps *m* d'entretien supplémentaire.
supply, mains s., secteur *m*, alimentation *f* secteur; **power s.,** alimentation *f*, source *f* d'énergie; **reference s.,** alimentation *f* de référence; **s. voltage,** tension *f* d'alimentation.
suppressed, s. carrier transmission, transmission *f* à suppression d'onde porteuse.
suppression, suppression *f*; **space s.,** suppression d'espaces; **transmission with partial sideband s.,** transmission *f* avec bande latérale partiellement supprimée, transmission *f* à bandes latérales asymétriques;

zero s., suppression de zéros.
suppressor, echo s., suppresseur *m* d'écho, éliminateur *m* d'écho; **parasitic s.,** éliminateur *m* de parasites, dispositif *m* antiparasites.
suspense, s. file, fichier *m* de relance.
swing, frequency s., excursion *f* de fréquence.
switch, 1. interrupteur *m*; 2. commutateur *m*; 3. aiguillage *m* de programme; **alteration s.,** inverseur *m*; **breakpoint s.,** inverseur *m* de point d'interruption; **call s.,** commutateur d'appel; **change-over s.,** commutateur; **control s.,** commutateur de commande, commutateur de contrôle; **crossbar s.,** commutateur crossbar; **cutout s.,** coupe-circuit *m*, interrupteur; **electronic s.,** commutateur électronique; **emergency s.,** interrupteur de secours; **programmed s.,** renvoi *m* multiple; **rotary s.,** commutateur rotatif; **sense s.,** inverseur *m*; **step-by-step s.,** commutateur pas-à-pas; **tape feed s.,** commutateur d'alimentation de bande; **toggle s.,** interrupteur à bascule; **s. core,** tore *m* de commutation; **s. insertion,** introduction *f* par commutateur; **s. room,** salle *f* de commutation; **s. storage,** mémoire *f* à commande manuelle.
switchboard, 1. commutateur manuel, standard *m*; 2. panneau *m* de commutation, panneau de commande; **telex s.,** commutateur télex.
switched, s. network, réseau commuté.
switching, commutation *f*; **automatic message s.,** commutation automatique de messages; **circuit s.,** commutation de circuit(s); **input/output s.,** commutation de canaux d'entrée-sortie; **line s.,** commutation de ligne(s); **message s.,** prise *f* en charge (*ou* commutation *f*) de messages; **packet s.,** commutation de paquets; **push-button s.,** commutation par bouton(s)-poussoir(s); **reperforator s.,** commutation avec retransmission par bande perforée; **s. centre,** centre *m* de commutation; **s. circuit,** circuit *m* de commutation; **s. control pilot,** onde *f* pilote de commutation; **s. network,** réseau *m* de commutation; **s. pilot,** onde *f* pilote de commutation; **s. relay,** relais *m* de commutation; **s. signal,** signal *m* de commutation; **s. space,** espace *m* de commutation; **s. threshold,** seuil *m* de com-

mutation; **s. time, 1.** temps *m* de commutation; **2.** temps *m* de changement d'état.

switchover, commutation *f.*

syllable, syllabe *f.*

symbol, symbole *m*; **abstract s.,** symbole abstrait; **breakpoint s.,** symbole de renvoi sur point d'interruption; **check s.,** symbole de contrôle; **external s.,** symbole externe; **flowchart s.,** symbole d'organigramme; **functional s.,** symbole fonctionnel; **graphic s.,** symbole graphique; **logic(al) s.,** symbole logique; **mnemonic s.,** symbole mnémonique; **special s.,** caractère spécial; **terminal s.,** marque *f* de fin de bloc (*sur bande perforée*); **terminating s.,** marque *f* de fin de bloc (*sur bande perforée*); **s. string,** chaîne *f* de symboles; **s. table,** table *f* des symboles.

symbolic, symbolique *adj.*; **s. address,** adresse *f* symbolique; **s. addressing,** adressage *m* symbolique; **s. assembly system,** système *m* d'assemblage symbolique; **s. code,** code *m* symbolique; **s. coding,** programmation *f* symbolique; **s. deck,** jeu *m* de cartes-programme en langage symbolique (*ou* en langage source); **s. instruction,** instruction *f* symbolique; **s. language,** langage *m* symbolique; **s. logic,** logique *f* symbolique; **s. name,** nom *m* symbolique; **s. notation,** notation *f* symbolique; **s. number,** nombre *m* symbolique; **s. programming,** programmation *f* (en langage) symbolique.

symmetric, s. difference, exclusion *f* réciproque, opération *f* de non-équivalence; **s. difference gate,** circuit OU exclusif.

symmetrical, symétrique *adj.*; **s. cyclically magnetized condition,** magnétisation *f* cyclique symétrique.

SYN (=**synchronous idle character**), caractère *m* de synchronisation.

sync., s. bits, bits *m* de synchronisation.

synch (*Am.*), signal *m* de début de bloc.

synchro, selsyn *m.*

synchronization, s. character, caractère *m* de synchronisation.

synchronize (to), synchroniser.

synchronizer, dispositif *m* de synchronisation; **tape s.,** synchroniseur *m* d'unités de bande.

synchronizing, s. pilot, onde *f* pilote de synchronisation; **s. pulse,** impulsion *f* de synchronisation.

synchronous, synchrone *adj.*; **s. computer,** calculateur *m* synchrone; **s. idle character (SYN),** caractère *m* de synchronisation; **s. machine,** machine *f* synchrone; **s. mode,** mode *m* synchrone; **s. operation,** fonctionnement *m* synchrone; **s. system,** système *m* synchrone; **s. transmission,** transmission *f* synchrone, transmission *f* isochrone; **s. working,** fonctionnement *m* synchrone.

synergic, synergique *adj.*

synergy, synergie *f.*

syntax, syntaxe *f.*

synthesis, synthèse *f.*

synthetic, synthétique *adj.*; **s. address,** adresse générée; **s. language,** langage *m* synthétique, langage artificiel.

system, système *m*; **accuracy control s.,** système de contrôle de précision; **adaptive control s.,** système à auto-contrôle; **addressed s.,** système adressé; **addressing s.,** système d'adressage; **all-relay s.** (*Am.*), système automatique tout à relais; **assembly s.,** système d'assemblage; **automatic data processing s.,** système automatique de traitement de l'information; **automatic s.,** système automatique; **basic operating s.,** système d'exploitation de base; **binary coded decimal s.,** système décimal codé binaire; **binary number s.,** système de nombres binaires; **bridge duplex s.,** système duplex à pont; **carrier s.,** système à courants porteurs; **computer s.,** système de traitement de l'information, système informatique, système de calcul; **crossbar s.,** système crossbar; **data processing s.,** système de traitement de l'information, système informatique; **data transfer s.,** système de transmission des données; **decimal numbering s.,** système de numération décimale; **decision feedback s.,** système détecteur d'erreurs avec demande de répétition; **detection s.,** système de détection; **disk operating s. (D.O.S.),** système d'exploitation sur disques; **ducol (punched card) s.,** système de perforation double par colonne; **duplex computer s.,** système à ordinateurs en double; **duplexed**

s., système duplexé; **duplex s.,** système duplex; **electronic data processing s.,** système électronique de traitement de l'information; **electronic funds transfer s.,** système automatique de transactions bancaires; **error-correcting s.,** système correcteur d'erreurs; **error-detecting and feedback s.,** système détecteur d'erreurs avec demande de répétition; **error-detecting s.,** système détecteur d'erreurs (sans répétition); **exception principle s.,** système de traitement par exception; **executive s.,** système d'exploitation; **feedback s.,** système correcteur d'erreurs par retour de l'information; **fixed-length record s.,** système d'articles en longueur fixe; **hybrid s.,** système (*ou* ensemble *m*) mixte; **information feedback s.,** système correcteur d'erreurs par retour de l'information; **information retrieval s.,** système de recherche de l'information; **information s., 1.** système informatique; **2.** système d'informations; **in-plant s.,** système intérieur; **input/output control s. (I.O.C.S.),** système de contrôle des entrées-sorties; **management information s.,** système intégré de gestion; **manual s.,** système manuel; **master/slave s.,** système à ordinateurs principal et asservi(s); **message switching s.,** système de commutation de messages; **monitor s.,** système d'exploitation; **multichannel s.,** système multivoie; **multiple-channel carrier s.,** système multivoie à courants porteurs; **multiple s.,** multicalculateur *m*, multiprocesseur *m*; **multiplex s.,** système multiplex; **multisequential s.,** système à multiprogrammation; **number representation s.,** système de numération; **number s.,** système de numération; **numeral s.,** système de numération; **numeration s.,** système de numération; **octal number s.,** système de numération octale; **offline s.,** système autonome, système non connecté; **online s.,** système connecté; **operating s.,** système d'exploitation; **out-plant s.,** système à terminaux extérieurs; **pilot s.,** système pilote; **polar direct-current s.** (*Am.*), transmission *f* par double courant; **polymorphic s.,** système polymorphe; **programming s.,** système de programmation; **pulse metering s.,** système de comptage par impulsions; **pulse transmission s.,**

système de transmission par émission d'impulsions; **quadruplex s.,** système quadruplex; **real-time s.,** système en temps réel; **relay automatic s.,** système automatique tout à relais; **remote computing s.,** système de télétraitement; **request repeat s.,** système détecteur d'erreurs avec demande de répétition; **semi-automatic s.,** système semi-automatique; **sequential scheduling s.,** système séquentiel de prise en charge de travaux; **shared files s.,** système à fichiers communs; **slave s.,** système asservi; **start-stop s.,** système arythmique; **step-by-step s.,** système pas-à-pas; **stepped start-stop s.,** système arythmique cadencé; **symbolic assembly s.,** système d'assemblage symbolique; **synchronous s.,** système synchrone; **tandem s.,** système en tandem; **tape-operating s. (T.O.S.),** système d'exploitation sur bande (magnétique); **tape plotting s.,** système traceur commandé par bande; **telemetering s.,** système de télémesure; **telephone carrier s.,** système de téléphonie par courants porteurs; **telephone s.,** réseau *m* téléphonique, liaison *f* téléphonique; **teleprinter s.,** système de téléimprimeurs, liaison *f* par téléimprimeurs; **time-shared s.,** système en temps partagé; **time-sharing monitor s.,** système superviseur du partage de temps; **transmitting s.,** système émetteur, système transmetteur; **two-way s.,** liaison bilatérale; **Uniterm s.,** système à Unitermes (*Recherche documentaire*); **variable length record s.,** système d'articles en longueur variable; **voice-frequency telegraph s.,** système de télégraphie harmonique; **Zatocoding s.,** indexation précoordonnée (*Recherche documentaire*); **s. check,** contrôle *m* de système; **s. disk,** disque *m* de système; **s. documentation,** dossier *m* d'application; **s. generation,** génération *f* de système; **s. input unit,** appareil *m* d'entrée du système; **s. library,** bibliothèque *f* (de programmes) d'une installation; **s. output device,** appareil *m* de sortie du système; **s. output unit,** appareil *m* de sortie du système; **s. reliability,** fiabilité *f* du système; **s. test,** essai *m* de système.

systematic, systématique *adj.*; **s. error checking code,** code *m* de contrôle systématique d'erreurs.

systems, card s., systèmes *m* à cartes; **s. analysis,** analyse *f* de systèmes; **s. analyst,** analyste *m ou f* de systèmes; **s. design,** conception *f* de systèmes, analyse fonctionnelle; **s. flowchart,** organigramme *m* de système(s).

T

table, table *f,* tableau *m*; **addition t.,** table d'addition; **Boolean operation t.,** tableau d'opération booléenne; **channel status t.,** table d'état des canaux; **decision t.,** table de décision; **external page t. (XPT),** table des pages externes; **frame t.,** table des cadres de page; **function t.,** table des fonctions; **header t.,** table des en-têtes; **output t.,** table traçante; **page frame t.,** table des cadres de page; **page t. (PGT),** table des pages; **plotting t.,** table traçante; **real storage page t. (RSPT),** table des pages réelles, table RSPT; **segment t. (SGT),** table des segments; **symbol t.,** table des symboles; **truth t.,** table de vérité; **t. block,** subdivision *f* de table; **t. look-up,** consultation *f* de table, recherche *f* dans une table; **t. look-up instruction,** instruction *f* de consultation de table.
tabular, t. language, langage *m* de traitement de tables (de décision).
tabulate (to), 1. disposer en tables (*ou* tableaux); 2. imprimer des totaux.
tabulating, t. equipment, matériel *m* classique, tabulatrice *f.*
tabulation, tabulation *f*; **t. character,** caractère *m* de tabulation.
tabulator, tabulatrice *f*; **digital t.,** tabulatrice numérique.
tag, 1. étiquette *f,* drapeau *m*; 2. ticket *m*; **t. converting unit,** unité *f* de lecture d'étiquettes; **t. format,** format *m* d'étiquette.
takedown, 1. démontage *m*; 2. manipulations *f* (*sur périphériques*); **t. time,** temps *m* de manipulations (*sur périphériques*).
take-off, t.-o. spool, bobine émettrice, bobine dérouleuse.
take-up, t.-u. reel, bobine réceptrice, bobine enrouleuse; **t.-u. spool,** bobine réceptrice,

bobine enrouleuse.
tally, bande imprimée (*de caisse enregistreuse, etc.*); **t. reader,** lecteur *m* de bandes imprimées (*de caisses enregistreuses, etc.*).
tandem, t. central office (*Am.*), central *m* tandem; **t. exchange,** central *m* tandem; **t. system,** système *m* en tandem; **t. working,** fonctionnement *m* en tandem.
tank, 1. réservoir *m*; 2. réservoir *m* à mercure; 3. circuit oscillant, circuit *m* bouchon; **mercury t.,** réservoir à mercure; **t. circuit,** circuit oscillant, circuit bouchon.
tape, bande *f,* ruban *m*; **amendment t.,** bande (des) mouvements; **blank t.,** bande vierge; **calibrating t.,** bande d'étalonnage; **carriage control t.,** bande pilote; **carriage t.,** bande pilote; **chadded paper t.,** bande perforée à confettis détachés; **chadless paper t.,** bande perforée à confettis semi-attachés; **change t.,** bande (des) mouvements; **control t.,** bande pilote; **father t.,** bande de deuxième génération; **fully-perforated t.,** bande perforée à confettis détachés; **grandfather t.,** bande de première génération; **instruction t.,** bande programme; **library t.,** bande (de) bibliothèque; **low t.,** indication *f* de fin de bande (*sur un perforateur*); **magnetic t.,** bande magnétique; **master instruction t. (M.I.T.),** bande d'exploitation; **master library t.,** bande (de) bibliothèque générale; **master program t.,** bande d'exploitation; **master t.,** bande maîtresse, bande principale; **numerical t.,** bande pour la commande numérique de machines-outils; **object t.,** bande programme en langage objet; **paper t.,** bande perforée; **perforated t.,** bande perforée; **program t.,** bande programme; **punched t.,** bande perforée; **scratch t.,** bande de manœuvre; **son t.,** bande de troisième génération; **teletypewriter t.,** bande perforée de téléimprimeur; **transaction t.,** bande (des) mouvements; **vertical format unit t.,** bande pilote; **virgin t.,** bande vierge; **work t.,** bande (magnétique) de manœuvre; **t. alternation,** travail *m* en bascule sur dérouleurs; **t.-bound,** subordonné au débit (binaire) des dérouleurs; **t. cable,** câble *m* ruban; **t. cluster,** groupe *m* de dérouleurs; **t. comparator,** comparateur *m* de bandes (per-

forées); **t.-controlled carriage,** chariot *m* automatique; **t. core,** tore enroulé; **t. deck,** unité *f* de bande magnétique, dérouleur *m* de bande magnétique; **t. drive,** (dispositif *m* d')entraînement *m* de bande magnétique; **t. feed,** alimentation *f* de bande; **t. feed switch,** commutateur *m* d'alimentation de bande; **t. file,** fichier *m* sur bande; **t. group,** groupe *m* de dérouleurs; **t. handler,** unité *f* de bande magnétique, dérouleur *m* de bande magnétique; **t. input,** entrée *f* par bande; **t. label,** label *m* de bande; **t. leader,** début *m* de bande, amorce *f* de bande; **t. library,** magnétothèque *f*, bibliothèque *f* de bandes magnétiques; **t.-limited,** subordonné au débit (binaire) des dérouleurs; **t. mark,** marque *f* de bande; **t.-operating system (T.O.S.),** système *m* d'exploitation sur bande (magnétique); **t. perforator,** perforateur *m* de bande; **t. plotting system,** système traceur commandé par bande; **t. punch,** perforateur *m* de bande; **t. reader,** lecteur *m* de bande perforée; **t. relay,** transit *m* par bande perforée; **t. reproducer,** reproducteur *m* de bande; **t. serial number,** numéro *m* de série du fabricant (*de bande*); **t. skip,** saut *m* de bande; **t. sort,** tri *m* sur bande magnétique; **t. station,** unité *f* de bande magnétique, dérouleur *m* de bande magnétique; **t. synchronizer,** synchroniseur *m* d'unités de bande; **t. thickness,** épaisseur *f* de bande; **t.-to-card converter,** convertisseur *m* bande (à) cartes; **t. trailer,** fin *f* de bande; **t. transport (mechanism),** (dispositif *m* d')entraînement *m* de bande magnétique; **t. unit,** unité *f* de bande magnétique, dérouleur *m* de bande magnétique; **t. verifier,** vérificatrice *f* de bande; **t. width,** largeur *f* de bande; **t. wound core,** tore enroulé.

tapped, **t.-potentiometer function generator,** générateur *m* de fonctions à potentiomètres à prises.

target, **t. computer,** calculateur *m* objet; **t. configuration,** configuration *f* objet; **t. language,** langage *m* objet, langage généré; **t. program,** programme *m* objet, programme résultant, programme généré; **t. routine,** programme *m* objet, programme résultant, programme généré.

tariff, tarif *m*.

task, **1.** travail *m*, tâche *f*, unité *f* de traitement; **2.** programme *m*; **t. control block,** zone *f* de contrôle (d'enchaînement) de travaux; **t. dispatcher,** distributeur *m* de tâches; **t. management,** supervision *f* des travaux; **t. queue,** file *f* d'attente des travaux (*ou* des tâches).

TDL (=**tunnel diode logic**), logique *f* à diodes tunnels.

teaching, **t. machine,** machine *f* à enseigner.

technique, technique *f*.

techniques, **information retrieval t.,** techniques *f* de recherche documentaire.

technology, **solid logic t. (S.L.T.),** technologie *f* des circuits logiques transistorisés et/ou miniaturisés.

teleautograph (*Am.*), téléautographe *m*.

telecommunication(s), télécommunication(s) *f*.

telegraph, **t. alphabet,** alphabet *m* télégraphique; **t. centre,** centre *m* télégraphique; **t. channel,** voie *f* de communication télégraphique, voie *f* (de transmission) télégraphique; **t. circuit,** circuit *m* télégraphique; **t. code,** code *m* télégraphique; **t. connection,** communication *f* télégraphique, liaison *f* télégraphique; **t. demodulator,** démodulateur *m* télégraphique; **t. distortion,** distorsion *f* télégraphique; **t. modulation,** modulation *f* télégraphique; **t. modulator,** modulateur *m* télégraphique; **t. relay,** relais *m* télégraphique; **t. service,** service *m* télégraphique; **t. signal,** signal *m* télégraphique; **t. signal element,** élément *m* de signal télégraphique; **t. speed,** vitesse *f* télégraphique; **t. word,** mot *m* télégraphique.

telegraphy, télégraphie *f*; **automatic t.** (*Am.*), transmission *f* automatique; **carrier (current) t.,** télégraphie par courants porteurs; **facsimile t.,** télégraphie facsimilé; **frequency-shift t.,** télégraphie par déplacement de fréquence; **multicircuit carrier t.,** télégraphie multivoie par courants porteurs; **voice-frequency (multichannel) t.,** télégraphie harmonique.

telemeter, télémètre *m*, appareil *m* de télémesure.

telemetering, télémesure *f*; **t. channel,** voie *f* de télémesure; **t. circuit,** circuit *m* de télémesure; **t. coder,** appareil *m* de codage

des télémesures; **t. receiver,** récepteur *m* de télémesure; **t. system,** système *m* de télémesure; **t. transmitter,** émetteur *m* de télémesure; **t. transmitter-receiver,** émetteur-récepteur *m* de télémesure.
telephone, t. amplifier, répéteur *m* téléphonique; **t. cable link,** liaison *f* téléphonique par câble; **t. carrier system,** système *m* de téléphonie par courants porteurs; **t. channel,** voie *f* téléphonique; **t. charge,** taxe *f* téléphonique; **t. circuit,** circuit *m* téléphonique; **t. connection,** communication *f* téléphonique, liaison *f* téléphonique; **t. current,** courant *m* téléphonique; **t. data set,** unité *f* de transmission téléphonique; **t. exchange,** centre *m* (*ou* central *m*) téléphonique; **t. frequency,** fréquence *f* téléphonique; **t. line,** ligne *f* téléphonique; **t. link,** liaison *f* téléphonique; **t. network,** réseau *m* téléphonique; **t. operator,** téléphoniste *m ou f,* standardiste *m ou f*; **t. rate,** tarif *m* téléphonique; **t. receiver,** récepteur *m* téléphonique; **t. relay,** relais *m* téléphonique; **t. repeater,** répéteur *m* téléphonique; **t. service,** service *m* téléphonique; **t. station,** poste *m* téléphonique; **t. subscriber,** abonné *m* au téléphone; **t. system,** réseau *m* téléphonique, liaison *f* téléphonique; **t.-telegraph circuit,** liaison *f* téléphonique-télégraphique; **t. traffic,** trafic *m* téléphonique; **t. transmission,** transmission *f* téléphonique.
telephony, téléphonie *f*; **multicircuit carrier t.,** téléphonie multivoie par courants porteurs; **multiple carrier t.,** téléphonie multiple à courants porteurs.
teleprinter, téléimprimeur *m,* téléscripteur *m,* télétype *m*; **t. channel,** voie *f* de téléimprimeur; **t. circuit,** liaison *f* par téléimprimeurs; **t. connection,** liaison *f* par téléimprimeurs; **t. for duplex operation,** téléimprimeur pour service duplex; **t. line,** ligne *f* de téléimprimeurs; **t. network,** réseau *m* de téléimprimeurs; **t. service,** service *m* de téléimprimeurs; **t. signal,** signal *m* de téléimprimeur; **t. system,** système *m* de téléimprimeurs, liaison *f* par téléimprimeurs; **t. traffic,** trafic *m* par téléimprimeur; **t. transmission,** transmission *f* par téléimprimeur; **t. transmitter,** émetteur

m de téléimprimeur.
teleprinting, liaison *f* par téléimprimeur.
teleprocessing, télétraitement *m,* télégestion *f.*
teleprocessor, téléprocesseur *m.*
teletype, téléimprimeur *m,* téléscripteur *m,* télétype *m*; **t. paper,** bande *f* de téléimprimeur.
teletypewriter, téléimprimeur *m,* téléscripteur *m,* télétype *m*; **perforated-tape t.,** téléimprimeur à bande perforée; **t. channel,** voie *f* de téléimprimeur; **t. tape,** bande perforée de téléimprimeur.
telewriter, téléautographe *m.*
telex, télex *m*; **t. call,** communication *f* télex; **t. call office,** bureau *m* télex; **t. channel,** voie *f* télex; **t. charge,** taxe *f* télex; **t. circuit,** circuit *m* télex; **t. communications,** communications *f* télex; **t. connection,** liaison *f* télex, raccordement *m* télex; **t. correspondence,** message *m* télex; **t. exchange,** centre *m* (*ou* central *m*) télex; **t. network,** réseau *m* télex; **t. rate,** tarif *m* télex; **t. service,** service *m* télex; **t. station,** poste *m* télex; **t. subscriber,** abonné *m* au (service) télex; **t. switchboard,** commutateur *m* télex; **t. traffic,** trafic *m* télex; **t. transmission,** transmission *f* télex; **t. user,** usager *m* du télex.
teller, t. terminal, terminal *m* de guichet.
template, 1. gabarit *m*; 2. organigraphe *m.*
temporary, t. connection, connexion *f* temporaire; **t. storage,** mémoire *f* de travail, mémoire *f* de manœuvre.
ten, complement on t., complément *m* à dix.
tens, t. complement, complément *m* à dix.
terminal, terminal *m,* tête *f* de ligne, centre *m* tête de ligne; **central t.,** concentrateur *m*; **conversational t.,** terminal conversationnel, terminal de dialogue; **CRT t.,** terminal (à écran) cathodique; **data communication t.,** terminal de transmission de données; **graphical output t.,** terminal de visualisation; **inquiry display t.,** terminal d'interrogation à visualisation; **intelligent t.,** terminal intelligent, terminal lourd; **job-oriented t.,** terminal spécialisé; **multiplex data t.,** terminal multiplex (de transmission de données); **remote data t.,** terminal à distance; **teller t.,** terminal de guichet; **t. device,** terminal; **t. equipment,** (équipement *m*) terminal; **t. impedance,** impédance ter-

minale; **t. installation,** installation terminale, terminal; **t. symbol,** marque f de fin de bloc (*sur bande perforée*); **t. unit,** terminal.

terminate (to), arrêter, terminer.

terminated, t. line, ligne bouclée.

terminating, t. symbol, marque f de fin de bloc (*sur bande perforée*).

ternary, ternaire *adj.*; **t. incremental representation,** représentation f par accroissements à valeur ternaire; **t. notation,** numération f ternaire.

test, essai m, épreuve f, test m; **acceptance t.,** essai de réception; **bias t.,** test de marges, contrôle m par marges; **busy t.** (*Am.*), test d'occupation; **compatibility t.,** essai de compatibilité; **crippled-leapfrog t.,** test saute-mouton partiel; **destructive t.,** essai destructeur; **diagnostic t.,** test de diagnostic; **dynamic t.,** contrôle m dynamique; **engaged t.,** test d'occupation; **functional t.,** essai de fonctionnement; **high-low bias t.,** contrôle m par marges, test de marges; **leapfrog t.,** programme m de test sélectif, test saute-mouton; **marginal t.,** test de marges, contrôle m par marges; **program t.,** essai de programme; **pulse t.,** méthode f d'essai par impulsions; **routine t.,** essai périodique, essai courant; **static t.,** contrôle m statique; **system t.,** essai de système; **volume t.,** essai de matériel avec données réelles; **t. board** (*Am.*), table f d'essais; **t. case,** jeu m d'essai; **t. data,** données f d'essai; **t. pack,** jeu m d'essai (*sur cartes*); **t. problem,** problème m de contrôle, problème-test m; **t. program,** programme m d'essai, programme de test; **t. routine,** programme m d'essai, programme de test; **t. run,** passage m d'essai; **t. section,** section f d'essais; **t. tone,** signal m d'essai.

testing, essai m, contrôle m; **bias t.,** test m de marges, contrôle par marges; **echo t.,** contrôle par écho; **marginal t.,** contrôle par marges, test m de marges; **program t.,** essai de programme; **remote t.,** essais à distance; **t. time,** temps m de mise au point.

tetrad, tétrade f.

tetrode, tétrode f.

text, texte m; **full t.,** texte intégral (*Recherche documentaire*); **start of t.,** début m de texte; **t. editing,** édition f de texte; **t. mode,** mode

m texte.

theory, théorie f; **automata t.,** théorie des automates; **group t.,** théorie des groupes; **information t.,** théorie de l'information; **probability t.,** théorie des probabilités; **queueing t.,** théorie des files d'attente; **set t.,** théorie des ensembles.

thermionic, thermionique *adj.*; **t. relay,** relais m thermionique.

thermistor, thermistor m.

thermocouple, thermocouple m.

thesaurus, thésaurus m (*Recherche documentaire*).

thickness, épaisseur f; **tape t.,** épaisseur de bande; **wrap t.,** épaisseur d'enroulement.

thin, t. film, film m mince; **t. film memory,** mémoire f à film mince; **t. film store,** mémoire f à film mince.

third, t.-generation computer, calculateur m de troisième génération; **t.-level address,** adresse indirecte à trois niveaux.

thirty-nine, t.-n. feature code, code spécial 0-39 (*par colonne*).

thrashing, emballement m, affolement m.

three-address, à trois adresses f; **t.-a. code,** code m à trois adresses; **t.-a. instruction,** instruction f à trois adresses; **t.-a. instruction format,** format m d'instruction à trois adresses.

three-bit, t.-b. byte, triplet m.

three-input, t.-i. adder, additionneur m à trois entrées; **t.-i. subtracter,** soustracteur m à trois entrées.

three-level, t.-l. address, adresse indirecte à trois niveaux; **t.-l. addressing,** adressage indirect à trois niveaux.

three-plus-one, t.-p.-o. address, à trois adresses d'opérande et une adresse de commande.

threshold, seuil m; **switching t.,** seuil de commutation; **t. element,** élément m seuil à entrées pondérées; **t. value,** valeur-seuil f.

throat, card t., filière f.

throughput (*Am.* **thruput**), 1. débit m; 2. rendement m.

throw, paper t., saut m de papier.

throw-away, t.-a. character, caractère nul, caractère m de remplissage (d'espace *ou* de temps).

thyratron, thyratron m.

ticket, t. converter, convertisseur m de tickets.

tie, **t. line**, ligne privée; **t. trunk** (*A m.*), ligne privée.

time, temps *m*, durée *f*, période *f*; **acceleration t.**, temps d'accélération; **access t.**, temps d'accès; **add t.**, durée d'addition; **add-subtract t.**, durée d'addition/soustraction; **available t.**, temps disponible; **average operation t.**, temps moyen d'exploitation; **awaiting repair t.**, (temps d')attente *f* de dépannage; **carry t.**, temps de report; **code checking t.**, temps de mise au point; **compilation t.**, durée de compilation; **computer t.**, temps machine; **connection t.**, heure *f* d'établissement (d'une communication); **corrective maintenance t.**, durée de dépannage; **cycle t.**, durée de cycle; **dead t.**, temps mort; **debatable t.**, temps non imputable; **decay t.**, période d'extinction; **deceleration t.**, temps de décélération; **development t.**, temps de mise au point; **digit t.**, temps élémentaire; **down t.**, temps de panne; **effective t.**, temps d'utilisation effective; **engineering t.**, temps de maintenance; **execution t.**, temps d'exécution; **fault t.**, temps de panne; **idle t.**, temps d'attente; **incidentals t.**, temps d'utilisation annexe; **ineffective t.**, temps de non-utilisation; **installation t.**, temps d'installation; **instruction t.**, 1. temps de prise en charge d'instruction; 2. temps d'exécution; **latency t.**, temps d'attente; **machine-spoilt work t.**, temps perdu par incidents machine; **maintenance standby t.**, temps de garde; **makeup t.**, temps de reprise; **mean repair t.**, durée moyenne de réparation; **mean t. between failures (m.t.b.f.)**, intervalle moyen entre les pannes, temps moyen de bon fonctionnement; **mean t. between overhauls (m.t.b.o.)**, périodicité moyenne des révisions; **mean t. to failure (m.t.t.f.)**, temps moyen jusqu'à la panne; **mean t. to maintain (m.t.t.m.)**, durée moyenne de l'entretien; **mean t. to repair (m.t.t.r.)**, durée moyenne de réparation; **multiplication t.**, durée de multiplication; **no-charge machine fault t.**, temps non imputable dû à une panne machine; **no-charge non-machine fault t.**, temps non imputable non dû à une panne machine; **non-scheduled maintenance t.**, temps d'entretien non périodique (*ou* non planifié); **operation t.**, temps d'exploitation, temps opératoire;

operation(al) use t., temps d'utilisation effective; **out-of-service t.**, temps de non-disponibilité, temps d'immobilisation; **percentage occupied t.**, coefficient *m* d'occupation (*d'un faisceau de circuits*); **preventive maintenance t.**, temps d'entretien préventif; **production t.**, temps d'exploitation réelle; **productive t.**, temps d'exploitation réelle; **program development t.**, durée de mise au point de programmes; **program testing t.**, durée d'essai de programmes; **proving t.**, temps d'essai; **pulse decay t.**, durée d'extinction de l'impulsion; **pulse rise t.**, durée d'établissement de l'impulsion; **read t.**, temps d'accès; **receiver response t.**, temps de réponse (d'un récepteur); **reference t.**, moment *m* de référence; **repair delay t.**, temps d'attente de réparation; **repair t.**, temps de réparation; **response t.**, temps de réponse; **rise t.**, temps de montée; **routine maintenance t.**, temps d'entretien périodique (*ou* courant); **routing t.**, durée d'acheminement; **run t.**, durée d'exploitation; **scheduled maintenance t.**, temps d'entretien périodique (*ou* planifié); **search t.**, temps de recherche; **serviceable t.**, temps disponible; **servicing t.**, temps de maintenance; **set-up t.**, temps de préparation; **start t.**, temps d'accélération; **stop t.**, temps de décélération; **supplementary maintenance t.**, temps d'entretien supplémentaire; **switching t.**, 1. temps de commutation; 2. temps de changement d'état; **takedown t.**, temps de manipulations (*sur périphériques*); **testing t.**, temps de mise au point; **training t.**, temps de formation; **transfer t.**, durée de transfert; **turn-around t.**, 1. (*en télétraitement*) temps de basculement, temps de retournement, temps de renversement; 2. temps d'exécution; **unscheduled maintenance t.**, temps d'entretien non périodique (*ou* non planifié); **unused t.**, temps inutilisé; **up t.**, temps disponible; **usage t.**, temps d'utilisation; **waiting t.**, temps d'attente; **word t.**, période de mot; **write t.**, durée d'enregistrement; **t. base**, base *f* de temps, rythme *m*; **t. constant**, constante *f* de temps; **t.-derived channel**, voie dérivée en temps, sous-voie *f*; **t.-division multiplex**, multiplex *m* par partage du temps; **t.-pulse**

distributor, distributeur m de rythmes, distributeur d'impulsions d'horloge; t. relay, relais temporisé; t. scale factor, échelle f des temps; t. series, série f dans le temps; t.-shared system, système m en temps partagé; t. study, étude f des temps.

time-out, délai m d'attente.

timer, 1. minuterie f, rythmeur m; 2. horloge f; 3. base f de temps; 4. générateur m de rythme; interval t., rythmeur.

time-sharing, partage m de temps, temps partagé; conversational t.-s., partage de temps conversationnel; t.-s. computer, calculateur m en partage de temps; t.-s. monitor system, système m superviseur du partage de temps.

timing, t. diagram, diagramme m de temps; t. mark, marque f de synchronisation; t. mechanism, dispositif m de synchronisation; t. pulse, impulsion f de synchronisation; t. track, piste f de synchronisation.

title, key word in t. (KWIT), mot-clé m dans le titre (Recherche documentaire).

toggle, t. switch, interrupteur m à bascule.

tolerance, tolérance f; frequency t., tolérance de fréquence.

toll (Am.), interurbain adj.; t. call (Am.), communication interurbaine; t. circuit (Am.), circuit interurbain; t. office (Am.), central interurbain; t. switching trunk (Am.), ligne f intermédiaire.

tone, tonalité f, signal m, son m; test t., signal d'essai; t. dialling, appel m par boutons-poussoirs.

tools, automatically programmed t., machines-outils f à programme (ou à commande) automatique.

torn tape, t. t. relay (Am.), transit manuel par bande perforée; t. t. switching centre, centre m de commutation par bande perforée, centre de commutation à bandes coupées.

torque, couple m, torsion f; t. amplifier, coupleur synchronisé.

T.O.S. (=tape-operating system), système m d'exploitation sur bande (magnétique).

total, total m; batch t., total par groupe; check t., total de vérification; control t., total de contrôle; gibberish t., total mêlé de vérification, total de contrôle; hash t., total mêlé de vérification, total de contrôle; in-termediate t., total intermédiaire; major t., total de niveau supérieur; minor t., total de niveau inférieur; proof t., total de contrôle.

trace, selective t., programme m d'analyse sélective; t. program, programme m d'analyse, programme de dépistage; t. routine, programme m d'analyse, programme de dépistage.

tracing, traçage m; t. routine, programme m d'analyse, programme m de dépistage.

track, 1. chemin m; 2. piste f (d'un tambour, d'un disque); 3. voie f; address t., piste d'adresses; card t., chemin de cartes; clock t., piste de référence, piste de base de temps; code t., voie d'information; ejection t., piste d'éjection; feed t., piste d'alimentation; insertion t., piste d'insertion; library t., piste de référence; magnetic t., piste magnétique; punching t., piste de perforation; reading t., piste de lecture; regenerative t., piste à régénération; revolver t., piste à régénération; timing t., piste de synchronisation; t. density, densité f en (nombre de) pistes; t. hold, verrouillage m de piste; t. pitch, entraxe m de pistes.

traffic, trafic m; telephone t., trafic téléphonique; teleprinter t., trafic par téléimprimeur; telex t., trafic télex; t. capacity, capacité f d'écoulement de trafic.

trailer, tape t., fin f de bande; t. label, label m fin (de bande); t. record, enregistrement m complémentaire, article m secondaire.

trailing, t. edge, bord m arrière; t. end, fin f (de bande).

train, train m; pulse t., train d'impulsions.

training, t. time, temps m de formation.

transaction, t. data, données f variables (ou de mouvement); t. file, fichier m (des) mouvements, fichier (de) détail; t. record, enregistrement m (de) mouvement, enregistrement (de) détail; t. tape, bande f (des) mouvements.

transceiver, terminal m émetteur-récepteur; card t., émetteur-récepteur m à cartes perforées.

transcribe (to), transcrire, recopier.

transcriber, appareil m de transcription.

transducer, transducteur m; active t., transducteur actif.

transfer, 1. transfert m; 2. branchement m; 3. transmission f; block t., transfert de bloc(s); **conditional (control) t.**, branchement conditionnel, saut conditionnel; **control t.**, branchement, saut *m*; **information t.**, transfert d'information; **parallel t.**, transfert parallèle; **peripheral t.**, transfert périphérique (*ou* entre périphériques); **radial t.**, transfert radial, opération *f* d'entrée-sortie; **serial t.**, transfert en série; **unconditional t.**, branchement inconditionnel, branchement «toujours»; **t. admittance**, admittance *f* de transfert; **t. card**, carte *f* de lancement (de programme); **t. check**, contrôle *m* de transfert (par répétition); **t. function**, fonction *f* de transfert; **t. instruction**, instruction *f* de branchement, instruction de saut; **t. interpreter**, traductrice reporteuse, reporteuse *f*; **t. of control**, branchement, saut *m*; **t.-of-control card**, carte *f* de lancement (de programme); **t. operation**, 1. opération *f* de transfert; 2. opération *f* de saut; **t. rate**, débit *m*, vitesse *f* de transmission; **t. time**, durée *f* de transfert.

transfer (to), transférer, transmettre.
transfluxor, transfluxor *m*.
transform (to), transformer.
transformation, transformation *f*; **signal t.**, transformation de signaux.
transformer, transformateur *m*; **mains t.**, transformateur d'alimentation (secteur); **pulse t.**, transformateur d'impulsions.
transient, transitoire *adj.*
transistor, transistor *m*; **field effect t. (FET)**, transistor à effet de champ; **germanium t.**, transistor au germanium; **insulated-gate field-effect t. (IG FET)**, transistor à effet de champ à grille isolée; **MOS (=metal oxide semi-conductor) t.**, transistor métal-oxyde-semiconducteur (MOS); **n-p-n t.**, transistor n-p-n; **n-p-n-p t.**, transistor n-p-n-p; **p-n junction t.**, transistor à jonction p-n; **p-n-p t.**, transistor p-n-p; **p-n-p-n t.**, transistor p-n-p-n; **unijunction t.**, transistor unijonction; **t.-t. logic (TTL)**, logique *f* transistor-transistor.
transistorized, transistorisé *adj.*
transition, t. card, carte *f* de lancement (de programme).
translate (to), 1. traduire; 2. convertir.
translating, t. program, programme traducteur; **t. routine**, programme traducteur.

translation, traduction *f*; **algorithm t.**, traduction algorithmique; **channel program t.**, traduction du programme canal; **dynamic address t. (DAT)**, traduction dynamique d'adresse; **error rate of a t.**, taux *m* d'erreur d'une traduction; **frequency t.**, transposition *f* en fréquence; **language t.**, traduction de langage(s); **machine t.**, traduction automatique; **mechanical t.**, traduction automatique; **t. algorithm**, algorithme *m* de traduction (*de langages*).
translator, 1. (programme *m*) traducteur *m*; 2. traducteur (-trice) *adj.*; **code t.**, convertisseur *m* de codes; **language t.**, traducteur de langages; **one-for-one t.**, traducteur un(e) pour un(e).
transliterate (to), translitérer.
transmission, transmission *f*, émission *f*; **analog t.**, transmission analogique; **asymmetrical sideband t.**, transmission à bandes latérales asymétriques, transmission avec bande latérale partiellement supprimée; **asynchronous t.**, transmission asynchrone; **automatic t.**, transmission automatique; **data t.**, transmission de données; **direct current t.**, transmission par courant continu; **double-current t.**, transmission par double courant; **double-sideband t.**, émission sur double bande latérale; **end of t. (E.O.T.)**, fin *f* de transmission; **independent sideband t.**, transmission à bandes latérales indépendantes; **non-simultaneous t.**, transmission non simultanée; **parallel t.**, transmission parallèle; **point-to-point t.**, transmission (directe) entre deux points; **pulse modulated t.**, émission modulée par impulsions; **serial t.**, transmission série; **simultaneous t.**, transmission simultanée; **single-current t.**, transmission par simple courant; **single sideband t.**, émission sur bande latérale unique; **start-stop t.**, transmission arythmique; **stream-oriented t.**, transmission en continu (*PL/1*); **suppressed carrier t.**, transmission à suppression d'onde porteuse; **synchronous t.**, transmission synchrone, transmission isochrone; **telephone t.**, transmission téléphonique; **teleprinter t.**, transmission par téléimprimeur; **telex t.**, transmission télex; **t. channel**, voie *f* de transmission; **t.**

control character, caractère *m* de commande de transmission; **t. control unit,** unité *f* de contrôle de transmission; **t. gain,** gain *m* de transmission; **t. level** (*Am.*), niveau relatif de puissance; **t. line,** ligne *f* de transmission; **t. link,** chaînon *m* de voie (de transmission *ou* de communication); **t. loss,** perte *f* de transmission; **t. performance,** qualité *f* de transmission; **t. speed,** vitesse *f* de transmission; **t. with partial sideband suppression,** transmission avec bande latérale partiellement supprimée, transmission à bandes latérales asymétriques.

transmit, t. operation, opération *f* de transfert.

transmit (to), 1. transmettre, émettre; 2. effectuer un transfert (d'information), transférer.

transmitted, t. sideband (*Am.*), bande principale.

transmitter, émetteur *m*, transmetteur *m*; **automatic t.,** émetteur automatique, transmetteur automatique; **automatic numbering t.,** numéroteur *m* automatique; **data t.,** transmetteur de données; **pulse t.,** émetteur d'impulsions; **telemetering t.,** émetteur de télémesure; **teleprinter t.,** émetteur de téléimprimeur; **t. distributor,** distributeur transmetteur; **t. start code,** code *m* de lancement de transmission.

transmitter-receiver, émetteur-récepteur *m*; **telemetering t.-r.,** émetteur-récepteur de télémesure.

transmitting, t. device, appareil *m* de transmission; **t. system,** système émetteur, système transmetteur.

transparent, t. mode, mode transparent.

transport, tape t., (dispositif *m* d')entraînement *m* de bande magnétique.

transportation, document t., alimentation *f* de documents.

transposition, transposition *f*.

transput, t. process, transfert radial, opération *f* d'entrée-sortie.

transverse, t. check, contrôle transversal.

trap, déroutement *m*; **channel t.,** déroutement par canal; **data transmission t.,** déroutement en transmission de données; **t. setting,** déclenchement *m* d'un déroutement.

trapezoidal, t. integration, intégration

trapézoïdale.

trapping, déroutement *m* (sur incident).

traverse, t. speed, vitesse *f* de défilement (*d'une bande*).

tray, chip t., bac *m* à confettis, tiroir *m* à confettis.

triad, triade *f*.

tributary, t. circuit, circuit *m* tributaire; **t. station,** station *f* tributaire.

trigger, monostable t., multivibrateur *m* monostable; **t. pair,** bascule *f*; **t. tube,** tube *m* de déclenchement.

trigger (to), déclencher, lancer (un programme).

triode, triode *f*.

triple, pulse t., groupe *m* de trois impulsions; **t. error,** erreur *f* triple; **t. precision,** triple précision *f*.

triple-length, t.-l. working, fonctionnement *m* en longueur triple.

triplet, triplet *m*.

trouble, t. location problem, problème *m* de localisation de panne.

trouble-shoot (to), 1. mettre au point (*un programme*); 2. dépanner.

trouble-shooting, 1. mise *f* au point; 2. dépannage *m*, recherche *f* des dérangements.

true, t. complement, complément *m* à la base, complément *m* à zéro.

true-time, t.-t. operation, fonctionnement *m* en temps réel.

truncate (to), tronquer.

truncation, troncature *f*; **t. error,** erreur *f* de troncature.

trunk, 1. (*Am.*) jonction *f*; 2. circuit *m* (télégraphique) de jonction; 3. ligne *f* auxiliaire; 4. voie principale, canal *m*; 5. interurbain *adj.*; **check t.,** voie *f* de contrôle; **common t.,** ligne commune; **digit transfer t.,** voie *f* de transfert de chiffres; **individual t.,** ligne individuelle; **recording t.** (*Am.*), ligne d'annotatrice; **tie t.** (*Am.*), ligne privée; **toll switching t.** (*Am.*), ligne intermédiaire; **t. call,** communication interurbaine; **t. circuit,** circuit interurbain; **t. exchange,** central interurbain; **t. junction,** ligne intermédiaire.

trunks, input/output t., voies *f* d'entrée-sortie.

truth, t. table, table *f* de vérité.

TTL (=transistor-transistor logic), logique *f*

transistor-transistor.
tube, tube *m,* lampe *f*; **acorn t., **tube gland; **amplifier t.,** tube amplificateur, lampe amplificatrice; **cathode ray t. (CRT),** tube à rayons cathodiques, tube cathodique; **display t.,** tube-écran *m,* tube d'affichage; **electrostatic storage t.,** tube d'accumulation électrostatique; **Nixie t.,** tube Nixie; **storage t.,** tube-mémoire *m*; **trigger t.,** tube de déclenchement; **vacuum t.,** tube à vide; **video t.,** tube vidéo.
tunnel, t. diode, diode *f* tunnel; **t. diode logic (TDL),** logique *f* à diodes tunnels.
Turing, T. machine, simulateur *m* mathématique de calculateur.
turn around, t. a. document, document circulant (*ou* tournant); **t. a. time, 1.** (*en télétraitement*) temps *m* de basculement, temps *m* de retournement, temps *m* de renversement; **2.** temps *m* d'exécution.
turning, page t., transfert *m* de page.
turn off (to), couper, mettre hors circuit.
turn on (to), brancher, mettre en circuit.
TV, TV camera scanner, analyseur *m* à caméra de télévision (*OCR*).
twelve punch, perforation *f* «douze».
twenty-nine, t.-n. feature code, code spécial 0-29 (*par colonne*).
twin, t. check, double contrôle *m.*
two, scale of t., notation *f* binaire; **t. scale,** notation *f* binaire.
two-address, à deux adresses *f*; **t.-a. code,** code *m* à deux adresses; **t.-a. instruction,** instruction *f* à deux adresses; **t.-a. instruction format,** format *m* d'instruction à deux adresses.
two-core-per-bit, t.-c.-p.-b. store, mémoire *f* à deux tores par bit.
two-input, t.-i. adder, additionneur *m* à deux entrées; **t.-i. subtracter,** soustracteur *m* à deux entrées.
two-level, t.-l. address, adresse indirecte à deux niveaux; **t.-l. addressing,** adressage indirect à deux niveaux; **t.-l. subroutine,** sous-programme *m* à deux niveaux.
two-out-of-five, t.-o.-o.-f. code, code *m* deux parmi cinq, code *m* quinaire.
two-plus-one, t.-p.-o. address, à deux adresses d'opérande et une adresse de commande; **t.-p.-o. address instruction,** instruction *f* à deux adresses d'opérande et une adresse de commande; **t.-p.-o. address in-** **struction format,** format *m* d'instruction à deux adresses d'opérande et une adresse de commande.
twos, t. complement, complément *m* à deux.
two-state, t.-s. variable, variable *f* binaire.
two-tone, t.-t. keying, télégraphie *f* à deux fréquences porteuses; **t.-t. modulation,** modulation *f* à deux fréquences porteuses.
two-valued, t.-v. variable, variable *f* binaire.
two-way, t.-w. system, liaison bilatérale.
two-wire, t.-w. channel, voie *f* à deux fils; **t.-w. circuit,** circuit *m* à deux fils.
type, 1. type *m*; **2.** caractère *m* d'imprimerie; **t. bar,** barre *f* d'impression, barre porte-caractères; **t. drum,** tambour *m* d'impression; **t. face,** œil *m* (du caractère) (*OCR*); **t. font,** fonte *f,* ensemble *m* de caractères, police *f*; **t. style,** style *m* du caractère; **t. wheel,** roue *f* d'impression.
type (to), dactylographier, taper (à la machine).
typesetting, composition *f*; **automatic t.,** composition automatique (des textes); **computerized t.,** composition automatisée (*ou* assistée par ordinateur).
typewriter, machine *f* à écrire; **console t.,** machine à écrire de pupitre; **input/output t.,** machine à écrire d'entrée-sortie; **interrogating t.,** machine à écrire d'entrée-sortie; **online t.,** machine à écrire connectée.

U

U format, format *m* en longueur indéterminée.
UHF (=ultra-high frequency), ultra-haute fréquence.
ultra-high, u.-h. frequency (UHF), ultra-haute fréquence.
ultrasonics, science *f* des ultrasons.
unary, u. operation, opération *f* à un (seul) opérande.
unattended, u. answering, réponse *f* automatique.
unblock (to), dégrouper.
unbundling, facturation *f* (*ou* tarification *f*) séparée, dégroupage *m* des tarifs.
unconditional, u. branch, branchement

inconditionnel, branchement *m*
«toujours»; **u. branch instruction,** instruction *f* de branchement sans condition; **u.
control transfer instruction,** instruction *f*
de branchement sans condition; **u. jump,**
branchement inconditionnel, branchement
m «toujours»; **u. jump instruction,** instruction *f* de branchement sans condition; **u.
transfer,** branchement inconditionnel,
branchement *m* «toujours»; **u. transfer instruction,** instruction *f* de branchement
sans condition.

underflow, dépassement inférieur de
capacité, dépassement négatif;
characteristic u., dépassement négatif de la
caractéristique.

underpunch, perforation *f* 1 à 9.

undetected, u. error rate, taux *m* d'erreurs
résiduelles.

undisturbed, u. one-output signal, signal
m de sortie «un» sans perturbation; **u. output signal,** signal *m* de sortie sans perturbation; **u. response signal,** signal *m* de sortie sans perturbation; **u. response voltage,**
signal *m* de sortie sans perturbation; **u.
zero-output signal,** signal *m* de sortie
«zéro» sans perturbation.

unexpected, u. halt, arrêt imprévu (*d'un
programme*).

uniform, u. random number, nombre *m*
aléatoire.

uniformly, u. accessible store, mémoire *f* à
accès direct, mémoire *f* à accès sélectif.

unijunction, u. transistor, transistor *m*
unijonction.

union, opération *f* OU; **u. gate,** circuit *m*
OU.

unipolar, unipolaire *adj.*

unipunch, perforatrice *f* à perforation
unique.

uniselector, commutateur rotatif.

unit, unité *f*, organe *m*, dispositif *m*, ensemble *m*, élément *m*; **AND u.,** élément ET;
answerback u., émetteur *m* automatique
d'indicatif; **anticoincidence u.,** circuit *m* de
non-équivalence; **arithmetic and logical u.
(A.L.U.),** unité arithmétique et logique;
arithmetic u., unité arithmétique; **assembly
u.,** 1. unité d'assemblage; 2. segment *m* (de
programme) assemblable; **audio response
u.,** unité de réponse vocale; **automatic
calling u.,** dispositif automatique d'appel;

automatic dialling u., dispositif
automatique de sélection; **binary u.,** unité
binaire; **card punch u.,** perforateur *m* de
cartes; **card reader u.,** lecteur *m* de cartes;
central control u., unité centrale de commande; **central processing u. (C.P.U.),** unité centrale de traitement; **central u.,** unité
centrale; **code element u.,** unité d'éléments
de code; **coincidence u.,** dispositif
d'équivalence; **comparing u.,** comparateur
m; **consistent u.,** élément cohérent; **control
u.,** unité de commande; **data adapter u.,**
adaptateur *m* de ligne(s); **data display u.,**
unité d'affichage de données; **disk drive u.,**
unité de disques; **display u.,** unité
d'affichage, unité de visualisation; **equality
u.,** élément d'égalité, comparateur *m*
d'égalité; **graphic display u.,** unité
d'affichage graphique; **identity u.,** élément
d'identité, comparateur *m* d'identité; **input
u.,** unité d'entrée, élément d'introduction;
input/output u., élément d'entrée-sortie,
dispositif d'entrée-sortie; **inquiry u.,** unité
d'interrogation; **linear u.,** élément linéaire;
logical u., unité logique; **magnetic tape u.,**
unité de bande magnétique, dérouleur *m* de
bande magnétique; **manual input u.,** dispositif d'entrée manuelle; **master u.,** unité
pilote; **monitor u.,** appareil *m* de surveillance (*ou* de contrôle); **multicomputing
u.,** multicalculateur *m*, multiprocesseur *m*;
online u., unité connectée; **output u.,** élément de sortie, unité d'extraction; **paper
tape u.,** unité de bande perforée; **peripheral
control u.,** unité de commande de
périphériques; **peripheral u.,** unité
périphérique; **plug-in u.,** plaquette *f* embrochable (*ou* interchangeable); **program
control u.,** contrôleur *m* d'exécution de
programme; **read punch u.,** lecteur-perforateur *m*; **system input u.,** appareil *m*
d'entrée du système; **system output u.,** appareil *m* de sortie du système; **tag converting u.,** unité de lecture d'étiquettes; **tape u.,**
unité de bande magnétique, dérouleur *m* de
bande magnétique; **terminal u.,** terminal *m*;
transmission control u., unité de contrôle
de transmission; **visual display u. (VDU),**
unité de visualisation (cathodique); **volume
u.** (*Am.*), unité de volume; **u. control word,**
mot *m* de commande d'unité; **u. distance
code,** code *m* à signaux à espacement uni-

taire; **u. element,** élément unitaire; **u. interval,** intervalle *m* unitaire; **u. record equipment** (*Am.*), matériel *m* classique; **u. separator,** séparateur *m* d'unités; **u. separator character,** caractère *m* de séparation de blocs; **u. string,** chaîne *f* unitaire.

Uniterm, U. indexing, indexation *f* par Unitermes (*Recherche documentaire*); **U. system,** système *m* à Unitermes (*Recherche documentaire*).

unmask (to), démasquer.

unmodified, u. instruction, instruction *f* sous forme initiale.

unpack (to), 1. décondenser; 2. dégrouper.

unscheduled, u. maintenance time, temps *m* d'entretien non périodique (*ou* non planifié).

unset (to), remettre à l'état initial, réinitialiser, rétablir, restaurer.

unused, u. time, temps inutilisé.

unverified, u. failure, défaillance non contrôlée.

up, u. time, temps *m* disponible.

up and down, u. and d. working, exploitation *f* à l'alternat.

update (to), mettre à jour.

updating, mise *f* à jour.

upper, u. curtate, portion *f* des rangées supérieures (*d'une carte*).

upper case, u. c. letters, (lettres *f*) majuscules *f*.

usage, u. time, temps *m* d'utilisation.

USASCII (=U.S.A. Standard Code for Information Interchange), code standard américain pour l'échange d'information.

use, joint u., utilisation *f* en commun.

user, 1. utilisateur *m*; 2. usager *m*; **telex u.,** usager du télex; **u.'s set,** poste *m* (d')utilisateur.

utility, u. program, programme *m* de service; **u. routine,** programme *m* de service.

utilization, u. ratio, taux *m* d'utilisation.

V

vacuum, vide *m*; **v. column,** puits *m* à vide; **v. tube,** tube *m* à vide.

validity, validité *f*; **data v.,** validité des données; **v. check,** contrôle *m* de validité.

value, valeur *f*; **absolute v.,** valeur absolue; **code v.,** combinaison *f* de code, élément *m* de code; **end v.,** valeur limite; **numerical v.,** grandeur *f* numérique; **r.-m.-s. v.,** valeur efficace; **threshold v.,** valeur-seuil *f*.

valve, lampe *f*, tube *m*; **amplifier v.,** lampe amplificatrice, tube amplificateur.

variable, variable *f* ou *adj.*; **based v.,** variable pointée (*PL/1*); **binary-state v.,** variable binaire; **binary v.,** variable binaire; **Boolean v.,** variable booléenne; **controlled v.,** variable contrôlée; **dependent v.,** variable dépendante; **independent v.,** variable indépendante; **logical v.,** variable logique; **machine v.,** variable machine; **manipulated v.,** variable élaborée; **two-state v.,** variable binaire; **two-valued v.,** variable binaire; **v. address,** adresse indexée; **v. block,** bloc *m* à longueur variable; **v. connector,** renvoi *m* multiple; **v. field,** champ *m* variable; **v. function generator,** générateur *m* de fonctions variables; **v. length record system,** système *m* d'articles en longueur variable; **v. logic,** logique programmée; **v. multiplier,** multiplicateur *m* analogique; **v.-point representation,** représentation *f* à virgule variable, numération *f* à séparation variable; **v. speed gear,** mécanisme intégrateur; **v. word length,** longueur *f* variable de mot.

variable-length, v.-l. record, enregistrement *m* en longueur variable; **v.-l. word,** mot *m* en longueur variable.

varioplex, varioplex *m*.

VDU (=visual display unit), unité *f* de visualisation (cathodique).

vector, vecteur *m*; **v. quantity,** grandeur vectorielle.

Veitch, V. chart, diagramme *m* de Veitch; **V. diagram,** diagramme *m* de Veitch.

Venn, V. diagram, diagramme *m* de Venn.

verge, v.-perforated card, carte *f* à perforations marginales; **v.-punched card,** carte *f* à perforations marginales.

verified, v. failure, défaillance contrôlée.

verifier, vérificatrice *f*; **automatic v.,** vérificatrice automatique; **card v.,** vérificatrice de cartes; **paper tape v.,** vérificatrice de bande perforée; **tape v.,** vérificatrice de bande.

verify, key v., vérificatrice *f* (de cartes) (à clavier).

verify (to), vérifier; **key-v. (to)**, vérifier (les perforations de cartes).

verifying, vérification f; **card v.**, vérification des (perforations de) cartes.

vertex, adjacent v., sommet adjacent; **v. degree**, degré m d'un sommet; **v. matrix**, matrice associée à un graphe.

vertical, vertical *adj.*; **v. feed**, alimentation verticale; **v. format unit tape**, bande f pilote; **v. tabulation character (VT)**, caractère m de tabulation verticale.

very, v. high frequency (VHF), très haute fréquence; **v. low frequency (VLF)**, très basse fréquence.

vestigial, v. sideband, bande résiduelle.

VF (=voice frequency), fréquence vocale, fréquence f téléphonique.

V format, format m en longueur variable.

V.F.U. (=vertical format unit) tape, bande f pilote.

VHF (=very high frequency), très haute fréquence.

video, v. circuit, circuit m vidéo; **v. tube**, tube m vidéo.

video-chip, micro-image f magnétique.

virgin, vierge *adj.*; **v. coil**, bobine f de bande vierge; **v. medium**, support m vierge; **v. paper-tape coil**, bobine f (*de bande perforée*) vierge; **v. spool**, bobine f (*de bande perforée*) vierge; **v. tape**, bande f vierge.

virtual, virtuel (elle) *adj.*; **v. address**, adresse virtuelle; **v. environment**, contexte virtuel; **v. equals real (V=R) storage**, mémoire virtuelle=réelle (*ou* V=R); **v. memory**, mémoire virtuelle; **v. storage**, mémoire virtuelle; **v. storage partition**, partition f de mémoire virtuelle; **v. storage region**, région f de mémoire virtuelle.

visible, v. record computer (VRC), machine f électro-comptable, ordinateur m de bureau.

visual, v. display unit (VDU), unité f de visualisation (cathodique); **v. scanner**, analyseur m optique.

VLF (=very low frequency), très basse fréquence.

voice, v. channel, voie f téléphonique; **v. frequency (VF)**, fréquence vocale, fréquence f téléphonique; **v. grade channel**, voie f à fréquence vocale; **v. input/output**, entrée-sortie vocale; **v.-operated device**, dispositif m à commande par fréquence vocale.

voice-frequency, v.-f. band, bande f de fréquence vocale; **v.-f. (multichannel) telegraphy**, télégraphie f harmonique; **v.-f. telegraph system**, système m de télégraphie harmonique.

void, défaut m d'encrage; **v. date**, date f de péremption.

volatile, v. memory, mémoire non rémanente; **v. store (or storage)**, mémoire non rémanente.

voltage, tension f; **disturbed response v.**, signal m de sortie avec perturbation; **partial disturbed response v.**, signal m de sortie en sélection partielle avec perturbation; **partial undisturbed response v.**, signal m de sortie en sélection partielle sans perturbation; **r.-m.-s. v.**, tension efficace; **supply v.**, tension d'alimentation; **undisturbed response v.**, signal m de sortie sans perturbation; **v. regulation**, régulation f de tension.

volume, v. test, essai m de matériel avec données réelles; **v. unit** (*Am.*), unité f de volume.

volume-contractor, automatic v.-c., compresseur m.

volume expander, automatic v.-e., extenseur m, expanseur m.

VRC (=visible record computer), machine f électro-comptable, ordinateur m de bureau.

VT (=vertical tabulation character), caractère m de tabulation verticale.

W

wafer, tranche f.

wait, w. condition, état m d'attente.

waiting, w. time, temps m d'attente.

warning, w. lamp, lampe f témoin.

waste, w. instruction, instruction f factice, instruction de remplissage.

wave, onde f; **carrier w.**, onde porteuse; **pulse modulated w.**, onde modulée par impulsions; **sawtooth w.**, oscillation f en dents de scie; **sine w.**, onde sinusoïdale.

waveform, forme f d'onde, onde f, signal m.

waves, interrupted continuous w., ondes modulées.

waveshape (*Am.*), forme *f* d'onde, onde *f*, signal *m*.

wear, w. resistance, résistance *f* à l'usure.

weight, poids *m*; **binary w.,** poids (d'une position) binaire; **card w.,** presse-cartes *m*.

weighted, w. area mask, masque *m* à zones pondérées (*OCR*).

weighting, w. factor, facteur *m* de pondération.

wheel, roue *f*; **character w.,** roue d'impression; **code w.,** disque *m* codeur; **print w.,** roue d'impression; **type w.,** roue d'impression; **w. and disk integrator,** intégrateur *m* à disque et plateau; **w. printer,** imprimante *f* à roues.

who, w. are you? (WRU), qui est là?

wideband, (à) large bande *f*; **w. amplifier,** amplificateur *m* à large bande; **w. circuit,** circuit *m* à large bande.

width, largeur *f*; **pulse w.,** durée *f* d'impulsion; **stroke w.,** largeur de segment; **tape w.,** largeur de bande.

winding, 1. enroulement *m*; **2.** fil *m*; **drive w.,** fil de commande; **sense w.,** fil de lecture.

wiper, balai *m*, curseur *m*.

wire, fil *m*; **connecting w.,** fil de connexion, fil de liaison, fil de raccordement; **drive w.,** fil de commande; **jumper w.,** cavalier *m*; **magnetic w.,** fil magnétique; **open w.,** fil (nu) aérien; **order w.,** circuit *m* de service; **read w.,** fil de lecture; **sense w.,** fil de lecture; **w. printer,** imprimante *f* à stylets, imprimante à (matrice d')aiguilles.

wired, câblé *adj.*; **board-w.,** à tableau de connexions; **w. program computer,** calculateur *m* à programme câblé.

wiring, câblage *m*; **w. board,** tableau *m* de connexions; **w. diagram,** schéma *m* de câblage.

word, mot *m*; **alphabetic(al) w.,** mot alphabétique; **call w.,** mot d'appel (*de sous-programme*); **channel address w.,** mot d'adresse de canal; **channel control w.,** mot de commande de canal; **channel status w.,** mot d'état de canal; **check w.,** mot de contrôle; **computer w.,** mot machine; **control w. (of subroutine),** mot de commande; **conventional telegraph w.,** mot télégraphique conventionnel; **data w.,** mot de données; **end of record w.,** mot de fin d'article; **fixed-length w.,** mot en longueur fixe; **half w.,** demi-mot *m*; **index w.,** mot d'index; **infor-**

mation **w.,** mot d'information; **instruction w.,** mot d'instruction; **key w.,** mot-clé *m*; **machine w.,** mot machine; **numeric(al) w.,** mot numérique; **parameter w.,** mot paramètre; **program status w.,** mot d'état de programme; **reserved w.,** mot réservé; **short w.,** mot incomplet; **telegraph w.,** mot télégraphique; **unit control w.,** mot de commande d'unité; **variable-length w.,** mot en longueur variable; **w. gap,** espace *m* entre mots; **w. indexing,** indexation *f* par mot-clé (*Recherche documentaire*); **w. length,** longueur *f* de mot; **w. mark,** marque *f* de mot; **w. organized store,** mémoire organisée en mots; **w.-oriented computer,** ordinateur *m* à mots; **w. period,** période *f* de mot; **w. processing,** traitement *m* de texte; **w. processing equipment,** matériel *m* de traitement de texte; **w. separator,** séparateur *m* de mots; **w. space,** espace occupé par un mot; **w. time,** période *f* de mot.

work, w. assembly, préparation *f* des travaux; **w. tape,** bande *f* (magnétique) de manœuvre.

work-flow, parallel w.-f., déroulement *m* des travaux en parallèle; **serial w.-f.,** déroulement *m* des travaux en série.

working, 1. fonctionnement *m*; **2.** exploitation *f*; **asynchronous w.,** fonctionnement asynchrone; **autonomous w.,** fonctionnement autonome; **closed-circuit w.,** transmission *f* par interruption de courant; **concurrent w.,** fonctionnement simultané; **double-length w.,** fonctionnement en longueur double; **multiple-length w.,** fonctionnement en longueur multiple; **offline w.,** fonctionnement (en) autonome; **online w.,** fonctionnement (en) connecté, fonctionnement en direct; **open-circuit w.,** transmission *f* par fermeture de circuit; **real-time w.,** fonctionnement en temps réel; **simultaneous mode of w.,** mode (d'exploitation) simultané; **synchronous w.,** fonctionnement synchrone; **tandem w.,** fonctionnement en tandem; **triple-length w.,** fonctionnement en longueur triple; **up and down w.,** exploitation à l'alternat; **w. area,** zone *f* de travail, zone de manœuvre; **w. memory,** mémoire *f* de manœuvre, mémoire de travail; **w. routine,** programme *m* de production; **w. space,** mémoire *f* de travail, mémoire de manœuvre; **w. store (***or***

storage), mémoire *f* de travail, mémoire de manœuvre.

wrap, enroulement *m*; **w. thickness**, épaisseur *f* d'enroulement.

wreck, card w., bourrage *m* de cartes.

writable, w. store, mémoire active.

write, écriture *f*; **gather w.**, écriture avec regroupement; **w. half-pulse**, impulsion *f* de demi-intensité d'écriture (*ou* d'enregistrement); **w. head**, tête *f* d'enregistrement, tête d'écriture; **w. inhibit ring**, anneau *m* d'interdiction d'écriture; **w. lock-out**, verrouillage *m* d'écriture; **w. (permit) ring**, anneau *m* d'autorisation d'écriture; **w. pulse**, impulsion *f* (de commande) d'écriture, impulsion d'enregistrement; **w. time**, durée *f* d'enregistrement.

write (to), écrire, enregistrer.

writer, output w., programme *m* d'écriture (de fichiers) de sortie.

writing, écriture *f*; **demand w.**, écriture à la demande; **read while w.**, lecture et écriture simultanées; **w. head**, tête *f* d'enregistrement, tête d'écriture; **w. pulse**, impulsion *f* (de commande) d'écriture, impulsion d'enregistrement.

W R U (=who are you?), qui est là?

X

xerographic, x. printer, imprimante *f* xérographique.

xerography, xérographie *f*.

X P T (=external page table), table *f* des pages externes.

X punch, perforation *f* «X», perforation *f* «11».

X-Y, X-Y plotter, traceur *m* de courbes.

Y

Y-edge, Y-e. leading, ligne *f* des «Y» en tête.

yield, rendement *m*.

Y punch, perforation *f* «Y», perforation *f* «12».

Z

Zatocode, Z. indexing, indexation précoordonnée (*Recherche documentaire*).

Zatocoding, Z. system, indexation précoordonnée (*Recherche documentaire*).

zero, zéro *m*; **binary z.**, zéro binaire; **non-return-to-z.** (N.R.Z.), non retour *m* à zéro; **return-to-z.** (R.Z.), retour *m* à zéro; **z. address instruction**, instruction *f* sans adresse; **z. address instruction format**, format *m* d'instruction sans adresse; **z. complement**, complément *m* à zéro, complément à la base; **z. condition**, état *m* «zéro»; **z. elimination**, élimination *f* des zéros; **z.-level address**, adresse immédiate, adresse directe; **z.-level addressing**, adressage immédiat, adressage direct; **z.-match gate**, circuit *m* NON-OU (*ou* NI); **z. relative address**, adresse calculée par rapport à zéro; **z. state**, état *m* «zéro»; **z. suppression**, suppression *f* de zéros.

zero-fill (to), garnir de zéros, remplir de zéros.

zeroize (to), (re)mettre à zéro, garnir de zéros.

zero-output, signal *m* de lecture «zéro»; **z.-o. signal**, signal de lecture «zéro».

zone, zone *f*; **minus z.**, zone «moins»; **neutral z.**, zone neutre; **plus z.**, zone «plus»; **z. bit**, bit *m* (d'information) complémentaire; **z. digit**, perforation *f* hors-texte; **z. punch**, perforation *f* hors-texte.